IN ROYAL FASHION

THE CLOTHES OF PRINCESS CHARLOTTE OF WALES

& QUEEN VICTORIA 1796–1901

IN ROYAL FASHION

THE CLOTHES OF PRINCESS CHARLOTTE OF WALES

& QUEEN VICTORIA 1796–1901

KAY STANILAND

museum of
LONDON

First published in Great Britain
in 1997 by the Museum of London,
150 London Wall, London EC2Y 5HN

ISBN 0 904818 55 1 (cased)
ISBN 0 904818 77 2 (limp)

Project manager: Suzie Burt
Editorial: Perilla Kinchin, Suzie Burt,
Mandi Gomez, Julie Targett,
Samantha Luckhurst
Design: Anne Brady
Photography: John Chase
Index: Christine Shuttleworth
Colour origination: Essex Colour

Printed and bound in Belgium by
Snoeck, Ducaju and Zoon

Frontispiece: Bonnets, 1845–55

FOR ANNE BUCK OBE

AND STELLA MARY NEWTON

What odd mortals we are,
& how little likely to be understood
or faithfully represented by those who
don't know us.

Princess Charlotte to
Mercer Elphinstone, 11 November 1814

Acknowledgements

To be able to explore the personalities and clothing of two such interesting and different royal women is a rare privilege, and I should like to thank Her Majesty The Queen for graciously permitting the costume loans made by her predecessors to remain in the Museum of London. It would otherwise have been impossible to become so well acquainted with them and have the time to uncover and investigate their hidden secrets and uncertain attributions. Use has been made of Royal Archives material already in print, but special permission has been graciously granted by Her Majesty for much important new information quoted, sometimes at length, throughout the text. The staff of the Royal Archives and of the Royal Collection have been most encouraging and have fielded with immense good humour and patience my intense quizzing, seemingly endless queries and persistent explorations of their collections. Particular thanks go to Hugh Roberts, Christopher Lloyd, Sheila de Bellaigue, Jane Roberts, Oliver Everett, Frances Dimond, Helen Gray, Caroline Paybody, Stephen Patterson, Theresa-Mary Morton and Gay Hamilton. Those of us involved in selecting illustrations for the book owe a particular debt to Gwyneth Campling for all the assistance she gave with the many photographs we sought from her department.

My thanks are also extended to the Governors and Director of the Museum of London for allowing this project to come to fruition and for their enthusiastic support. And to Valerie Cumming, Deputy Director of the Museum, whose idea the publication and associated exhibition were, and my Heads of Department, Nicola Johnson and Catherine Ross. All who enjoy the stories that unfold throughout the course of this book must also be grateful to the numerous generous donors who, since 1912, have placed so many cherished royal mementos into the care of the Museum.

Research into the history of the dresses and accessories has led me into many libraries and museum stores. I should like to thank numerous colleagues, particularly those at the Brighton Museum & Art Gallery, the Gallery of English Costume (Manchester), the Museum of Costume (Bath), the Royal Museum of Scotland, and the Victoria & Albert Museum for showing me items in their collections. Anne-Marie Benson (Phillips) and Susan Mayor (Christie's South Kensington) drew items to my attention, enabled me to examine them at my leisure or helped me contact owners. I am grateful to colleagues at Exeter City Museums & Art Gallery, Liverpool Museum, Norfolk Museum Service, Northampton Museum & Art Gallery, Shrewsbury Museum Service, the Western Australia Museum (Perth) and the Power House Museum (Sydney) for sending information and photographs of items in their collections which it was not possible for me to examine.

The staff of the Public Record Office were unfailingly helpful during my weeks of research under their famous dome, and Mrs Lang at Bristol City Record Office unearthed invaluable information about local shoemakers which confirmed a reattribution. I should also like to acknowledge the help and encouragement of colleagues in the Guildhall Library, and the splendid provisions of the London Library, the Institute of Historic Research and the Inter-Library Loan Service.

I am indebted to Anne Buck, Charlotte Gere, Santina Levey, Natalie Rothstein and June Swann, for their expert identification of many pieces in the collection and for patient technical advice as writing progressed. Françoise Tétart-Vittu (Musée de la Mode et du Costume, Paris) provided valuable information about a number of Queen Victoria's Paris suppliers, and Marie-Jo de Chaignon (Musée Historique des Tissus, Lyon) sent information about silk firms known to have carried out royal commissions. Sylvia Hopkins (National Army Museum) and Captain David Horne (The Guards Museum) were my saviours in the field of royal military uniforms; any mistakes in the text are solely due to my own lack of grasp of this complex subject. David Meschutt (Westpoint Museum) kindly drew my attention to Thomas Sully's unpublished journal and I am most grateful to Meredith Ward for supplying relevant extracts, and to Hirschl & Adler Galleries (New York) for allowing some of these to be published for the first time.

I am grateful to innumerable colleagues, friends and contacts for stimulating ideas suggesting further sources of information. The Countess of Sutherland, for example, sent me information and photographs of surviving family robes when I tried to locate those claimed as perks by Harriet Leveson-Gower as Mistress of the Robes to Queen Victoria. Sally Brookes, Ann Coleman, Hazel Forsyth, Jean Hunnisett, Sacha Llewellyn, Joanna Marschner, Harry Matthews, Heather Meiklejohn, Geoffrey Munn, Naomi Tarrant and Alex Werner also provided background details.

Only rarely can quantities of historic dress be conserved, mounted and photographed to such high standards. I am deeply grateful to the large team of Museum staff and consultants who contributed to this immense task. My special thanks go to Edwina Ehrman who liaised, cajoled and placated the team from start to finish, to Jill Spanner who mounted the costumes with such attention to detail, and to Barbara Heiberger, Zenzie Tinker, Poppy Singer, Annabel Wylie, Frances Hartog, Kim Leath, Mie Ishii, Robert Payton, Patricia Mahony and Johann Hermans who wrought miracles in their conservation studios. The figures of Princess Charlotte, Queen Victoria and her family were created in conjunction with Garry Hall and Chris Gomm (H & H Sculptors), and Barbara Burrows (wigs), with contributions from Martin Adams (jewellery), Jennie Adey (caps), Carol Hersee (underdresses), Dave and Jo McCabe (shoes) and Barbara Owen (underwear). Their exceptional patience and hard work helped me realise what had long been a dream.

For their hard work on the book I should like to thank Suzie Burt and her colleagues: Anne Brady, John Chase, Mandi Gomez, Julie Targett, Stewart Drew and Donna Hughes. The exhibition design by Barry Mazur provides an elegant setting for the costume, and I am grateful to Karen Eyre, Head of Production Services, and Jayne Davis, exhibition graphic designer, for their part in realising a display of such fine quality.

My final thanks go to Nikki Cross for typing and retyping the manuscript for me with infinite patience and heart-warming enthusiasm; to Perilla Kinchin, a terrier-like editor who helped so much to clarify my thoughts and pull them together, and who gave such encouragement when the flesh was lagging; and to the Department of Opthalmology at Sidcup Hospital who made it possible for me to complete the marathon in time. Princess Charlotte and Queen Victoria have introduced me to many fascinating aspects of their lives and times; I am keen to follow up a number of threads left neglected or only partially disentangled.

Kay Staniland, 21 March 1997

Contents

List of illustrations

Every effort has been made to contact the original copyright holders. The publishers would be pleased to make good any errors or omissions brought to our attention in future editions. The illustrations may not be reproduced without permission from the copyright holders.

Royal Clothing:
its survival and display

The dress of the British Royal Family has always attracted public interest. During the last ten years it has excited a universal attention which has been unprecedented in the history of the monarchy. This has been a stimulating background to the work of a museum curator charged with the care and display of a large collection of historic royal dress. The theme of this book, and the exhibition related to it, is a backward glance at the lives of two important royal women in the nineteenth century, examining their surviving clothing, their fashion tastes and influence, and their patronage of home textile industries. Inevitably, similarities and contrasts with the present day will suggest themselves to author and reader from time to time: this is one of the fascinations of history and of institutions such as monarchies with long histories.

For the last two hundred years, descriptions and illustrations of royal ceremonial or wedding dresses and trousseaux have appeared in the press. Several generations of British princesses have been featured by the fashion press as examples of stylish dressing and without doubt they have exerted some influence in this area. But in recent years perceptions of royal dressing styles have suddenly sharpened; publishers have flooded the market with popular illustrated books devoted to the 'younger royals' and their dress, and public interest and expectations have been raised. Such interest in royal dress is not new, of course, and has always been both a spur and a bane to its subject. Inevitably some circumstances and characteristics remain the same, but others have changed dramatically. The emergence of a highly organised and influential fashion industry, coupled with an assertive fashion press and a rapidly expanding communications network, has intensified public interest in the dressing styles of women in the public eye – actresses, fashion models, pop stars and princesses alike: this interest has also been responded to. *In Royal Fashion* concentrates its attention on a period when the seeds of this phenomenon were just beginning to germinate and take root outside the confines of court society.

Royal clothing has altered radically in form and intention during the last five hundred years. The fine clothes which were the prerogative of the upper echelons of society were enormously expensive, far more so than they have been in recent times: costly fabrics, imported silks and furs, jewelled ornaments, lace and fine linen were worn in substantial quantities by all at the royal court. This was a competitive arena where visual dominance was paramount, especially when the full court gathered to celebrate church feasts, for royal births, marriages and deaths, or out of political necessity. A king had to make

1 *George III,* 1760–1, by Allan Ramsay (1713–84). (Royal Collection)

Ramsay's portrait of the young King in his coronation robes shows the traditional form of these ceremonial garments which had to be modified for Queen Victoria in 1838. The robes are lavishly trimmed with ermine and gold lace: the King wears underneath a fashionably styled suit of a richly patterned cloth of gold. These imposing state portraits demonstrate something of the lavishness of earlier royal dress which relied upon quantities of expensive imported textiles and furs to provide the monarch with a commanding regal image.

himself the centre of attention by whatever means were in his power, and his clothing, together with his castle furnishings, plate and horses, were employed to this end. The novelties of fashion were accommodated within this practice: new garments and tailoring styles, new silks, trimmings or embroidered ornament. As far as we know no budget was set for this apparel and it was funded out of the monarch's considerable personal revenues. Although courtiers or political commentators might criticise, kings were free to indulge their individual preferences. Fine, but not necessarily ornate, apparel was expected as a norm and clothing was replaced throughout the year. In a society which lacked other material indicators of wealth and power, clothing and textiles occupied a much more important place than they do today. The 'old' royal clothing was a valued possession akin to gold or silver plate or jewels, and was used as gifts to friends, courtiers, ambassadors or the Church, or to reward personal service. Through centuries of custom some garments became perquisites of office which were likely to be turned into cash by the recipient. The textile furnishings of a medieval or Tudor palace cost considerably more than the building they adorned, and they frequently featured as costly gifts in international diplomacy, or rewards to courtiers. On occasion clothing was used in this way too.

Changes in the status and financing of the monarchy in the later eighteenth century caused this ancient system to begin to break down: expenditure on dress now came within the political domain, budgeted and controlled by Treasury officials. The early Hanoverian kings had already introduced and encouraged a more bourgeois approach to dress at court, turning away from or modifying ornate fashionable dress. As far as we know George III (illustrations 1, 16) was little concerned by constraints on his wardrobe, but they caused problems to Queen Charlotte precisely because of continued public expectations that she would maintain something of the old rich style of dress on court occasions. Her personal attendants also expected to continue to receive cast-off clothing in the old way, as a perk of their position. Many of George III's sons were less accommodating and large tailors' bills were always prominent amongst the huge debts they accumulated towards the end of the eighteenth century. These princes looked to public funding to clear such debts, but wily governments insisted upon politically acceptable marriages in return: legitimate heirs to the throne were a priority.

The Prince of Wales (later George IV) was the most inveterate transgressor of all in this respect (illustrations 2, 22). Lacking any conscience about the huge debts he accrued he indulged himself, and his brothers and sisters, in all manner of fashionable and fancy dress which at first entranced and amused the public. But once it was realised that his expensive whims would have to be paid for eventually by the public purse, ill humour set in and the Prince and his family were increasingly subjected to harsh criticism and satire. They had long ago ceased to be leaders of fashion. The Prince's largesse did not extend to his daughter Princess Charlotte of Wales who, as she approached adulthood, faced many difficulties in maintaining the appearance expected of one in her elevated social position. After her early death, history repeated itself when, as Regent, the Prince refused to grant an income to his brother's widow, the Duchess of Kent and her daughter, Princess Victoria. His flamboyant spending resulted in severe repercussions on the clothing allowances granted to Princess Charlotte and Queen Victoria by successive governments – and in the officious implementation of these limits by minor Treasury officials in Victoria's reign. It also imbued both with a horror of debt and a natural reticence about fashionable dress, a conservatism that is a well-recognised characteristic of the latter.

2 *The King attended by the Eight Eldest Sons of Peers who held the Train of his Crimson Mantle as he processed to the Abbey,* engraving by E. Scriven after J. P. Stephanoff, published in Whittaker's *Coronation of George IV,* 1823. (MoL 70.23/1)

George IV was intimately involved in the design of the ceremonial robes worn at his coronation by himself, his ministers and household officers, and also by the nobility. He discounted much that was traditional and instead used as his model the ornate robes worn by the Emperor Napoleon at his coronation in 1804.

Queen Victoria's dress allowance remained at £6000 per annum from her succession in 1837 to her death in 1901, and she rarely overspent; when this happened very occasionally she found the additional finance herself.

The skills of generations of portrait painters have recorded with great accuracy the features and characteristics of a succession of kings and queens, princes and princesses. These reveal the fine silks and furs, jewels and elaborate hairstyles which were the usual trappings of royalty in the past, and are a perennial source of admiration and interest to the public. However, it is the surviving artefacts which most stir the public imagination. For example, the immense popularity of the display of the Crown Jewels at the Tower of London, together with the more recent successful opening of Buckingham Palace, demonstrate this continuing fascination with the history and possessions of the British monarchy. It is an irony that the lifestyle and spending which once attracted so much reproach from a disadvantaged public should now attract so much money and attention from a public so critical of its own monarchy. Films and television dramas have also contributed to this glamorisation of past royal personalities, endowing them with the characteristics of fictional heroes, heroines or villains, and distancing them from the reality of their lives.

Historic royal clothing of any period holds a fascination for the visiting public, who approach such relics with a mixture of curiosity and reverence. Once again it offers an actual contact with its original owner, an outer skin which is still strongly permeated with the bodily characteristics of that personality. Often originally preserved for quite other reasons, a number of such royal relics still survive, now carefully conserved and often publicly displayed. The heraldic tunic of the Black Prince, suspended with his other 'achievements' over his tomb in Canterbury Cathedral since his funeral there in 1376, for example, is one of the oldest and most famous of these relics. Although long exposure has reduced it to little more than a mass of grey dust encased in net, it remains on display, an object of interest and veneration to Cathedral visitors, its original colourful form now conveyed by a modern copy. At Westminster Abbey can still be seen the famous 'ragged regiment' of royal and aristocratic funeral effigies which has been displayed to an inquisitive public since 1606. These figures, dating from the fourteenth to the early nineteenth centuries, include Edward III, Henry VII, Mary Tudor, Elizabeth I, James I, Charles II, and Mary II; they are mostly dressed in original garments and have recently undergone costly conservation and redisplay precisely because they continue to attract interested, paying visitors to the Abbey. [1]

Royal images were also popular exhibits at several waxworks in eighteenth-century London, although the nineteenth-century entrepreneur Marie Tussaud has become synonymous with these popular entertainments. Those who benefited most from Madame Tussaud's earliest displays in Britain lived in or close to provincial towns which she visited with her touring exhibits between 1803 and 1834; she settled in London permanently in 1835. Figures of George III and Queen Charlotte 'taken from the life' were early added to her original stock featuring the deposed French royal family; by 1808 the twelve-year-old Princess Charlotte of Wales also appeared in the exhibition, with her mother the Princess of Wales. Through these popular displays a large proportion of the public must have become familiar with the likeness of their young heir, possibly the first, and perhaps the only, close likeness of her that many would see. No description of the 1808 figure of Princess Charlotte now exists, but it (or an updated version) continued to feature in the exhibition and she is still listed in a catalogue of the 1880s. With unerring showmanship Marie Tussaud presented her astonishingly life-like wax portraits against impressive backdrops. Another characteristic of her displays appears to have been a meticulous attention to detail: she used original clothing where possible, or good copies in their stead. The most famous piece of royal clothing she owned was George IV's magnificent embroidered red velvet coronation robe of 1821 which she acquired at a public auction of his clothing after his death in 1830 (illustration 2). She had already mounted her first impressive coronation tableau in 1821, a practice she was to repeat for all subsequent coronations.

Apparently Princess Victoria did not feature in the displays until 1836. She is traditionally said to have visited the new Baker Street premises in this year to view a recent portrait of her uncle, the Duke of Sussex: if the story is true, this may have provided Marie Tussaud with the opportunity to create the portrait 'from life' of the Princess which was advertised shortly afterwards. She certainly went on to exploit the new Queen in changing displays highlighting her coronation, marriage and young family. Advertisements in 1840 for the 'marriage group' claimed to show 'Her Majesty in her nuptial robes of Honiton Lace, by Miss Bidney, manufacturer of the whole of the lace for Her Majesty's bridal attire' (illustrations 3, 123–5). Newspaper reports at the time had claimed that the Queen's lace had cost between £1000 and £1500, and it is disappointing not to have a more detailed description of the lace used on the Tussaud's version to know how close a copy it was. In recent times the company was allowed to acquire copies of the wedding dresses of the Princess of Wales and the Duchess of York, but it seems unlikely that Queen Victoria would have allowed any direct copies to be made of her own unique wedding lace. Perhaps the commercially-minded Jane Bidney cleverly persuaded Madame Tussaud to purchase a similar suite of lace from her? Although this would have been costly, the new tableau must have formed a successful attraction and would have soon recouped the expense. The dress itself would not have been difficult to reproduce, nor would Prince Albert's Field Marshal's uniform (illustration 169).

Marie Tussaud's early posters reveal that one of the curios in her displays was a shirt of Henry IV (of France), and although similar relics came into her possession from time to

3 Queen Victoria's wedding dress, 1840.
(MoL D325, Royal Collection)

Jane Bidney, the supplier of the Queen's wedding lace, is reported to have destroyed the designs herself to foil attempts to make exact copies. The lace was so expensive that few brides could have attempted to copy it closely, following the reports in the daily press and fashion journals.

4 London Museum display, 1912.

An early showing of the 1902 coronation robes of Edward VII and Queen Alexandra, in the Presence Chamber at Kensington Palace. The destructive effect of strong light on displayed costume was not understood and much damage was inflicted on all costumes on public display here and at the Museum's next home at Lancaster House.

time this aspect of her exhibition was never developed to form a museum of such curios. This, interestingly enough, was left to the Royal Family itself to foster.[2]

When Queen Victoria died in 1901 Edward VII inherited a lifetime's accumulation of his mother's personal possessions, quite apart from the magnificent art collections, library and other historic royal material spread through several royal palaces, as well as in the homes of her own creation at Osborne and Balmoral. Nostalgia for earlier happy days and an intense emotional attachment to the possessions of her husband and children had led her to preserve a great deal of what would now be classed as personalia. There was, it seems, a large collection of her own clothes, plus garments which had belonged to her mother, her husband, and her children. Virtually everything from her current wardrobe, including all her underwear and nightwear, appears to have been distributed to her family and household staff. A quantity of the earlier clothes were kept by Queen Alexandra and Queen Mary. In 1911–12 the establishment of the London Museum in the State Apartments at Kensington Palace offered a solution to the problem of this embarrassment of riches (illustrations 4–6). The display of the King's and Queen's coronation robes proved extremely popular with visitors, who for the first time were able to see these impressive ceremonial garments at close quarters. A large deposit of historic royal clothing was then placed on long-term loan with the Museum and this has remained in its care ever since. The hazards of display were apparent at an early date and therefore only a selection has been displayed at any one time. This in turn has attracted many donations of royal clothing, contemporary as well as historic, from both royal and private sources. Comprehensive collections of ceremonial and court uniforms and dresses were subsequently developed to complete the representation of court life in London. Much of the royal loan is now being transferred to the recently-established Royal Ceremonial Dress Collection at Kensington Palace administered by the Historic Royal Palaces Agency. However, many items will remain at the Museum of London as

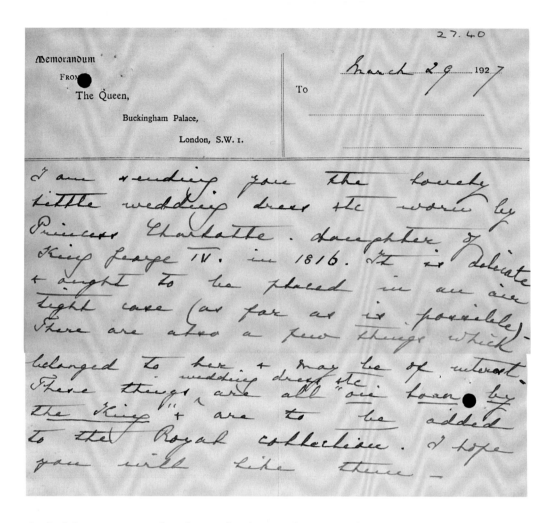

5 Memorandum, 29 March 1927. (MoL 27.40/1)

Many of the costume items received by the London Museum from Queen Mary were accompanied by notes in her own handwriting giving attributions and history; sometimes she requested that items be returned to her. Such notes are often the sole source of information about royal loans and few now survive.

6 London Museum display, c.1920.

An early display showing a dress associated with Queen Victoria's wedding, but possibly slightly earlier. It has a noticeably smaller waist measurement than the wedding dress. The dress is now frail and discoloured and is not included in this publication.

the link between capital and court has been a dominant element in London's history for centuries.

The starting point for this study has been the old London Museum's collection of royal clothing and ceremonial robes. Much material that was dispersed by Queen Victoria through her own lifetime, coupled with many pieces from her last wardrobe, has gradually joined the original nucleus. Many pieces, but mostly dating only to the end of the Queen's life, are to be found in several other British costume collections; others, treasured family heirlooms transported in the baggage of migrants, can now be found in a number of Commonwealth and North American museums. Dresses belonging to Princess Charlotte were not received from royal sources until 1927 and there is nothing to reveal whether any had formed part of Queen Victoria's 'hoard' or had meanwhile been acquired from elsewhere. Queen Mary's own acquisitive powers are well known and the sources of the steady stream of royal memorabilia which she directed to the London Museum throughout her lifetime were rarely revealed (illustration 5). A sizeable collection of dresses and accessories once owned by Princess Charlotte was acquired by the Museum in 1964 and these, together with clothing traditionally associated with her from a variety of sources, form the second largest group of nineteenth-century royal clothing to survive. Only eighteen months divide the lives of these two cousins whose own lifetimes extend over more than one hundred years (1796–1901). Their clothes cover the period 1800 to 1900, and represent many of the styles and changes in fashionable dress during this remarkably diverse period.

These two groups of clothing do much more than simply represent fashions of the

7 Group of display figures.

Individual fibreglass figures have been made for each of the garments illustrated in this book and this motley assembly shows the diversity of shapes required. They were made smaller than actual size so that a final covering of polyester wadding could provide the nuances needed to give the correct touches to the final outline.

nineteenth century, finely crafted and attractive though so many of them are. They offer a unique opportunity to explore the wardrobes of two significant royal women and through this clothing to look at the very different personalities and life experiences of Princess Charlotte and Queen Victoria. Certainly once the dresses were properly mounted on their specially sculpted figures (illustration 7) for photography they sprang to life in the most remarkable way, transformed from limp garments on hangers into utterly distinct personalities with commanding presences. In museum displays it is more usual to focus on the craftsmanship or social context of objects, and only rarely do such large cohesive groups of clothing, previously worn by a known individual, survive. In contrast, exhibitions with a biographical intention normally bring together a mixture of artefacts – portraits, letters and other documents, and an assortment of personal possessions – to illustrate a particular individual and his or her life, but rarely is it possible to reconstruct that individual in the third dimension, through their outer skin, their clothing. These two groups of clothes offer that opportunity. *In Royal Fashion* follows a chronological course so that the dresses, portraits and other personalia can be placed in the context of their owners' lives.

Because of the magnitude of the subject, some aspects of the lives have been omitted completely or sketched in very lightly, for example, the discordant relationship between the Prince and Princess of Wales, including Princess Charlotte's own changing relationship with her mother. In the same way much of Queen Victoria's life and interests, as well as discussion of her husband and their large family, has had to be passed over. These are all very adequately covered in a number of biographies and related studies. Most quotations from Queen Victoria's Journal and letters are from published extracts, and much relevant material must still await discovery by diligent researchers in the Royal Archives. Nor has it been possible here to make adequate reference to the Queen's extensive network of over four hundred textile and accessory suppliers, a fascinating topic which it is hoped will form the central theme of a complementary volume.

The re-creations of Madame Tussaud were immensely popular because she avoided glamorising her subjects, preferring to reproduce their features accurately from carefully recorded measurements, and even life casts, when permitted; the use of original clothing or accurate copies added to the final sense of reality. It has not been the intention of the present project to follow her example exactly. Royal dresses and ceremonial robes were traditionally displayed by the London Museum and the Museum of London on headless tailors' dummies which recreated the original form of the torso; the garments were viewed as curios, divorced from their original wearers, and good portrait heads were beyond the limited budget (illustrations 4, 6, 14). This tradition has now been set aside and abstracted likenesses have been specially created to reflect the appearances of Princess Charlotte and Queen Victoria; these draw upon portraits and photographs and use realistic wigs and accessories to complete the likeness (illustrations 7, 8, 9). This has proved a challenging and revealing process, adding immeasurably to a sense of the personalities of the subjects as well as to our understanding of their physiques, tastes and dressmakers' and tailors' skills.

Where appropriate, aspects of this process have been integrated into the narrative of this book as they throw so much light on the personal characteristics of Princess Charlotte and Queen Victoria, sometimes offering a new perspective or new evidence not known from any other source. For example, it has been possible to determine hair colourings more closely by matching the hair for the wigs with the tiny locks of royal hair still preserved in royal cupboards or set into jewellery. The various hair colourings represented in portraits of Queen Victoria, for example, both in the originals and in book reproductions, are unreliable and confusing. The expansion of Queen Victoria's waistline as she progressed through her childbearing years has long been a recognised factor in the dating of her dresses and uniforms. Like that of any of her subjects, her figure aged and changed, and one of the most notable aspects of this project has been the ability to follow these changes so intimately. Her lack of height was frequently commented upon by those who met her or came into her presence, but this impression was soon forgotten once her commanding personality made itself felt. It is apparent that court portrait painters and photographers usually devised compositions which cleverly modified the contrast in height between the Queen and Prince Albert, although the Queen had never developed a complex about her lack of inches. The Prince's exact height does not now appear to be recorded, but his uniform trousers suggest a height of 6ft (1.83m) which was particularly striking when his completed display figure was placed beside that of his wife (illustration 169). Another feature of the Queen's figure that has emerged from mounting her dresses is the considerable loss of height she had experienced by the end of her life. This is not a surprising feature in an eighty-year-old suffering from rheumatism, but the loss appears to amount to at least 4in. (10cm) and is not otherwise recorded, even by her last physician Sir James Reid. Her last dresses also reflect the elderly Queen's mobility problems. Loops with corresponding buttons are a distinctive feature on the skirt fronts, and when fastened raised the front of the dress so that she could walk safely without tripping (illustration 196).

Princess Charlotte's dresses have similarly provided practical details about her physique, showing that she must have been about 5ft 7½in. (1.71m) high. Size has played an important part in trying to establish a chronological sequence to her surviving dresses: coming from a variety of sources these lack the certainty of attribution which normally makes Queen Victoria's dresses less problematic. Those associated with the last months of the Princess's life reflect her pregnancy, and reveal how the usual construction of fashionable dresses could be modified to cope with this state at a time when identifiable 'maternity' dresses are not known to have existed (illustrations 54, 66). It is clear from her letters that the Princess gained and lost weight in the years leading up to her marriage, a state of affairs which adds further complications to the process of assigning dates to her surviving dresses. The detailed practical work on these dresses also revealed that one of Princess Charlotte's breasts was larger than the other, a trait she shares with a great many women. This has now been detected in four dresses (illustrations 36, 54, 55, 66). Unfortunately, alterations and past conservation attempts have destroyed this valuable evidence in the other dresses traditionally associated with the Princess.

The main purpose of this book is to share something of this exceptionally rich royal heritage with the public. Surprisingly, this has not been attempted before, despite the fact that the royal costumes have been on public display for three-quarters of a century. A catalogue of the whole of the Museum's costume collection first published in 1933 listed the royal dresses then in the collection, whilst one of a set of specialist catalogues published between 1970 and 1973 outlined the Museum's extensive holdings of ceremonial robes associated with English coronations.[3] In recent years the mixture of mostly unrelated royal garments that previously satisfied public curiosity has been replaced by a number of thematic exhibitions highlighting coronation robes, wedding

8 Detail of wig and replica wedding wreath.

Dressing the display figures' heads has revealed many subtleties of the Regency and Victorian hairdresser's art. Queen Victoria's wedding wreath, for example, was placed on her head before her front hair was draped back and fixed into a small nape chignon.

9 Detail of wig of Princess Charlotte.

The wigs are made of natural hair handknotted on to a shaped net base. All are based on contemporary portraits of the subjects and from time to time it has been necessary to 'invent' back details when portraits fail to supply the relevant views.

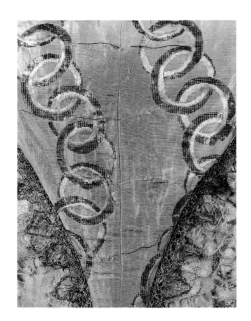

10 Detail of silk dress shown in
illustration 155.

As the result of prolonged display the deep
pink of this silk has faded considerably. The
original colour can still be discerned behind
the bows, as shown in this photograph taken
during conservation treatment.

dresses, children's clothing and Queen Alexandra. This new initiative is therefore a
natural and more elaborate progression in the display of historic royal dress.

One of the most disconcerting aspects of the research for *In Royal Fashion* has been
the problems of attribution which have continually arisen as each garment has been
subjected to careful scrutiny. The traditional associations of many of the items were
rarely supported by documentary evidence when they entered the Museum's collection.
This has always been the case with royal loans or donations, whilst material handed
down within families often seems to have been subjected to a process very like the
child's game of 'Chinese Whispers', whereby information is misunderstood or altered
unintentionally as it is passed on. Accurate feedback on new acquisitions is a problem
which frequently confronts museum curators, and uncovering 'new' information about
long established accessions is usually impossible. Disentangling fact and fiction, reliable
and unreliable attribution, and establishing a more satisfactory dating sequence has
absorbed a great deal of energy during the preparations for this project and it has proved
impossible to resolve all questions. For example, Princess Charlotte's dresses have few
parallels in British costume collections, and examination of European and American
collections would without doubt help to identify similar examples and throw more light
on the dresses of the upper classes. The varying construction of the Princess's dresses has
posed considerable problems, particularly as they must, if authentic, fit into her brief
adult life between 1814 and 1817. Discussion of many of these problems has been
included in the main text, and not relegated to endnotes, for they are an integral part of
the history of each item. The traditions and mythologies which have become associated
with a number of these garments can now be seen as inaccurate and misleading, and
these need to be examined and explained fully. Happily, the process of exploring the
construction and possible use of many dresses and accessories has given rise to a much
richer understanding of their origins and the part they may have played in the royal
wardrobe. A few groups of these costume relics do retain fuller histories, usually
involving strong royal household associations. These have been particularly valuable in
helping to construct a broader picture of the processes by which these royal possessions
became widely scattered, and in determining the authenticity of garments where
documentation has been lost.

Perhaps more than any other museum item, including furniture, clothing is likely to
have been subjected to alteration by its first owner; a succession of owners might then
change it considerably. Dresses may have been brought up to date, lengthened or
shortened, let out or taken in, have had trimmings removed or added, necklines altered,
sleeves shortened or replaced; skirts were often removed and used entirely separately,
whilst charades and fancy dress balls in later decades have left their own forms of
devastation. The dresses of Princess Charlotte and Queen Victoria have been subject to
many of these processes either during their wearers' lifetimes or at the hands of later
owners. It is often not possible to restore garments to their original form – which cannot
always be ascertained for sure anyway – and the current practice is to leave well alone,
allowing necessary restoration or additions to be discreetly apparent, whilst the
conservation processes are reversible and have been recorded carefully by photography
and in detailed reports.

The fragile state of a number of the earlier dresses means that future display or
handling cannot avoid inflicting further damage and will therefore be unwise. The net
and lace dresses are all in advanced stages of deterioration, for the moment held together

as a result of mounting on a modern net in the 1960s; they cannot survive long even in this state (illustrations 11, 31, 36, 48). Fur can also be a short-lived component of fashionable and ceremonial dress. It is attractive as a breeding ground for moth larvae and the thin layer of skin retained by furriers dries out quickly, becoming brittle and liable to tear (illustration 12). Ermine, the pre-eminent royal fur, is the winter coat of the stoat and has a particularly thin skin. It was so expensive that white squirrel ('pured' miniver) or, more recently, white rabbit and mink have been used instead for Parliament and state robes. The conditions which preserved so many of these dresses and robes during the nineteenth century, stored in dark drawers or chests, rarely disturbed and never exposed to strong light, have been replaced by less satisfactory circumstances: museum stores, public access and long periods of display are not conducive to the well-being of fragile old textiles. Short periods of display under strictly-controlled conditions must suffice to satisfy public demand if this unique group of costumes is to survive. The research, mounting and photography carried out as part of this project will therefore be of immense importance in the future when display is no longer possible or must be severely curtailed.

The way that such royal clothing has survived deserves further discussion. Beds in which Elizabeth I allegedly slept still abound, as do a number of gloves and other accessories associated with her. She was a long-lived and famous English queen and it is not surprising that such mementos should have been preserved for four centuries. Any reverence which may originally have attached to these relics has surely long since vanished and they have simply joined the mass of curios of past ages which now fill our museums and historic houses. Her massive collection of jewels and clothes was carefully inventoried in 1600 and we therefore know exactly what must have passed to her successor James I when he arrived from Scotland in 1603 to ascend the English throne. What became of this amazing textile treasure is not precisely known, but James's consort Anne of Denmark is traditionally believed to have reused a number of the dresses for her own purposes. Some are thought to have been turned into costumes for court masques, whilst others must surely have been dispersed as gifts to favourites of the new monarch. Nothing from this inheritance is now known to have survived: it was almost certainly viewed as another inherited asset, just like the late Queen's paintings, plate and jewels, which could be utilised by her successors as whim dictated. Preserving any dresses seems never to have been on the Stuart agenda.[4] A quite different textile heritage has descended from James's son Charles I, whose beheading in Whitehall in 1649 has given him a special place in English history. His martyrdom inevitably ensured that items of his clothing became revered keepsakes. Many of these are associated with that momentous day in Whitehall: some are believed to have been handed to those who witnessed his execution whilst others were removed from his corpse and shared amongst those who remained loyal in his last months. Not all of the garments associated with this event can be authentic, but owners of such memorabilia are often reluctant to relinquish the colourful anecdotes associated with their cherished possessions.

Princess Charlotte's unexpected death in 1817 unleashed an unprecedented national mourning and instantly made her a national heroine. Public interest in the Princess had intensified when she married, and her death just eighteen months later resulted in a flood of cheap souvenirs and many eulogistic biographies. To her family and close associates, her possessions, particularly her clothing, retained something of her engaging personality and consequently much was preserved. In contrast, the wardrobes of her

11 Detail of embroidered net dress, 1814–16.

The fineness of the silk threads used in the construction of this net make them particularly vulnerable to damage and decay. This close-up of the fabric of the dress in illustrations 31, 38, 39 reveals the very frail state of the net, splitting and disintegrating all over. This delicate fabric was immensely popular during the Regency period, but few examples now survive.

12 Detail of ermine lining of Parliament mantle, 1838.

The mantle has had to be completely taken apart and reassembled to rectify many problems. For example, much of the ermine was splitting, and the small pelts were coming apart where stitching threads had rotted. The problem was increased by the great weight of the mantle itself. This conservation work alone took some 440 hours. See also illustrations 152, 153.

13 Lady Gardiner, 1861. (Royal Archives)

Queen Victoria's interest in photography led her to have many record photographs taken of her homes, staff and companions, and these now form an invaluable archive. Lady Gardiner was Woman of the Bedchamber between 1837 and 1859. She told the Queen that Princess Charlotte would have turned into an authoritarian monarch had she lived and succeeded to the throne. The preservation of many of Princess Charlotte's dresses was the result of her intervention and care.

mother and father were put on sale shortly after their deaths in 1821 and 1830 respectively and almost nothing has survived.[5]

It seems certain that Prince Leopold could not bring himself to dispose of his wife's possessions in such a public manner. We know that in the 1820s, when Princess Victoria visited Claremont with her mother, the cloak and bonnet Princess Charlotte wore for her last walk with him still hung on the screen just as she had left them. In 1838 a quantity of her clothes were still in the possession of her loyal and beloved dresser Mrs Louisa Louis when she died at Buckingham Palace. After 1817 she had remained at Claremont as housekeeper and had become 'dear old Louis' to Queen Victoria, who noted her death with great regret in her Journal. Her will reveals that in 1838 she still had possession of the Princess's wedding dress which she now bequeathed – 'a silver Tissue Dress covered with silver net worn by her late Royal Highness the Princess Charlotte on her marriage' – to Lady Gardiner, Woman of the Bedchamber to Queen Victoria (illustration 13). Sir Robert Gardiner had been principal equerry to Prince Leopold between 1816 and 1831, and had been at Claremont when the Princess died; he and his wife had continued to live on the estate and she had early entered the Queen's service.[6] Documents which have descended from the Gardiners show that in 1838 Lady Gardiner took upon herself the task of discreetly selling the remainder of Princess Charlotte's clothes in Mrs Louis's estate to a small circle of royal ladies or close associates, to benefit the deceased's German relatives. Queen Victoria, the Duchess of Kent, the Duchess of Gloucester and the Queen of the Belgians (Prince Leopold's second wife) were amongst the purchasers, but the fate of these garments is not known.[7]

Lady Gardiner passed down to her descendants a generous assortment of Princess Charlotte's dresses and accessories, but it is not clear how much of this was acquired in 1817 and how much in 1838. These now form the most important group of the Princess's personalia in the Museum's collection and, apart from one small exception (a misidentified intrusion, presumably from a member of the Gardiner family), the most undeniably authentic material. The dress that is now called Princess Charlotte's wedding dress is not part of this group and it is not possible to trace its history between 1838 and 1927 when, together with several other dresses associated with the Princess, it was lent to the London Museum by Queen Mary. Did Lady Gardiner give it to Queen Victoria during her lifetime or might it have been a gift when she herself died in 1876? Or could Queen Mary have acquired it much later from the family or some other source? It seems unlikely that this mystery will ever be resolved.

The other dresses that came with the wedding dress in 1927 demonstrate the problems in ascertaining the authenticity of such personalia. The so-called 'Russian' dress was also included in this royal loan. It is the only surviving dress which the Princess is shown wearing in a portrait and consequently presents no problems of authenticity (illustrations 65, 66). However, it is much more difficult to be so certain about the two other dresses which came with this group and their problems reflect those which affect all the other dresses, drawn from different sources, which are associated with Princess Charlotte. One of these 1927 dresses is discussed and illustrated below (illustrations 46–9), but the authenticity of a second, a small white cotton dress with a coarsely embroidered hem claimed to have been worn by the Princess in childhood, is still uncertain (illustration 14). The construction of the dress and its embroidery suggest a date that does not comfortably accord with the size the Princess should have been at this time. In the past it was assumed that royal personalia lent or given by members of the royal family were family possessions inherited through several generations. Questions were not asked and the attributions which arrived with the garments were accepted as genuine. It now seems likely that a number of such relics could have been acquired at a later date through presentation by acquaintances or the public, or even by purchase. In the 1840s and 1850s Queen Victoria occasionally repurchased old family lace for use on her dresses and the eventual fate of this lace is unknown.

The most beautiful of the dresses associated with Princess Charlotte is the most problematic to date and authenticate (illustrations 11, 31, 38, 39). It was given to the Museum by the late Princess Marina as part of a group of later royal clothing items whose authenticity was apparent, and no further information was sought about the origins of the dress. Is this another of the dresses sold off from Louisa Louis's estate by Lady Gardiner, or has it descended by some other route? Its form as a Continental-style court dress opens up the question of Princess Charlotte's first trousseau in 1814, which was abandoned and was perhaps too out-dated in 1816 to be reused in her second trousseau. Was this distributed to family and friends, or might it have been discreetly sold off through one of Queen Charlotte's dressmakers? The continuous process of thinning these royal wardrobes via gifts to staff and intimates has ensured the survival of a number of other pieces associated with the Princess, but they can also pose problems of authentication similar to those of items received directly from royal sources. For example, one assemblage of such relics was early discounted because most pieces date to the middle years of the eighteenth century and can have had no part in the Princess's life. The items were allegedly housed in an attic chest marked with the Princess's name and an incorrect link was made between container and contents.

Problems like these occur only occasionally in connection with Queen Victoria's clothing. She appears, as has already been explained, to have been responsible for preserving a sizeable quantity of her own dresses before 1861, and also for keeping many mementos of her children when they were small. Following Prince Albert's death it is said that she would not allow his wardrobe to be dispersed, but almost nothing of this now survives. A large quantity of her clothes will have been shed from her own wardrobe throughout her lifetime but only a few of these gifts or perks have survived intact. Those from her married years often arrive with good oral explanations of descent from servants in the royal household. Most of these gifts by the Queen must have been put to practical use, as indeed she intended they should be, altered and worn anonymously far away from the royal circle: these are now lost to posterity. Only one of her earlier widowhood dresses now survives and this was accidental, at least in the first place: it was lent to an artist for a portrait, never returned and obviously after some time took on the air of a revered curiosity (illustrations 180–3). This artistic oversight was repeated some thirty years later, but obviously the late 1890s large black dress preserved on this occasion is of far less historic interest: however the incident has preserved the only known example of one of the Queen's famous widow's caps (illustrations 204–6).

A further artist, the American Thomas Sully, revealed in a diary entry something of the compulsive urge which must so often have overcome other visitors to royal palaces, and which has been the means of saving many inconsequential royal mementos. When visiting London in 1837–8, with a commission to paint the new Queen's portrait, he was granted several sittings at Buckingham Palace (illustration 15). After the first sitting he noted in his diary of the visit how: 'When left alone I cast my eyes about to find some trifle that I might bring away as a relic – an old pen, a Card – but nothing presented itself

14 Muslin dress, 1800–5.
(MoL 27.40/4, Royal Collection)

Opinions are divided about whether Queen Mary's attribution of this dress to Princess Charlotte is correct. It is not possible to fix an exact year for the dress now, but its construction and decoration suggest that it must belong to the period when the Princess was between four and nine years old. The dress is considerably smaller than any of the other dresses associated with her. Was she already tall for her age or is this an attribution which cannot be upheld?

15 *Queen Victoria, c.*1838, by Thomas Sully (1783–1872). (Wallace Collection, London)

During a visit to London in 1837–8 the American artist Thomas Sully painted this half-length study of Queen Victoria in her Parliament robe so that it could be engraved. The main purpose of his visit was a full-length portrait commissioned by the 'Society of the Sons of Saint George' in Philadelphia. He kept a diary during his visit recording his impressions of London and his sitters: David Wilkie advised him to 'Dress, as if going to a party' when going to the Palace, whilst Alfred Chalon confirmed that his black garments were 'quite in the right and fully respectful'. His daughter Blanche accompanied him to one sitting to model the circlet and Orders, a procedure which much amused the Queen.

but her foot-muff; out of which I plucked a little of the wool'. At a later sitting Sully was given an infinitely more valuable historic souvenir by the redoubtable Baroness Lehzen: a length of tape giving exactly the young Queen's height. 'The Queen says if you show this measurement when you return to America, they will say what a little Queen the English have got', the Baronesss reported to him. Presumably he did show the tape on his return, but it is now uncertain whether it has been preserved in the artist's scattered papers.[8]

Men were of course not the only ones to have this collecting urge. Three small exercise books containing samples of Queen Victoria's dresses have come to light in the last few years, in three quite separate collections. One book appears to have been compiled by an employee in the workroom of the Queen's earliest dressmaker, Mary Bettans, whilst a second includes many of the same samples in a much broader collection of textile and wallpaper snippets associated with many other historical personalities (illustrations 16,

110, 137). This second volume appears to have been the work of a later collector of such small historical relics, possibly a client of Mary Bettans's apprentice. A third book, presented to Queen Mary in the 1930s by a descendant of the original compiler, contains a totally different selection of samples, again of the earliest years of Queen Victoria's reign, which must have come from yet another of her dressmakers. Indeed many small samples of the Queen's dresses were saved over the years by many individuals, most notably by the silk weavers in Spitalfields responsible for weaving special silks and velvets for ceremonial robes and the Queen's wedding and jubilee dresses. Some samples of silks are to be found in the archives of English and French firms commissioned by the Queen to weave special lengths for her, whilst the shops which supplied her have also been the source of these small personal curios.

Those who worked for the Queen in her various homes were, of course, in the best position to acquire small personal mementos of their mistress, although this was no doubt strongly discouraged. As already explained, some early examples of the Queen's clothing, given as perks to her staff, have been carefully preserved by their descendants. The Museum holdings apart, by far the largest quantity of the Queen's clothing to survive must be the contents of her wardrobe at her death. These are now widely scattered, but examination of many small collections confirms that a distribution of the Queen's wardrobe did indeed take place after her death, within the confines of her family and staff, although there is now no record of this in the royal archives. Curiously enough, in nearly all cases any account of the source of the relics has been lost within one or two generations. One account relates that the items were distributed according to rank within the household, the least significant being the lot of the most junior household servant. How much truth there is to this tale is impossible to discover today. These late mementos are particularly distinctive through their shape, size, fine materials and workmanship: they were perhaps more difficult to use for practical ends, and may also have been regarded with greater reverence for a generation or two. Perhaps the most bizarre souvenirs are the fragments of the dead Queen's laying-out clothes and coffin, discarded scraps apparently picked up by one of the staff at Osborne House shortly before the Queen made her final journey to Windsor in February 1901. These are matched by a sample of the purple mourning drapes from Buckingham Palace, inserted at a later date into the sample book associated with the apprentice of the royal dressmaker Mary Bettans.

Although to many people today Princess Charlotte and Queen Victoria appear to have lived in two very different eras, they in fact share links quite beyond their inherited relationship. The circumstances of their births, upbringing and education, adult lives and personal characters offer comparisons and contrasts which are particularly relevant to any discussion of their surviving clothing. Both obviously took an interest in the passing novelties and changes in fashion, but neither can be shown to have had the beauty, outstanding taste, or that pervasive passion for dress which would distinguish them as leaders of fashion in their time. This they share. Indeed, if such quantities of their clothing had not survived it is unlikely that either would ever have been selected as subjects for an exhibition or book about royal fashion! It is now impossible to treat any of their contemporaries or near descendants in like manner since no similar groups of garments have been preserved. The two also held similar attitudes to their own body images, to dress appropriate to their royal status, to the world of fashionable dressing, and to any influence they might exert through the patronage of British textile industries. These themes are in fact common to the experience of most British queens and

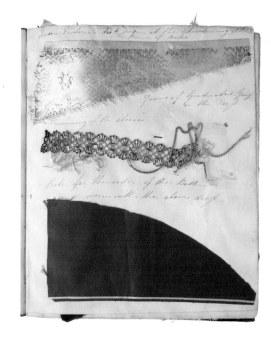

16 Dress cuttings book, 1837–44. (MoL 80.424/1, Private Collection)

This page from one of two books associated with Mary Bettans's workshop includes a piece of the white and silver dress worn by Queen Victoria at the christening of the Prince of Wales in 1841. The books also contain fragments of dresses made for Queen Adelaide, the Duchess of Kent and Baroness Lehzen, and a tiny fragment of a court dress worn by Queen Victoria before she ascended the throne. See also illustrations 110, 137.

princesses since the beginning of the nineteenth century, and have been particularly relevant to recent members of the royal family.

Princess Charlotte of Wales (1796–1817) is little known today even though her sudden death in childbirth when only twenty-one years old caused a national sensation and a succession crisis. Her dresses belong exactly to the period of Jane Austen's last novels, works which have suddenly enjoyed an unprecedented success in film and television adaptations during the course of this project. She was the child of an arranged marriage which was an almost instantaneous disaster, and lived in the care of each parent at different times in her life; each in turn failed her as the result of their own impaired personalities and flamboyant lifestyles. But she was fortunate that her status enabled her to be brought up in a separate establishment with attendants who could offer her a little of the stability she lacked in her family relationships. After an arranged engagement, which she broke off herself amidst strong family disapproval, she at last found happiness in 1816 when she married Prince Leopold of Saxe-Coburg, a husband of her own choosing. It was a tragically short-lived happiness. She died a little over eighteen months later and the loss of an already popular heir to the British throne brought widespread grief. It also returned the country to the succession problems which her birth in 1796 had been expected to remedy.

Queen Victoria (1819–1901) is better known than her cousin, but it is her image later in her life – a very small, rotund black figure – that now seems immutably fixed in the public memory. It is true that she spent the last forty years of her life in black after the death of Prince Albert in 1861, but the forty years which preceded that traumatic event witnessed a full and fruitful life, far more attractive and absorbing than the later black years. Her childhood was more stable than that of her cousin, and the early loss of her father was compensated for by the affectionate and generous figure of her Uncle Leopold, Princess Charlotte's widower. Unlike her cousin, Princess Victoria lived long enough not only to succeed to the throne when she was eighteen, but also to enjoy one of the longest reigns in British history. Her marriage, also to a man of her own choosing, was equally happy and she was able to supply an adequate succession to the throne. Her death brought customary widespread national mourning for a familiar, but now distant, regal figure who had been the only monarch in the lifetime of many of her subjects. It also opened the twentieth century and brought to the throne an ageing heir apparent.

The Court of George III

The culture of the English royal court in the eighteenth century was to be formative in the lives and attitudes of Princess Charlotte and Queen Victoria. Queen Charlotte and the Prince of Wales, the Prince Regent, in particular had brought with them into the nineteenth century a formidable inheritance which they maintained by a rigid insistence upon court etiquette and constant reference to past precedents. Although so much of their childhoods were lived away from the court itself, both royal princesses were well versed in its culture. As heirs presumptive they were trained to become key figures in the future court and it was necessary for them to understand its history and etiquette. Knowing what clothes were appropriate to this role was part of this preparation, although both, through observation and reaction, would develop their own individual approaches to the problems of changing fashions and the changing court cultures.

The eighteenth century had witnessed the increasing separation of the public and private lives of the English Royal Family. This was a trend promoted by George III and Queen Charlotte, who made Windsor Castle their main residence. The King's levees and the Queen's Drawing Rooms, held at St James's and Buckingham House respectively, remained the principle parade ground for sartorial finery in London and the Royal Family continued to appear at them in rich apparel, which was duly described in the pages of the press. The King gleaned little pleasure from this ritual, however, and his own lack of interest in clothes was well known. It had become the practice for courtiers to wear striking new outfits at Drawing Rooms held to commemorate the birthdays of the king or queen, but it is said that George III took so little notice of this expensive compliment that people lost heart and the tradition gradually died out. Disappointment and disdain drew harsh comments on his 'ill-made coats and general antipathy to the fashion' from the most illustrious courtiers, and created a vacuum which his son the Prince of Wales was to fill with enthusiasm – and at great public expense.[1]

However, George III did make one notable contribution to the royal wardrobe through his invention of the Windsor uniform in the late 1770s (illustration 17). This grew out of the advent of military uniforms which, with their precise system for differentiating rank in the services, provided a particularly appropriate alternative to fashionable dress for wear at court functions. Not only did they offer a means of denoting status, but they also exuded authority and masculinity. George III, and later all his sons, enthusiastically adopted various forms of military and naval uniforms, 'improving' existing forms or devising entirely new ones. Resplendent with gold buttons and lace,

17 *George III,* 1807, by Peter Edward Stroehling (1768– after 1826). (Royal Collection)

The elderly King is shown on a terrace at Windsor Castle in his Windsor uniform with the ribbon and star of the Order of the Garter, and the badge of the Order of the Bath.

and with the insignia of the Orders of knighthood, such uniforms made an exciting addition to the splendour of the English court. Massed together at the all-male levées they presented a remarkably impressive sight, whilst at the Queen's Drawing Rooms they provided an excellent foil to the richly embroidered or diaphanous lace and gauze confections of the court ladies.

The Windsor uniform, of 'blue turned up with red', was devised by the King as a private royal household uniform to be worn only by himself, his family and favoured gentlemen when the court was in residence at Windsor. For a short time after its introduction the Queen and princesses wore versions of the uniform, but this practice soon died out and was only briefly reintroduced by Queen Victoria at the beginning of her reign (p103). The uniform became a coveted mark of royal favour limited to a few distinguished recipients, and continues in use within the Royal Family today.[2]

Information about royal and court dress was once spread by word of mouth, the reports of ambassadors or the letters of courtiers, but the growth of the press during George III's reign encouraged an interest in court affairs, which embraced the fashions paraded before the King. These soon found a natural home in the earliest women's journals, which carried monochrome engravings of the latest fashions. At this point it was the descriptions of dresses worn at court which yielded the richest copy, and these clearly served a valuable purpose in disseminating news of London fashions far and wide. Those not privileged to appear at court were still avid for such information, whilst those who did attend court functions doubtless also read these reports; it was important for them to see and be seen, but also to keep abreast of details not observed because of the crush on such occasions. Thus quietly, almost insignificantly, was born the fashion press, which in the twentieth century has become so powerfully interested in royal clothing, and so influential in the formation of the public's concept of royalty as leaders of fashion.

18 *Inconveniences of a Crowded Drawing Room,* engraving by George Cruikshank (1792–1878); published by G. Humphrey, 27 St James's Street, 6 May 1818. (British Museum)

Although overstated, this satirical print conveys something of the discomfort involved in attending one of the Queen's Drawing Rooms, and the considerable inconvenience caused by the ungainly hoops of the ladies' court dresses. By 1818 one courtier noted that: 'The crowds are so great & so little decorum attended to, that people's clothes are litterally torn to pieces'. (George, IX, p836.)

A typical example of this early reporting describes the dress worn by the Queen on 4 June 1792 at a Drawing Room held to mark the King's birthday.

> Her Majesty upon this occasion, was dressed with more magnificence than we remember to have ever seen her before. The petticoat was of green silk, entirely covered with Brussels point, thrown very fully over it, with a loose drapery of lilac silk, covered also with lace, and drawn up in festoons with large bouquets of diamonds, each bouquet consisting of one large rosette, from which rise bending sprigs in imitation of snowdrops. From each rosette fall two large diamond chains and tassels; and upon each festoon of the drapery is a chain of large diamonds.
>
> At the bottom, a flounce of fine lace, headed with rows of large diamonds. The robe and train white and silver silk, trimmed round with a border of lilac silk covered with lace. The cap blond, with bandeaus, and girdle of diamonds. Each bouquet of the petticoat has a central stone in the rosette valued at £2,000; the rosette, including this stone, is valued at £3,000; and the bouquets, of which there are six, at £8,000 each. Adding to the amount of these that of the other diamonds upon the petticoat, and those upon the head-dress and stomacher, the dress worn by Her Majesty could not be worth less than an hundred thousand pounds; and the task displayed in the arrangement of the whole was well suited to such an expenditure.

How such information was procured is not known, but royal mantua makers and milliners were probably persuaded to supply details to representatives acting as court correspondents. It is also possible that impecunious members of the nobility, with the entrée to these exclusive gatherings, became involved in the process.[3]

The conservatism which had brought into being the rich and colourful ceremonial dress of the eighteenth-century English court had to be flexible to survive. Discreet modification was also necessary to avoid the ludicrous and inappropriate. Queen Charlotte's unyielding insistence that the ladies attending formal court functions continue to wear unwieldy hoops long after they had gone out of fashion produced just such an extraordinary outmoded form of dress (illustration 18). In 1786 Jane Austen's sister-in-law was daunted by the prospect of standing for two hours at a Drawing Room 'loaded with a hoop of no inconsiderable weight', whilst in 1818, almost at the end of the reign, the newly arrived United States ambassador, Richard Rush, flatteringly compared court ladies to 'beautiful architecture, the hoops the base, the plume the pinnacle . . . like old English buildings and Shakespeare they triumph over criticism'. Such outmoded dress had long been discarded in France: here an elegant train completed elaborate fashionable gowns. The Prince Regent did not relax the rule on court hoops until he himself came to the throne in 1820.[4]

Queen Charlotte (illustration 20) shared her husband's preference for a simple private life away from the stiff formality of court life. In 1791 or 1792 Mrs Harcourt reported from Weymouth that 'Even the Queen walks about with only a lady and goes into the shops'. Numerous similar anecdotes tell of the King visiting shops in Windsor or Pall Mall: this was considered extraordinary for one who could command the attendance of all tradespeople at his palace (illustration 19). His granddaughters, Princess Charlotte and Queen Victoria, were also to delight in visiting shops, a rare treat for these palace-bound princesses.[5]

A valuable intimate description of the Queen's daily dressing routine was recorded in her diary by the novelist Fanny Burney, who in 1786 was appointed a second keeper of

A MILLINER's SHOP.

the Queen's robes. It is all the more interesting as we do not have such information for Princess Charlotte or Queen Victoria. Their dressing routines, like those of all noble women, must have followed a similar pattern and indeed occasional comments in Queen Victoria's Journal suggest that little had changed. Queen Charlotte rose early and her hair was dressed by Mrs Thielky, her wardrobe woman, before Miss Burney was called, usually at about 7.30am, to help dress her.

> No maid ever enters the room while the Queen is in it. Mrs Thielky hands the things to me, and I put them on. 'Tis fortunate for me I have not the handing of them! I should never know which to take first, embarrassed as I am, and should run the prodigious risk of giving the gown before the hoop, and the fan before the neckerchief.

The Queen was not attired in her formal dress until 1pm when Miss Burney and Mrs Schwellenberg (the senior dresser) 'help her off with her gown, and on with her powdering thing, and then the hairdresser is admitted. She generally reads the newspapers during that operation.' The Queen then moved to her state dressing-room where:

> her dress is finished … and I see no more of her until bedtime … Between 11 and 12 my last summons usually takes place, earlier and later occasionally. Twenty minutes is the customary time then spent with the Queen, half an hour, I believe, is seldom exceeded … I then come back & after doing what I can to forward my dress for the next morning, I go to bed – and to sleep, too, believe me.[6]

Of all the large family which Queen Charlotte bore George III, it is their eldest son the Prince of Wales (the Prince Regent, later George IV), father of Princess Charlotte, who is best known today (illustrations 2, 22). His inordinate interest in clothes was

19 *A Milliner's Shop,* engraving by Henry Kingsbury (active 1775–95), published by S. W. Fores, No. 3 Piccadilly, 24 March 1787. (British Museum)

No aspect of royal life was considered sacrosanct by satirists, and this print focuses on George III's and Queen Charlotte's habit of visiting shops at Windsor with their daughters. It is a rare and interesting view of an eighteenth-century shop interior: Jane Austen would have visited just such a shop when purchasing items for her own dresses, but until this time it was unusual for royalty to visit shops. The fictitious name given to the Queen's milliner is a reference to her supposed miserliness.

20 *Queen Charlotte,* 1781, by
Thomas Gainsborough (1727–88).
(Royal Collection)

There is a report that the drapery of this
dress was painted in one night by the artist
and his nephew Gainsborough Dupont so
that it could be exhibited at the Royal
Academy. Whatever the truth, this is a
masterly portrayal of a fashionable gauzy
dress just as it began its slow transformation
into the slim, soft Empire-line of Princess
Charlotte's lifetime. The hoops which had
supported the heavy stiff silks fashionable in
the previous two decades were already
becoming irrelevant and would soon be
abandoned in fashionable circles.

apparent at an early age: in 1779, for example, when sixteen, he sent patterns and pieces of cloth from his tailor to his current amorosa Mary Hamilton requesting that she indicate her recommendations by marking them with pins. By 1782 he had already incurred debts of £60,000. Although he was awarded an annual civil list allowance of £50,000, in addition to the Duchy of Cornwall revenues, his spending continued to be reckless. By 1791 he had built up further enormous debts: of £31,912, for example, solely to his various tailors – Weston of Old Bond Street, Schweitzer & Davidson of Cork Street, Louis Bazalgette, and Winter & Co. He owed £1875 to his breeches makers White & Thomas.[7] It was to extricate himself from financial disaster that in 1795 he married his cousin Princess Caroline of Brunswick.

Princess Caroline herself was to say of her husband's obsession with clothing '[I] ought to have been the man and he the woman to wear the petticoats . . . he understands how a shoe should be made or a coat cut, . . . and would make an excellent tailor, or shoemaker or hairdresser but nothing else.' The sculptor John Rossi was kept waiting for three hours one day while the Prince tried on 'at least forty pair of boots' and conducted 'many trials of patterns and cuttings'; on the previous day he had been kept waiting for five hours![8] The evidence for this preoccupation is more than anecdotal: the Prince carried out countless commissions for his brothers when, stationed abroad, they hankered after the sartorial luxuries which it seemed only London could supply. Amongst these were some of the uniforms which the Prince and his brothers delighted in. Criticised by George III for his huge bills, the Prince commented to his brother Frederick (later Duke of York): '. . . the King is grown so stingy with regard to himself yt. he will hardly allow himself 3 coats in a year'.[9]

21 *Caroline of Brunswick, Princess of Wales*, 1795, by Gainsborough Dupont (1754–97). (Royal Collection)

George III himself commissioned this portrait of his daughter-in-law in her wedding dress, wearing a coronet and, fastened at her breast, a miniature of the Prince of Wales. *The Gentleman's Magazine* described the dress as 'A royal robe; silver tissue petticoat, covered with silver Venetian net and silver tassels . . . sleeves and tippet fine point lace, and the bands of the sleeves embroidered with plumes of feathers; a royal mantle of crimson velvet, silver cord and tassels, trimmed with ermine.'

22 *George IV when Prince of Wales*, 1798, by Sir William Beechey (1753–1839). (Royal Collection)

The Prince of Wales is shown in the striking uniform of the Tenth Light Dragoons, wearing the star of the Order of the Garter. This subtly updated copy of 1803 was commissioned by the Prince as a gift to his brother the Duke of Kent.

In 1794, once it had been decided that the Prince of Wales would marry his cousin, Queen Charlotte took on the task of assembling a trousseau, including a wedding dress, to supplement her future daughter-in-law's (illustration 21). How she went about this is revealed, sporadically, in the Queen's correspondence with her son. Like Fanny Burney's diary, these occasional insights into practical aspects of royal life are of immense value – especially since there are no similar records of the assembling of Princess Charlotte's trousseau in 1816.

An exact date for the marriage had not been set, but on 30 October 1794 the Queen reported to her son that that morning she had been 'buying linen and petticoats, ordering Mr. Kg. [William King, silk mercer, of Pall Mall] to be here on Tuesday morning with plain silks, & Mrs Barber & the agreable Nonini with all kind of muslin dresses.' By spending time with other suppliers on Monday and Tuesday, she believed, 'we shall settle a great deal'. Establishing the size of her daughter-in-law was a problem, and 19 November found her commenting to her son:

> I received yesterday the pattern of the Princesses nightdress which is very elegant & pritty, but nothing else. Pray be so good as to enquire of Princess Sophia of Gloucester if she has a pattern glove & if so send it to me. What to do about shoes, I do not know & feel very sorry about it . . . I have also spoken to the Kg. about the robe. He says that the Princess may be married in a gown and petticoat if you like it, also that he had no objection to a robe. I beg therefore a determination upon that subject. The <u>Gazette</u> of 1736 will tell exactly how it was.

A letter she wrote later that day told the Prince that 'Princess Sophia has a shoe [of Princess Caroline's] & if you wish Taylor [shoemaker of Cockspur Street] to make them pray bespeak them yourself or send him down to Windsor with the shoe.'[10]

Royal bridal dresses followed a centuries-old tradition of being made of silk cloths enriched with gold or silver, according to status, and precedents were still examined carefully to ensure that appropriate dress was worn. George III himself had been reading 'papers to make himself master of every etiquett, that he may give directions . . . and was so kind as to direct me about getting all proper information concerning the Princesses dress', the Queen reported to her son, and went on to explain:

> I have appointed Mrs Beauvey & Spilsbury . . . to meet me at the Queen's House [Buckingham House] . . . with a doll. The former is to undertake the whole for Madame La Future [Princess Caroline], as the only person capable to command as many hands as we shall want to accomplish it in time.[11]

This is an extremely rare and important reference to a fashion doll. It presumably wore a miniature version of the proposed dress, or was used to work out the form of the dress before expensive and time-consuming work began on the dress itself. Madame Beauvais was one of the Queen's milliners at this period. Princess Caroline was still in Brunswick and in fact did not arrive in London until 5 April.

The ceremony took place at 8pm on 8 April 1795, in the Chapel Royal, St James's Palace, in the presence of the King and Queen and their family, and senior members of the court. A Drawing Room was held immediately afterwards but already, so eyewitnesses reported, there was a coolness between the bride and groom. Their only child, Princess Charlotte, was born nine months later.

Girlhood, 1796–1812

Princess Charlotte was born early on 7 January 1796 at Carlton House, the London home of her father, the Prince of Wales. Shortly afterwards, at 9.45am, he wrote to his mother Queen Charlotte to announce the event:

> The Princess [of Wales], after a terrible hard labour for above twelve hours, is this instant brought to bed of an <u>immense girl</u>, and I assure you notwithstanding we might have wish'd for a boy, I receive her with all the affection possible, and bow with due defference and resignation to the decrees of Providence.[1]

The delighted grandmother had already been making her own preparations for this important arrival and on the following day she sent a note to her son via her principal milliner (her dressmaker):

> Madame Beauvais, who is the bearer of this, is ordered to deliver into yr. hands the cradle for Thursday next which I beg leave to present upon this happy occasion. The Christning suit accompanies this, which is trimmed with the Princesses [? of Wales'] lace, as also the cushion and sheet of the cradle. You will be so good as to have it delivered into the hands of Ldy Dashwood by Madame Beavais that it may not be tumbled before it is wonted. I regret that my finances will not allow me to offer more…[2]

Lady Dashwood had been appointed Governess of the Royal Nursery at Carlton House the previous October. The christening ceremony took place in the Audience Chamber at Carlton House on 11 January in the presence of members of the Royal Family, the Lord Chancellor and household officials. George III and Queen Charlotte, and the Duke and Duchess of York acted as sponsors, and the baby was named Charlotte Augusta after her two grandmothers.

As the mother of fifteen children Queen Charlotte had considerable experience of running a royal nursery and she seems to have maintained a sharp eye on her son's new establishment, advising him and Lady Dashwood when early problems arose. On her advice he issued a set of *Rules Respecting Princess Charlotte of Wales* to Lady Dashwood and Miss Garth, her sub-governess, towards the end of January. This lengthy list of dos and don'ts essentially regulated the hours and activities of the nursery staff – Mrs Bower (the wet nurse), the two rockers and the nursery maid, as well as the 'two Governesses' – and controlled admittance into the nursery to 'prevent the possibility of infection'. For the same reason contact with other members of the Prince's household was limited.[3] Mrs Bower was:

23 (Above) *Princess Charlotte of Wales*, 1812, by Charlotte Jones (1768–1847). (Royal Collection)

This artist painted an unique series of miniatures of the Princess throughout her life. Some are derived from the work of artists like Cosway and Lawrence but for others she was able to portray from life. Earlier miniatures show the Princess with her hair cropped or in childish curls, but now, aged sixteen, she wears it carefully dressed in a more adult style.

24 *Caroline, Princess of Wales, and Princess Charlotte*, 1800–1, by Maria Cosway (1760–1838) and Sir Thomas Lawrence (1769–1830). (Private Collection)

This portrait was originally painted from life by the talented wife of the artist Richard Cosway. The following year Lawrence, a friend of the Princess of Wales, retouched and altered the heads before the portrait was given to Lady Glenbervie; it was she who later criticised the way that Princess Charlotte sat revealing so much of her drawers.

The PRESENTATION — or — The Wise Men's Offering.

The Princess Charlotte was born on the 7th of January 1796. Mrs Fitzherbert is here presenting her to the Prince of Wales Sheridan and Fox are kissing the child's behind.

PRINCESS CHARLOTTE AUGUSTA

25 *The Presentation – or – The Wise Men's Offering*, engraving by James Gillray (1756–1815), published by H. Humphrey, New Bond Street, 9 January 1796. (British Museum)

The satirical prints which were such a feature of the period marked Princess Charlotte's birth on 7 January 1796 with this rather cruel, fantastical, evocation of her first meeting with her father (right) at Carlton House. The Prince's friends and political allies, Charles James Fox and Richard Brinsley Sheridan, obsequiously kiss the royal baby's backside, whilst Michael Angelo Taylor brings in a cradle ornamented with the Prince's crest. The title of the engraving is said to have caused proceedings against Gillray in the Ecclesiastical Court.

26 *Princess Charlotte Augusta of Wales*, 1797, engraving by Francesco Bartolozzi after a pencil drawing by Richard Cosway (1742–1821). (National Portrait Gallery, London)

Several drawings of Princess Charlotte as a baby were made by leading artists of the day, and this engraving was probably the first likeness to be circulated publicly. Richard Cosway was Principal Painter to the Prince of Wales and a personal friend, and was no doubt given special access to the Princess's nursery.

to breakfast at half past eight, dine at two, tea at six, sup at nine, and all attendants to be in bed at eleven and to rise early … The Princess [was] to be moved in her cradle into Lady Dashwood's room when the nursery is cleaned … Her Royal Highness can only be accompanied by one of her Governesses and her nurse in her airings [at half past twelve] … [and the] infant must on no account be kept sleeping out of her cradle or be out of her nursery later than three o'clock …[4]

The birth of Princess Charlotte heralded the breakdown of her parents' brief marriage.[5] They soon began to live separate lives, the Prince's hostile attitude to his wife driving her from Carlton House. Princess Charlotte's nursery was maintained there, but for much of her life she lived separately from both her parents, and was only allowed visits from her mother. In her teenage years she was settled in Warwick House, adjoining Carlton House. The volatile and self-absorbed personalities of her parents and their antagonistic relationship were to blight the young princess's life, and they form a constantly shifting and complex backdrop to the person herself and her clothes. The Prince could be very negligent of his daughter whilst his estranged wife's imprudent behaviour gradually brought about the isolation of Princess Charlotte from anything resembling a family environment. Ageing grandparents, frustrated aunts, and disreputable uncles formed her family background beyond the governesses, tutors and personal staff responsible for the young princess's care and education.

The earliest surviving item associated with Princess Charlotte is a pair of white cotton baby shoes, presumably preserved out of sentiment by her family or attendants (illustration 27).[6] She was a plump and fair-haired small child, already exhibiting her Hanoverian ancestry, who much engaged the affections of the inhabitants at Windsor Castle. To Queen Charlotte she was 'the little beauty', 'the dear little girl', while George III – always at his best with small children – was happy to play on the carpet with his grandchild. In 1797 it was her aunt Princess Elizabeth who reported to her brother the first cutting of his daughter's hair and her baby utterance 'it's all gone'. On her first birthday her aunts sent her bracelets, a necklace, a fan, a doll and a silver rattle.[7]

There is very little information about the dress of the Princess during her childhood but it seems likely that much of the time she wore the simple and practical clothing of cotton, linen or wool then fashionable for children and ubiquitous in portraits of the time (illustration 24). The high quality of the materials, trimmings and sewing would, of course, have distinguished her apparel from that of most children outside the court circle: silk and more elaborate trimmings were probably only resorted to for formal occasions. In 1797, for example, she was dressed in 'a silver [?embroidered] muslin Frock trick'd with silver net' for a visit to her grandmother, whilst in 1804 the Baroness Bunsen described the eight-year-old Princess Charlotte dressed for a similar visit in pale pink covered with lace, and wearing a pearl necklace and brilliants – 'a very pretty and delicate-looking child . . . [who] has the manners of a little queen, though she is as natural as possible'. She could be exuberant and naughty too. Her sub-governess Ann Hayman wrote how she tore 'her caps with showing me how Mr. Canning takes off his hat to her as he rides in the park and I hold up her Royal Highness to the Summer House window'.[8]

A set of accounts for the Princess's household in the years 1800–5 are the only details now surviving about expenditure on her dress in her lifetime.[9] They reveal that her nurses were now pensioned off, and in addition to her governess, sub-governess and dresser Princess Charlotte had an under-dresser, Madame Victoire Petite, who taught her small charge French and music. There was also a sempstress, Miss Pohl. The expenditure on the Princess's wardrobe was relatively modest. Not a great deal is known about the small group of London firms which supplied her clothing and accessories during this early period. Almost certainly some already supplied the Princess of Wales, for whom no clothing accounts now survive, and a few are found in Queen Charlotte's accounts; others may have been recommended by ladies of the court.

The Princess's dress accounts provide only a fragmentary picture of her wardrobe at this early period, when she was between six and nine years old. There are mantua makers and milliners, stay and corset makers, a collar maker, a clear starcher, hatters, glovers, shoemakers, mercers and a linen draper, a hair cutter and a toyman. It is possible that the sempstress Miss Pohl may have made the Princess's body linen (ie underwear and nightwear) from linen supplied by William Londell, the linen draper; his bill of £36 18s 6d is the highest in the accounts, and he may also have supplied fine linen or muslin for Princess Charlotte's dresses. An attractive winter image of the five- or six-year-old is conjured up by the payment of five guineas to Solomon Lange, furrier in Holborn Bars, in 1802 for a muff and tippet. One or two names stand out as of particular interest. 'R. Vandervell, shoemaker', for example, was the maker of Princess Victoria's earliest tiny shoes some fourteen years later, whilst 'Crook & Co., haberdashers' figure as suppliers of socks and then stockings to this same cousin of Princess Charlotte (illustration 79).

Surviving in the Royal Archives are a number of Princess Charlotte's childhood letters in the bold and painstakingly formed script typical of such early essays in letter writing. One written when she was five – presumably under the close supervision of her governess Lady Elgin – is of particular interest as it accompanied an early example of Charlotte's handiwork, a present to her grandfather George III (illustration 28):[10]

27 Baby shoes, 1796.
(MoL 27.40/6, Royal Collection)

The shoes are of soft twilled cotton trimmed with a satin ribbon rosette; they have soles of fine white linen. Their history before they arrived in the London Museum in 1927 is not known, but their style is acceptable for 1796 and their authenticity need not be doubted.

26th of Augst 1801

I hope you are well My Dear Grandpapa and that Dear Grandmamma is so too, I hope you will accept of the Cape String which I have made for you, I wish it were better but it is the first I have ever done.
I am busy at the foot stool for my dear Grandmamma and hope I shall see her soon and Dear Aunts pray come back soon to Kew [Palace] and send for Eggy and me.
I am Dear Grandpapa,
Your Dutiful Child.
Charlotte.

The proffered 'Cape String', a neat plait of fine golden yellow silk threads, was carefully preserved with the letter; wisely, considering its delicate nature, it was never put into service! The King's granddaughter was clearly being introduced to the usual feminine occupations, but there is no evidence that she gained any pleasure from sewing or embroidery or continued to practise either, despite the industrious example set by her grandmother and aunts at Windsor Castle. She became a very able linguist and derived intense pleasure, especially in later unhappy years, from music and reading. Like Princess Victoria she had a drawing tutor but unlike her cousin appears not to have been much interested in this activity; she does seem, however, to have inherited her father's eye for the fine arts, and became a collector of prints.[11]

Unlike Princess Victoria, Princess Charlotte appears not to have kept a journal and instead it is her correspondence with her close friend Mercer Elphinstone (illustration 30), daughter of Lord Keith, that one turns to for details about her life and thoughts from 1811 onwards.[12] At the beginning of the correspondence the Princess was fifteen and Mercer twenty-one. The Princess spent much of her time at Lower Lodge, Windsor and consequently only saw her friend when she was in London. Their correspondence, although Mercer's replies do not survive, therefore took on the exchange of family, political and social news, and, for the Princess, provided a much needed outlet for her unhappiness and confusion. In return Mercer offered sympathy, wise advice and a consistent concern which the Princess otherwise lacked in her life. The letters contain much of historical importance, giving an insider's view of both family and national politics, as well as forming an important source of information about the Princess until her death in 1817. Realising their potential historic value Mercer refused to give up the letters to Prince Leopold after Princess Charlotte's death: without doubt they would have been destroyed.

Early in June 1811 when Mercer, an heiress in her own right, sent the Princess a 'beautiful gown', Charlotte responded in heartfelt gratitude:

> It was a great surprise to me … and indeed I want words to express the <u>warmth</u> of my feelings for so new and unexpected a kindness … put it on that evening [at Windsor] and they [the Queen and her aunts] were all in raptures. Sophy [her aunt Princess Sophia] is so delighted that she intends to have one like it … The Prince [of Wales] was there who <u>hardly spoke to me</u> AT ALL, and when he did his manner was <u>so cold</u> that it was very distressing.

Her father's treatment of her was often unpredictable in this way. [13] A great dandy who delighted to organise the uniforms and dresses of his brothers and sisters, he yet appears never to have taken a similar interest in his daughter's wardrobe, apart from occasional gifts of jewellery.

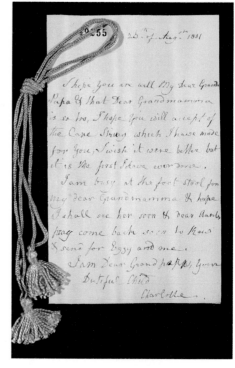

28 Letter and cape string, 1801.
    (Royal Archives)

An early letter from Princess Charlotte to her grandfather George III enclosing her gift of a cape string.

29 Doll with bearing cloth, 1800–10.
    (MoL A25315)

This doll is traditionally known as 'the great doll's baby' and is said to have been given by Princess Charlotte to a childhood playmate, Anne Barnard, the niece of the Prince of Wales's coachman. The story continues that in 1817 Anne was to have become wet nurse to Princess Charlotte's baby. The doll has a wax head attached to a stuffed cloth body. It 'wears' what is in fact a child's pocket over its dress.

30 *The Hon. Mercer Elphinstone (as Miranda),* by John Hoppner (1758–1810). (Marquess of Lansdowne)

The heiress Margaret Mercer Elphinstone, daughter of Admiral Keith, became Princess Charlotte's most trusted confidante following their meeting in 1809, and the Princess's letters to her provide an invaluable insight into her private life and most intimate thoughts. Mercer's friendship and marriage (in June 1816) with Napoleon's aide-de-camp, Comte Flahaut, strained their friendship.

It is disappointing that Princess Charlotte does not otherwise refer to her own dress or that of those around her in this correspondence, leaving us to infer that it perhaps held little interest for her. Certainly the events surrounding her were of great moment, although she herself took small part in public life. There are no parallels to the critical interest and admiration expressed in Princess Victoria's Journal at the same age for the stars of the stage or beauties of the court. Charlotte seems not to have been provided with any companions of her own age. Her dull or disreputable uncles paid irregular visits: Ernest, Duke of Cumberland, for example, sometimes took her riding and one day came and waltzed with her and her sub-governess. She also received visits from her father's mistress, Lady Hertford. There were, of course, her mother's regular visits and also visits from her father; she shared musical accomplishments with both and her father liked hearing her play the piano. He sent musicians from his band so that she could play piano trios, and she particularly enjoyed playing pieces by Mozart and Haydn.

Happily in 1812 she found her own solution to her boredom and unhappiness. 'Studdy, from disliking it, … is now my greatest resource', she informed Mercer. 'Reading is now a great passion of mine, and I read a great deal both serious and light.' She appears to have been allowed to read widely, perhaps exploring her father's library at Carlton House. Her new found devotion to 'studdy' however did little to improve her erratic spelling, which continued to attract severe reprimands from her tutors. On 22 January 1812 she reported her latest literary adventure to Mercer:

> Sence and Sencibility I have just finished reading; it certainly is interesting, and you feel quite one of the company. I think Maryanne and me are very like in disposition, that certainly I am not so good, the same imprudence, &c, however remain very like. I must say it interested me much.

Jane Austen's novel had been published anonymously the previous year and indeed it is easy to see characteristics in Marianne Dashwood with which Princess Charlotte – a year younger than Marianne when the novel opens – might identify. Disarmingly, Charlotte acknowledged her similarly passionate and impulsive nature, and she had likewise turned to books and music as distractions in periods of unhappiness. While the society depicted by Jane Austen was far removed from the glitter and privilege of the Regent's court, Princess Charlotte evidently responded as warmly as readers do today to the novelist's acute observation and characterisation: she would have been all too familiar with the self-indulgent hypocrisy and assiduous flattery which feature so prominently in *Sense and Sensibility*.[14] She doubtless had too a strong emotional response to the romantic escapism of such novels, in which the heroine eventually finds love and security in marriage to the right man. That after all its misery her own life would bring her a similarly happy ending, however briefly enjoyed, was in the circumstances an unexpected blessing.

Engagement, 1812–16

The establishment of the Regency in 1811 as the result of the severe illness and debility of George III brought Princess Charlotte one stage nearer the throne. Despite this, and despite the fact that in January 1812 she turned sixteen, her father continued to treat her as a child, refusing to grant her a more appropriate adult establishment with her own ladies-in-waiting; she was not allowed to be confirmed or to appear at court. When she retaliated by complaining to the Lord Chancellor, Lord Liverpool, a compromise was negotiated which brought to her side, as lady companion, Ellis Cornelia Knight, one of her grandmother's favourite ladies-in-waiting.

Miss Knight's *Autobiography* is a valuable source of information about the Princess's life, and a useful supplement to the Princess's letters during the next four years. She commented that the Regent seemed to have a 'plan of keeping the Princess as long as possible a child'.[1] When in February 1813, although now seventeen, Princess Charlotte was still not allowed to attend the Queen's Birthday Drawing Room, Cornelia Knight noted how greatly the Princess was hurt by her father's harsh disregard. He did, however, allow her to attend a ball he gave at Carlton House the following evening in honour of her grandmother's birthday. It was one of the most glittering events of the season and from the columns of the *Magazine of Fashion* we learn that his daughter wore 'a superb dress of white lace richly embroidered in lama, body and sleeves bordered to correspond, worn over white satin. Her Royal Highness wore a profusion of the finest diamonds. Her dress had altogether a most brilliant and elegant effect.' Miss Knight recalled that it was the first occasion on which the Princess wore court feathers. We might have expected the Princess herself, writing two days later to her friend Mercer, to comment upon her unusually fine appearance but she preferred instead to list her dancing partners and to reveal more of the difficulties and tensions of her existence. As the fifty-one-year-old Regent's own health gave cause for concern, the position of Princess Charlotte was of considerable political importance and the way she was treated by the royal family caused concern to Ministers of State and leading figures at court: they could not, it seems, intervene. The Princess was so much kept from court that she knew only a handful of people at this ball and reported to Mercer the kindness of Lady Jersey who 'danced a great deal <u>for her</u>, and kept as near to me as she could to tell me who the people were &c.'

Closer to the throne than her aunt Mary, Princess Charlotte felt publicly slighted in that 'Pss. M[ary] opened the Ball, tho' it was given for me and was <u>always the cupple above me</u>, as <u>jealous</u> & ill natured the whole night as she could be. I did not care, as I am

31 Embroidered net dress with court train, 1814–16. (MoL 66.79/1)

This dress is an exquisite example of the Regency dressmaker's art. No comparable examples have so far been found which help to confirm the date of the dress or indicate where it was made, nor have any been found illustrated or described in fashion journals. For the moment its origins and association with Princess Charlotte must remain uncertain. What is certain, however, is that it was an extremely costly dress, intended for wear at one of the courts of Europe by a lady of high social status.

not quite so mean as to care about trifles.'[2] She clearly believed that the ball was a compensation for not being allowed to appear at court. No wonder, then, that in her distress she failed to mention her own glittering dress. Kind Lady Jersey, she did allow, 'was very well dressed' and so we know that Charlotte was scrutinising the dresses around her.[3]

The Princess's appearance at this Carlton House ball was later described in some detail by Captain Gronow, the socialite and MP:

> This was the first day that her Royal Highness the Princess Charlotte appeared in public. She was a young lady of more than ordinary personal attractions; her features were regular, and her complexion fair, with the rich bloom of youthful beauty; her eyes were blue and very expressive, and her hair was abundant, and of that peculiar light brown which merges into the golden: in fact, such hair as the Middle-Age Italian painters associate with their conceptions of the Madonna. In figure her Royal Highness was somewhat over the ordinary height of women, but finely proportioned and well developed. Her manners were remarkable for a simplicity and good-nature which would have won admiration and invited affection in the most humble walks of life. She created universal admiration, and I may say a feeling of national pride, amongst all who attended the ball.[4]

The Princess was said closely to resemble her father and her strong Hanoverian features gave her a striking rather than delicately feminine appearance. Lady Rose Weigall, her nineteenth-century biographer, has exactly described an interesting feature of the Princess's face, 'that there was a total lack of shade'.[5] Elsewhere the Princess is reported to have had fair, almost white, eyebrows and eyelashes and light eyes, all set against a rather pale complexion. Her long nose was a distinctive feature of the profile preferred by her portrait painters (illustrations 43, 65). Her hair was usually dressed simply, drawn up from the nape at the back, in a plait or a chignon, with her front hair drawn forward in curls on each temple in the popular style (illustrations 41, 58, 65, 67).[6] For formal occasions it was dressed more elaborately on the top of her head and ornamented with flowers or jewels. The Princess's partiality for wreaths of fresh roses was commented upon by several contemporaries. Her dresses certainly reveal her to have been tall, about 5ft 7½in. (1.71m). The earlier dresses were made for a slighter frame, which became more ample with her marriage.

When in London the Princess lived in Warwick House, adjacent to Carlton House: a very unroyal residence, 'miserably out of repair, and almost falling to ruins', Cornelia Knight thought. The Princess had only a drawing room, bedroom and dressing room (in which her maid slept), on the first floor. Miss Knight's small sitting room and even smaller bedroom adjoined it. Yet despite all its drawbacks this establishment was preferred by the Princess to her lodgings at Windsor where she was even more isolated and had recourse only to the uncertain tempers of her grandmother and aunts. In London she received more visitors, occasionally visited the theatre and exhibitions, and may also have visited the shops of some of her suppliers in nearby Pall Mall.

One reason for the Princess's apparent lack of interest in her dress was that she had a limited income and seems to have preferred to spend it on pictures and other *objets d'art*: 'she loved nothing so much as making presents of valuable trinkets to her young friends', as Cornelia Knight recalled. Her annual dress allowance was £800 and, Miss Knight continued, 'now that balls and birthdays necessarily took up so much money for dresses,

32 Handkerchief, 1815–17.
(MoL 74.100/3)

This large fine lawn handkerchief has embroidery in each corner, garlands of roses alternating with urns of flowers; the embroidery is carried out in stem and satin stitch with needle-made fillings.

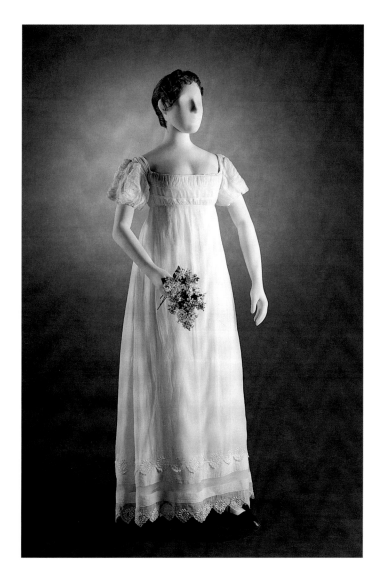

33 & 34 Muslin dress, *c*.1814. (MoL 27.40/3, Royal Collection)

This dress, of a very fine white cotton relieved with ruched panels of cotton and net, has hand-embroidered edgings of flowerheads. It appears to have been lengthened at the hem by discreet net inserts and bands of pleated cotton between two embroidered edgings and may represent a sudden late spurt in growth on the Princess's part. It is noticeably smaller round the upper torso than the Princess's later dresses, and therefore the date of 1814 seems reasonable.

which the Prince and Royal Family expected should be new and splendid, the difficulties were great'. Such difficulties were somewhat overcome by the skills of the Princess's second dresser, Mrs Louis, whose 'contrivances with respect to her Royal Highness's wardrobe, to which she gave the appearance of novelty at a very trifling expense, were truly praiseworthy in a situation where extravagance and airs are so apt to characterise the menial servants of Princesses'.[7] Mrs Louis, German by birth, served the Princess loyally and was given much, if not all, of her wardrobe after her death.[8] A dress which may have belonged to Princess Charlotte at this date, or a little later, bears signs of skilful alterations which it is tempting to attribute to Mrs Louis: it comes from a royal source and the association seems likely although it cannot be proved (illustrations 33–4).[9]

If her father continued to treat the Princess as a child, by the time she was sixteen the government was regarding her as an important political asset. To strengthen the Anglo-Dutch alliance, a marriage to Prince William of Orange (1792–1849) was proposed in 1812, but the Princess was not informed of the plan until February 1813. She was well aware that she was likely to marry a man she was not in love with. 'In our situation we do not marry as others', she acknowledged later, in 1815, to her uncle the Duke of York: '... A marriage with us must always be to <u>covenance</u>.'[10] But she had entertained hopes that as heir presumptive she might be able to remain in England amongst her future subjects: this her father was adamantly opposed to. In December 1813 Miss Knight described how 'we passed the evening at Carlton House. A print of the hereditary Prince was placed on a chair to be looked at, and Princess Charlotte thought it not ugly.' Shortly afterwards, she met the Prince for the first time at a dinner at Carlton House, 'dressed in violet satin trimmed with black lace', and returned home engaged.[11]

The Regent proposed that the marriage should take place the following spring and preparations appear to have begun immediately. Evidence for this is scattered, and Cornelia Knight, who lived so closely with Princess Charlotte during this period, was discreet about what she revealed in her *Autobiography*. The ordering of an elegant yellow landau from the carriagemakers Birch & Son, announced in the *Morning Chronicle* early the following February, drew complaints from the Regent's coachmakers and Miss Knight had to explain the circumstances to the Regent. 'He [also] mentioned Princess Charlotte spending too much with jewellers, and said it was fruitless to conceal anything from him, for tradespeople would talk, and it came to his knowledge.' In 1815 letters to Lord Liverpool from Henry Norton Willis her Comptroller (the manager of her household) mention debts of 'somewhat more than £2000 ... to different Jewellers and Dressmakers', and eventually revealed that in fact they amounted to £14,651 0s 3d. From Mr Willis's long and most elegant explanation it appears that the debts may have built up over a period of years.[12] Although her father certainly knew of these debts he does not appear to have taken any action. The largest sum owed was to the jeweller Thomas Gray of Sackville Street, Piccadilly, on whose premises Elinor Dashwood first encountered the dashing Robert Ferrars in *Sense and Sensibility*: they, like Rundell & Bridge (another creditor), carried out much work for the Regent and must have revealed something of his daughter's spending to him. The Princess also owed money to Colnaghi & Co., print sellers at 23 Cockspur Street, for prints and statuary busts.[13]

That a trousseau was prepared for the Princess also seems certain from a remark of Miss Knight's: 'The Queen bought her [Princess Charlotte's] wedding clothes, and told her she need have only one court dress, as hoop petticoats were not worn in Holland'. The Princess herself described a revealing conversation with her grandmother the following September in a letter to Mercer Elphinstone:

> The Queen entered into money concerns with me, asked who was to pay for the linnen she had allowed me out of the trousseau. When I told her I did not know, she was all surprise, but said she should ask the P.R. She heard from Garth he had no money, and that there was none given him for expences &c. She then hears also that Willis had none either, that my allowance had never been paid, and asked if it was true. I could not deny it. She asked me what it was. I told her. She quite clasped her hands together with astonishment, & said severely, 'I wish the P.R. was not gone. I would have spoke to him. It is no joke.'[14]

The Princess's engagement brought her the official recognition which many felt was greatly overdue. Her long-delayed confirmation was carried out in October 1813 and as her eighteenth birthday approached the King commanded that she be considered of age.[15] Clearly, however, whilst her father controlled so much of her life and household there was neglect regarding its proper running and finance. It seems that no official announcement of the marriage plans had been made by April 1814, and, when news gradually percolated through to English papers from Holland, questions were asked in Parliament.[16] A further advancement for the Princess came in June 1814 when her

HER ROYAL HIGHNESS THE PRINCESS OF WALES

35 *The Princess of Wales in Court Dress,*
4 June 1807. (MoL Z250)

This fashion plate from the women's journal
La Belle Assemblée of July 1807 shows the
hooped dresses and long trains which Queen
Charlotte insisted be worn at formal court
occasions. The style of these dresses changed
little in the next ten years and Princess
Charlotte's court dresses must have looked
very similar. Dressmakers were only
infrequently credited but happily it is
recorded that this dress was made by 'Mrs.
Webb of Pall Mall'. Mrs Webb is known to
have been supplying goods, perhaps dresses,
to the eleven-year-old Princess Charlotte at
exactly this time.

father finally allowed her to be presented formally into court society at a Drawing Room
held by her grandmother. It was an occasion tinged with sadness as the Regent had
publicly banned his wife from attending: Princess Charlotte, still fond of and
sympathetic to her wayward mother, had entertained thoughts of not attending herself.
The Prince Regent furthermore imposed another of his slights on his daughter who 'was
not allowed to dress at home, lest it should be considered that she was going in state, and
… it was proposed that she should dress in Princess Elizabeth's apartments at the top of
the Queen's house'.[17] Consequently her finery, with her dresser Mrs Louis, had to be
transported to Buckingham House (now Palace) and the large crowd which had
gathered to see the Princess in her magnificent court dress had to wait until she left, later
in the afternoon. As was habitual, the press carried extensive descriptions of the rich
formal dresses and suits worn on the occasion, and magnificent the Princess's certainly
appears to have been from the description in the *Lady's Magazine*:

> *The Princess Charlotte of Wales* – An elegant petticoat of rich white satin, with a superb
> border of the same, and a wreath of silver laurel-leaves tastefully intermixed with white
> roses; draperies of rich embroidered patent lace, in silver lama, with superb borders

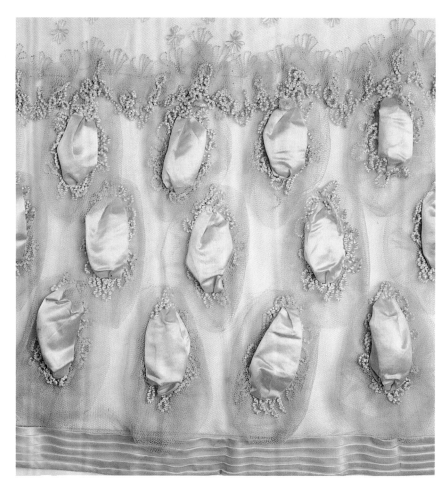

36 Silk net dress, c.1814–16.
   (MoL A15589)

This attractive dinner or evening dress is made of a fine cream silk net with hand-embroidery in floss silk. It is a small dress, and may therefore have been worn by Princess Charlotte at the time of her first engagement, or may even have formed part of her first trousseau. It was acquired by the London Museum in 1915–16.

37 Skirt border of dress shown in illustration 36.

The deep and ornate hem of this dress would normally suggest a later date, nearer 1820. However, English fashion journals of 1814–16 reveal a shortlived fashion for this feature just before the conclusion of the Napoleonic wars. Such decoration was a natural means of changing the outline, heralding fuller skirts; it appears to have been abandoned and then reintroduced towards 1820. The rosettes are formed from puffs of satin ribbon surrounded by net and twisted and coiled silk thread.

formed in festoons, and ornamented in an elegant style with wreaths of silver laurel-leaves and white roses, with rich silver cord and tassels; train of rich striped and fringed silver tissue, tastefully trimmed with silver lama border and rich silver blond lace, and ornamented with beautiful diamonds. Head-dress, a profusion of most beautiful diamonds and ostrich feathers; necklace, ear-rings, armlets, and broach, to correspond.[18]

Altogether the *Lady's Magazine* described over two hundred of these ornate confections, meticulously listed according to rank, but still omitting 'a considerable number of other ladies, who advantageously displayed their taste on this remarkable occasion'. At the end of the exhausting proceedings the Princess was handed into her coach by the Prince of Orange himself.

A matter of days later on 16 June 1814 Princess Charlotte broke off her engagement with the Prince of Orange. Officially her reasons were that both of them needed to reside in their own countries (it had been intimated to her that she would need to accompany the Prince on campaign on the Continent), and that she felt she must stay in England for her mother's sake, none of which she felt was conducive to 'domestick happiness'. In fact the Princess had met and fallen in love with her cousin Prince Frederick of Prussia eight or nine days before. She resisted all her family's efforts to reinstate her engagement.[19] When her father reacted by dismissing every member of her household, she fled to her mother's house but was eventually persuaded to return to Carlton House; her father then sent her to Cranbourne Lodge, in the depths of Windsor Great Park, where she lived in seclusion amongst her new attendants. She was allowed no visits from friends and her correspondence was restricted.

Early in September 1814 Princess Charlotte retired to Weymouth. The conflicts and stress which followed the breaking off of her engagement had made her health a matter of concern.[20] Here, she reported to Mercer, 'It is no small amusement to me whilst dressing to look out of the window and see the ladies dip [in the sea], which I do from here'. Later in the month she described the treatment she herself was receiving:

> Yesterday I went into the bath … at 84, lowering it 10 degrees, and tomorrow is to be my last of the tepid, as it is lowered again to 75, and then I am to bath in the open sea, wh. has always agreed with me, and I have great faith in its doing my general hea[l]th a great deal of good.[21]

Weymouth offered a further diversion: 'a smuggler … who sells most delightful French silk at 5 shillings a yard. I am going to be after him.' Unfortunately we hear no more of this shady character and there is no way of knowing whether the Princess conducted any business with him. The products of the French looms were banned because of the Napoleonic wars and problems in the English silk-weaving industry.[21]

The chaotic state of the Princess's finances was now discovered by her grandmother. 'With regard to the finances', Charlotte confided to Mercer, 'I have not said a word of them, but I fancy some tradespeople at W[indsor] have spoken out, … it has opened their eyes'. The muddle continued and in December she reiterated her concern for her creditors: 'I could not endure the thought of keeping so many people from their money which was their due, & feeling that everything I bought was getting me deeper into debt.' However, as we have already seen, Henry Willis was still trying to resolve these debts in the spring of 1815.[22]

Christmas 1814 found Princess Charlotte back at Windsor, again incarcerated in Cranbourne Lodge. She was still out of favour with her father, although she appears to have celebrated her birthday with him at Brighton in January 1815. Life was dull once more and her future uncertain. She was still under pressure to reconsider the match with the Prince of Orange, and at the same time coming to realise that there was little hope of an alliance with Prince Frederick of Prussia. To be buried 'in the country, to be seen by nobody, and to be thought of by no one' was preferable, she explained to Mercer, 'for I am hurt & disappointed with many things & unhappy and miserable at the life I spend'.[23]

Clearly at this point she had little use for the grand trousseau of the previous summer and its fate is not known. Its existence, however, adds to the difficulties of ascribing dates to the surviving dresses associated with the Princess, and to proving attributions with reasonable certainty. Pinpointing the exact year of manufacture and wear is perilous and usually impossible. Were any of the 1813–14 trousseau dresses subsequently worn by the Princess, and have any survived (illustrations 14, 36)? As the alliance was broken off so suddenly, no descriptive list of the trousseau was published, and there are no detailed payments listed in Queen Charlotte's household accounts which might have provided helpful clues.

Perhaps surviving from this trousseau or a little later is a very attractive silk net dress, which was probably white originally, with a matching court train, from a royal source, which poses great problems of authentication (illustrations 14, 31, 38, 39).[24] The long

train suggests a court dress, but the form of the dress itself, only slightly altered, is simply incompatible with the immense hoops still worn at the English court. The lack of hoops suggests a continental usage. Hoopless court dresses were included in the Princess's 1814 trousseau: some would contest such an early date for this dress and it has been suggested that it may have been made early in 1817 when the Princess may have planned a visit to the French court. However, if her biographers' eulogies have any factual basis, then for patriotic reasons the Princess would not have worn a dress of foreign manufacture in 1817 (p72). It is exactly the form the Princess's hoopless wedding dress must have taken, but does not link up satisfactorily with any of the dresses in her 1816 trousseau (see Appendices 2a & b). Like her other net dresses, this is now extremely fragile, disintegrating and posing considerable conservation problems. It has been altered at the waist and the train unpicked and reassembled, perhaps for wear by an early recipient or later for fancy dress; it is currently shown over a replica satin underdress.

In April 1815 the Prince Regent allowed his daughter to return to London and to resume her place in its social life. He had promised her 'a box at the Play & Opera to go to properly, & … it should not be his fault if I was not much amused this year in town.' But she was still not to have an independent establishment or income. The Prime Minister Lord Liverpool had told her father 'that the Civil List was swelled up to so enormous a sum that he could not presently seek to add more demands on it'.[25]

38 Detail of hem of dress shown in illustration 31.

The ornamentation on this dress absorbed an immense amount of skilled labour. The bellflowers are made using silk-covered wire and net ornamented with silk thread darning. The tiny bellflowers scattered over the net were also handmade: they were stamped out of thin card and wrapped with silk thread before being applied to the net.

39 Back view of dress shown in illustration 31.

Long trains were usual in dresses intended for formal court functions. Their length emphasised the status and importance of the wearer, but they needed to be handled with special skill in crowded gatherings. Many ladies had their trains stepped on and torn! Originally this train would have been attached by a belt with a jewelled buckle.

Riots which broke out in London in March had delayed the Princess's return to London. They were a reaction to the Corn Laws which were passing through the Houses of Parliament at the time. One of the Queen's Drawing Rooms was cancelled because of the violence and Princess Charlotte cautioned Mercer to 'remain at home & not think of going out any where'. Graffiti threatened the Regent, she was told, and he 'was very low & half-frightened'. To add to these fears 'Bony [Napoleon Bonaparte] being landed [from exile in Elba] was a fine source of conversation' at the Windsor dining table.[26]

By 13 April 1815 the worst of the rioting had blown over and Princess Charlotte was able to attend the Queen's resumed Drawing Room. To avoid inciting further trouble she had to forego a carriage ride to Buckingham House in her ornate court dress, which was again noted with admiration, although no detailed description appears to have been published. At the next Drawing Room, on 5 May:

> The Princess Charlotte of Wales went in state with two carriages, and was received with all the high distinctions due to her rank. Her dress on this occasion was exquisitely beautiful. Gold lama and white draperies over a petticoat of rich white satin; beneath the draperies a trimming of superb blond lace, headed with a wreath of white satin and gold twisted trimming; train of rich figured white satin, body elegantly trimmed with rich gold and blond lace; head-dress, plume of ostrich feathers, with a beautiful diadem of brilliants; necklace and ear-rings of diamonds.[27]

It is frustrating that not a single one of these glamorous outfits survives. Today many people assume that dresses of rich silks, ornamented with expensive lace or embroidery, formed the everyday attire of royal princesses. The press descriptions published at the time certainly detail very ornate clothing, whilst many portraits of royal ladies also seem to confirm this assumption. To Princess Charlotte they must have offered a brief diversion from the uncertainties and unhappiness of her daily existence, although in her letters she never alluded to meetings with her dressmaker to plan or to have fitted these extraordinary ceremonial dresses. What became of any of her dresses from 1814 and 1815 is not known, and none of the surviving dresses can, with absolute assurance, be ascribed to this period. Still living on the limited income allowed by her father she must have found them a considerable expense and it is not clear whether they were worn again. It is very likely that most of the time she continued to wear simple muslin or plain silk dresses, much like those of Jane Austen's chief characters, dresses which saw much service and alteration as she grew or gained or lost weight.

Marriage, 1816

A further suitor for Princess Charlotte's hand, however, was already waiting in the proverbial wings. He had proposed marriage in the summer of 1814, immediately after she had so dramatically broken off her engagement to the Prince of Orange. His proposal annoyed the Prince Regent, who was still intent on the Orange alliance. It also annoyed Princess Charlotte: totally infatuated with her cousin Prince Frederick of Prussia, she had no time for this extremely handsome and personable new suitor. Six years older than Charlotte, Leopold of Saxe-Coburg was a younger son of the ruler of a small German principality. He had already made a successful career in the Russian army and in the summer of 1814 had come to London in the suite of the Tsar Alexander I during the visit of the Allied sovereigns.

Princess Charlotte's letters to Mercer Elphinstone during the following six months reveal how, presumably prompted by her friend's wise advice, she gradually came to accept that marriage with Prince Frederick was not a practical proposition. They were both heirs to the thrones of their respective countries, and leaving England was not part of the Princess's plans. By November 1814 Charlotte could see that Prince Leopold was 'the next best thing … [and] I should not scruple, knowing from you what his sentiments and feelings are, to <u>propose him</u> myself to the P.R. This appears very odd, all of it, does it not?', she commented. 'That I should be as wholly occupied & devoted as I am to <u>one</u>, & yet think & talk & even provide for another would appear unnatural in the highest degree if it were written in a novel, & yet it is <u>true</u>, it is not <u>overstrained</u>.'

Her reasoning was entirely practical, however, since she recognised her own need for 'a good tempered man with good sence, with whom I could have a reasonable hope of being <u>less unhappy and comfortless</u> than I have been in a single state'.[1]

By the following January she was able to report to Mercer: 'I have perfectly decided and made up my own mind to marry, and the person I have as decidedly fixed upon is Prince Leopold'. Her hopes were now pinned on 'the Leo' as 'the most eligible connexion for me now'. He had no responsibilities to demand his presence in Saxe-Coburg and was 'perfectly unconnected with the affairs of the Continent & a man of no party in this country', who would therefore be 'more likely than any other Prince to have the interest of it at heart'.[2] Some were critical of the handsome Prince's ingratiating manner and impoverished gentility. 'People say he has only £200 a year, which they calculate is just enough to buy him two coats and a dozen shirts', Cornelia Knight recorded in her diary.[3]

40 *Leopold, Prince of Saxe-Coburg, later King of the Belgians, c.1816,* by Louis-François Aubry (1767–1851). (Royal Collection)

Prince Leopold is believed to have given this tiny miniature to Princess Charlotte around 1816: it is set in a gold locket engraved with the arms of Saxe-Coburg.

41 *Princess Charlotte Augusta of Wales,* watercolour by Richard Woodman c.1816. (National Portrait Gallery, London)

The ostentatious way in which the Princess's left hand is raised to show her wedding ring suggests that this small watercolour portrait was probably painted shortly after the Princess's marriage in May 1816. On her left wrist the Princess wears the diamond bracelet given to her as a wedding present by Prince Leopold.

When it was reported to Princess Charlotte that her father had been heard to praise Prince Leopold, her hopes rose. However, he continued to urge his daughter to marry the Prince of Orange. 'The P.R. <u>must</u> have gone quite mad if he goes on <u>persecuting me</u> with <u>his abominable Du[t]ch man</u>', the Princess exploded to Mercer in March 1815, 'for I hate him more than ever, a nasty insignificant thing that is <u>not worth thinking of once more, much less twice</u>.' Unable to persuade her father she prevailed upon first the Duke of York, and then the Prime Minister, to intervene on her behalf. The Prince Regent was by now preoccupied with political negotiations in the aftermath of Bonaparte's defeat at Waterloo in June 1815. He was irritated by his daughter's latest manoeuvre and refused to consider her request immediately. Familiar with her father's obstinacy, and no doubt guided by wise counsels, she desisted from urging her case for the moment. Her frustrations, however, were poured out to Mercer:

> nothing can be so selfish, so mean, so inconsiderate, so careless of one's comfort, wishes
> or happiness than the P.R. is in everything. He tries one's temper and patience beyond
> anything … Oh what a blessing to be <u>rid</u> of <u>any yoke so galling</u>.[4]

Recognising that she was powerless to alter her father's decision and obviously advised that her best policy was to bide her time, Princess Charlotte had retreated to Weymouth again, for the autumn of 1815. It was 'very dul yet … <u>quiet</u> here … after London and its <u>vicinity</u> wh. never could allow my enjoying an hour in comfort … I think I really could be very comfortable here'.[5]

Princess Charlotte's patience paid off, for when she joined her family at Windsor that Christmas she was delighted to be told that her marriage to Prince Leopold could go ahead. The Regent gave his formal consent after a Privy Council meeting in January 1816 in Brighton and Prince Leopold was invited to return to England in February. After such a long period of unhappiness and uncertainty, Princess Charlotte's life was suddenly transformed. She had 'the happiest face imaginable', her grandmother informed the Prince Regent, and had a calm and reasoned approach to her forthcoming marriage.[6]

Already plans for the wedding were beginning to be made, and on 1 February the Princess informed her friend that she expected to be married at Carlton House '<u>as the Prince of Wales's daughter & not</u> as <u>heiress presumptive</u> to the Crown. It seems as if there would be as little fuss as possible made, & as little delay.' Queen Charlotte was already at work on a new trousseau. 'She was here today to consult and show me some fine lace &c. wh. she would not secure before I had decided about it. She seems very anxious that nothing <u>in her department</u> or on <u>her part</u> should be wanting or delayed', Princess Charlotte told Mercer on the very day that Prince Leopold landed at Dover.[7] He arrived in London on 21 February 1816 and almost immediately joined the Prince Regent at Brighton. Presumably in the ensuing days he and the Regent were able for the first time to get to know each other, and then after a few days they were joined by Queen Charlotte, her daughters and granddaughter. It was the first meeting between Princess Charlotte and Prince Leopold since the tumultuous summer of 1814. 'I find him quite charming', she reported immediately to Mercer, '& I go to bed happier than I have ever done yet in my life. We have had a delightful e[venin]g together, full of long conversations on different subjects interesting to our future plans of life &c.'[8]

Although a biographer writing just two years later might be suspected of undue flattery, it does seem likely that Prince Leopold was a popular choice for the young heir to

A German Suitor at the Court of Wales.

42 *A German Suitor at the Court of Wales,*
engraving by Charles Williams
(*fl.*1797–1830); published by J.
Sidebotham, No. 96 Strand, March
1816. (British Museum)

Most caricaturists chose to portray Prince
Leopold in his smart military uniform,
which made him instantly recognisable.
Here a gouty Prince Regent introduces him
to Princess Charlotte. The numerous
'credentials' he carries include one drawing
attention to the generous government
settlement on the couple which had
attracted so much public censure. Behind
Princess Charlotte are her grandmother and
three of her spinster aunts.

the throne. From being a supernumerary in the train of the Tsar of Russia, this twenty-four-year-old Prince suddenly found himself the focus of attention in London. His hotel, we are told, 'was crowded with grandees, and besieged with the less exalted'. Naturally he was courted by sections of the nobility keen to make the acquaintance of this potentially influential royal consort, whilst 'the common people were anxious above all things to have the pleasure of cheering and huzzaing him'.[9]

Such a royal alliance could be expected to have little effect upon the social unrest and economic difficulties which engulfed England and were so visible in the capital at that time. Yet it offered hope for the future. The extravagant and immoral lifestyles of the Regent and his brothers were resented by the populace and cruelly caricatured. In contrast the twenty-year-old heir to the throne displayed no inclination to follow in their footsteps, nor to emulate her mother's equally unseemly lifestyle. Although still kept out of the public eye by her father, Princess Charlotte had already become a popular figure, and was known to be resolute in her desire to remain in England amongst her future subjects. Prince Leopold's exceptional looks, military record, and impecunious and apolitical background all hinted at a personal attachment which captured the public imagination.

Events now moved rapidly. The date for the wedding ceremony was set at 4 April 1816. A financial settlement for the pair proved troublesome, although the outcome was generous: £60,000 a year 'to maintain an establishment which without being either extravagant or profuse' would be 'suitable to their rank and station.' In addition there would be a one-off government grant of '£40,000 for furniture, plate, etc., £10,000 for personal equipment and £10,000 for jewells'. Neither bride nor bridegroom had the personal resources to set up home for themselves: 'if we were to furnish everything for ourselves we should be ruined', the Princess noted. It is obvious that both she and Prince Leopold were averse to living beyond their means, frequently having to counter the Regent's ideas for staffing beyond their income.[10]

The Princess's trousseau was already well advanced, in the capable hands of the Queen. By 13 March Charlotte was able to tell Mercer that

> the trousseau ... is entirely done. The things are given out to be made, so that there is no further trouble about that. She [Queen Charlotte] has bespoke me a very fine diamond necklace, but waits the Regent's further orders as to what more jewels she is to get ...

This is the sum total of the Princess's comments on the fine array of dresses currently being made for her in the fashionable workrooms of London! Her grandmother probably followed a process similar to her preparation of a trousseau for Charlotte's mother in 1794–5. Her suppliers in 1816 are not known, but the mercer William King held an official appointment to Princess Charlotte's household and it is reasonable to assume that he provided some of the fine silks for her trousseau. Work on the Princess's trousseau seems to have been divided between two London dressmakers. Mrs Triaud made her wedding dress, going-away outfit and eight dresses, whilst Mrs Bean, whose work was often illustrated in Ackermann's *Repository* at about this time, was responsible for twenty-six dresses. She may also have provided the eighteen lace-trimmed caps, of both English and continental lace, which were included in the trousseau (Appendix 2a).[11]

Jewellery was of first importance in any aristocratic wardrobe. Jewels were vastly more expensive than the dresses they complemented and, as is still the case today, demonstrated more than anything else their owner's rank and wealth. Careful selection was therefore imperative. Queen Charlotte's love of jewels is well attested and the large and valuable collection she amassed in her lifetime was much worn and loved by Queen Victoria until in the 1850s she was finally forced to relinquish them to her uncle the King of Hanover.[12] The jewellery which the Regent had acquired in 1814, anticipating his daughter's marriage to the Prince of Orange, still seems to have been in his possession in February 1816, when Princess Charlotte reported to Mercer:

> The 15 thousand pounds worth of Orange jewels I find are to be sold. [Princess] Elizabeth is going to bye the fine emerald cross & broach to it ... & I am going to see what remains yet of the perls, that I may retain some for myself out of my own money, as I have no perls belonging to me, & I suppose the P.R. will give me the fine diamonds, he intended before, but wh. he returned to Bridge, who, however, has not sold them as yet.[13]

In March we find the Regent quizzing his daughter about her mother's jewels,

> as wanting to know what was become of them ... as he wished to get them & give them to me. This I dissuaded him from as highly indelicate, tho' I told him I believed the box's containing them were at Drummonds [bank] where they used all to be kept. He suspects she has taken them abroad & sold them.[14]

During the same conversation in March the Regent revealed his new intentions regarding his daughter's wedding jewels:

He intends to give me a diamond necklace, but at my request, not the great, large ugly thing he had fixed upon when I was going to marry P.O., as I don't wear earings & bracelets are not seen. The money for them is to be given for one of the pearl necklaces & bracelets that I had chosen for the 15 thousand pound of the P.O. I am not to get any of the other jewels tho' they are all there still to be disposed of. I shall get the prices of them all for C[oburg – ie Prince Leopold], who wishes to give me something very much, but does not know what, or what is customary or proper.

Her fiancée, she continued, 'has a great horror of debt & I have had a good lecture upon economy & extravagance already'. In the end Prince Leopold is reported as having given his bride a diamond bracelet. None of her other jewellery is identifiable in her portraits.[15] In a later letter she reported that

> the diamond necklace is done, & very handsome for 3,000 pound. I am also to have the diamond belt & 2 head ornaments <u>we ordered together</u>, & the 2 strings of perls for perl bracelets, wh., with what I have in jewels, will do very well, as I would rather less money were spent on them, & more upon plate, furniture & such like things.[16]

As the weeks passed it must have become apparent to the young Prince of Saxe-Coburg that he had embarked upon a challenging undertaking. Had he been adequately warned? Princess Charlotte's letters show that he was already establishing his authority with her as head of their household, a relationship her grandmother had been trying to prepare her for. Thus she had already been persuaded to relinquish riding:

> <u>he</u> [Prince Leopold] <u>does not much like</u> a ladies <u>riding</u>, he thinks it too violent an exercise, & so I have [given] over to him my saddle horses & grooms & riding master who is to break in horses for him &c. … L. says we shall walk a great deal together, & that he intends to have me a great deal, & for <u>very long</u>, & that if there are parties he could go to & that I could not, why that he should decline them, preferring to stay with me & not leave me alone.

His future wife, who had ever been ready to flout authority when her own wishes were denied, was now happy to comply with Prince Leopold's bidding, so enthusiastic was she about him. 'I think him very talented, with a 1000 resources – musick, singing, drawing, agriculture, farming & botany – besides all he is a capital Italian scholar, so I have <u>everything</u> almost I could <u>wish</u> & <u>desire collected in one</u>.'[17]

Something of the prospect facing the Prince was reported by his friend Archduke John of Austria in a letter to the Austrian foreign minister Prince Metternich, written in March 1816:

> She surprises everybody who has not been told beforehand of her ways. A well-set, young, beautiful woman with the features of a man in her conversation, intelligence, knowledge and wit: for the rest unrestrained merriment, disingenuousness, even a bluntness that is astonishing. She seems to have a good disposition, but is self-willed and quite indifferent to the knowledge that is required of a woman of distinction. A curious mixture.
>
> … The Princess has no regard for her father, grandmother, and many of her uncles and aunts. So Prince Leopold stands between the Princess and the many who are devoted to her, on the one side, and her father, grandmother, and aunts and uncles on the other. He has to deal differently with each. He has the difficult task of keeping peace and unity. I certainly do not envy him.[18]

43 *Princess Charlotte Augusta of Wales*, 1816, by Peter Turnerelli (1774–1839). (National Portrait Gallery, London)

Princess Charlotte is recorded as having given a two hour sitting for this bust on her wedding morning; it is apparently a good likeness and displays well the Princess's inherited Hanoverian features. There is a companion bust of Prince Leopold in the Royal Collection and also one of the Princess made by Turnerelli in 1801–2, just after his appointment as Sculptor in Ordinary to Queen Charlotte and the Royal Family. He taught sculpture to the Princess's mother.

A BRIGHTON HOT BATH, or Preparations for The WEDDING!!

His future father-in-law posed quite other problems for the Prince, who was fast discovering the difficulties of life within the English royal establishment. April came and the wedding ceremony was postponed at least twice. One postponement, the Regent would have Leopold believe, was entirely due to a bilious attack of Princess Charlotte's, but it was actually caused by the Regent's severe gout. Then he attempted to influence Leopold's attitude to the Princess's friends, a move which vexed the Prince and put him on his guard with his father-in-law. Knowing her father so well the Princess was concerned that Leopold would succumb to his bullying ways. Although kept very much apart, and meeting only with chaperons present, the couple were wholeheartedly in agreement about their future. Prince Leopold had for the time being retired to Weymouth, preferring its quiet to the crowds and attentions of London.

Eventually the date of 2 May 1816 was decided upon. The Princess had been disappointed by her father's insistence that the ceremony be private, an evening affair at Carlton House, with only family, political and court officials present. 'I am aware like you of the Regent's unpopularity', she commented to Mercer, '& if this is a <u>smuggled</u> wedding it will <u>put</u> the <u>finishing stroke</u> to it all.'[19] Her dilemma was that raising objections could produce further delays and therefore, to escape from her father's restrictive dominance, she offered no resistance on this point. Much of the court, as well as the populace, was thereby deprived of any opportunity to witness this important and glamorous occasion.

Meantime much consideration was being given to suitable homes for the Princess and her husband. It was eventually settled that Claremont, Lord Clive's old home near Esher in Surrey, would be purchased for the couple by the government as a country residence.[20] Accommodation in London was less easy to resolve and as a short-term measure Camelford House, fronting Oxford Street, at the top of Park Lane, was leased for the first year of their

44 *A Brighton Hot Bath, or Preparations for the Wedding!!*, engraving by George Cruikshank (1792–1878); published by J. Sidebotham, No. 96 Strand, April 1816. (British Museum)

Cruikshank, one of the most famous satirists of his day, used this scene of the bathing of Prince Leopold before his marriage to refer obliquely to the Regent's own unhappy marriage. There was already public concern about the outcome of the forthcoming royal marriage and this is alluded to in the picture on the wall anticipating a fight between the couple, wielding bellows and a sausage; sausages were frequently used as symbols of sexual innuendo. Queen Charlotte pours hot water on Leopold, whilst Lord Chancellor Eldon uses his wig to scrub him.

marriage. The Princess included few details about the equipping of these two residences in her letters and little is now known about their decorative features, furniture or paintings. On the day before her wedding the Princess is reported to have visited Camelford House with Prince Leopold, Queen Charlotte, and Princess Mary, and to have spent about two hours inspecting it – and finding it not altogether suitable for her new role in society. The Queen and Princesses then viewed Princess Charlotte's trousseau, a visit which is reported in a single source.[21] This was presumably at Warwick House or Carlton House.

Although the Prince Regent had insisted that the wedding ceremony be conducted privately within Carlton House, Princess Charlotte's position as granddaughter of the King and daughter of his heir the Regent still required that she have a 'bridal dress' befitting her rank. Resolving the niceties of precedence and rank was not the sort of thing the Prince Regent could bring himself to deal with promptly and decisively, a trait which infuriated his aged mother and, no doubt, his household officials.

Clearly the Queen continued to advise her son and to make a great many arrangements for the ceremony, just as she had done for his own marriage twenty-one years earlier (p33). In March 1816 she reported to him the precedents of his aunt Princess Augusta when she married the Duke of Brunswick in 1764 in the Great Drawing Room at St James's: 'it being a Private wedding H.R.H. was dressed in the usual Court Dress'. The notebook of Robert Chester, Assistant Master of Ceremonies, confirms that discussions about the status of Princess Charlotte's wedding ceremony had been taking place. He seems to have scampered backwards and forwards among the protagonists in this mini-drama, exploring precedents, advising, negotiating, explaining, and no doubt pacifying – making the multitude of behind-scenes administrative arrangements and agreements necessary to bring the ceremony into being. He eventually recorded that those invited were to be 'in full dress, but the Ladies without Hoops. The Ceremony will take place at nine o'clock'.[22]

Very similar descriptions of Princess Charlotte's wedding trousseau appear in several contemporary fashion journals; these in turn seem to be the source for the lengthy descriptions in the biographies published just after her death. It is possible that originally there was a common source, the forerunner of later official press handouts. These reports do not, however, provide information about the dressmakers, milliners and other London craftworkers and tradespeople who helped to assemble the Princess's trousseau. As we have seen, she rarely touched upon such matters in her letters, and no accounts or bills now survive to provide this information.[23] (See Appendix 2a.)

Reporting the royal wedding in their 1 June 1816 issue *La Belle Assemblée* claimed to have been 'gratified with a sight of the wedding dresses [the trousseau] of this amiable and illustrious female', and went on to give the following description of 'the bridal dress':

> silver lama on net, over a silver tissue slip, embroidered at the bottom with silver lama in shells and flowers. Body and sleeves to correspond, elegantly trimmed with point Brussels lace. The manteau was of silver tissue lined with white satin, with a border of embroidery to answer that on the dress, and fastened in front with a splendid ornament.

The dress associated with Princess Charlotte's wedding is now exceptionally frail (illustrations 47–9). The bodice and skirt are of a fine silk net now disintegrating through age and the effects of long periods of display. Evidence of numerous alterations has prompted a reappraisal of each of the components which make up the present dress – separate bodice, skirt, train and underskirt. Careful comparison of this dress with the various reports in fashion journals, coupled with inconsistencies in the dress itself, suggest that at some distant time, presumably before the dress entered the London Museum's collection in 1927, it was assembled from a group of unpicked parts (illustration 49). Almost certainly these elements came from two, and perhaps three, different dresses. They have fitted together so well, reflecting the generalised representation of Princess Charlotte in her 'bridal dress' that accompanied *La Belle Assemblée's* description, that the inconsistencies have not previously been questioned or examined.

La Belle Assemblée's report, like those of other fashion journals, implies that shell ornaments formed an integral part of the decorative scheme of the whole dress, and were to be found in the ornamental hem of the dress as well as edging the mantle. Shells certainly still ornament the bodice, whilst a sizeable length of shell edging survives attached to a strange 'apron' front to the dress (illustrations 46, 49). This extraordinary crude addition, with roughly cut sides hidden under the train, is entirely without historical precedent and can only be interpreted as a much later reuse of the original 'manteau' edging.

The present skirt and train, having a completely different design in silver embroidery, must have belonged to another dress of similar standing to the 'bridal dress'. An obvious possibility might be one of the other 'wedding dresses', but it is difficult to find a satisfactory match amongst these descriptions (Appendices 2a & b). One has an associated 'manteau' but descriptions of the embroidered designs fail to match up conclusively. Was this, instead, one of the Princess's few formal dresses from before or after her marriage? Could it, indeed, be a survivor from the 1814 trousseau?[24] The will of Princess Charlotte's dresser Louisa Louis, made in 1838, specifically mentions the Princess's wedding dress: 'I also give and bequeath to Lady Gardiner the wife of Sir Robert Gardiner a silver Tissue Dress covered with silver net worn by her late Royal Highness the Princess Charlotte on her marriage'.[25] The history of the dress between 1838 and 1927 is not known.

There is no reason to doubt the association of all the individual parts of the present ensemble with Princess Charlotte. Dresses of this distinction and high quality were less easy to recycle than utilitarian day dresses which were more readily passed on to others, altered, and eventually worn out. Boxes of unpicked complete or, much more often, incomplete dresses are to be found in many private attics and public collections, and re-assembling them or determining their original form is a frequent task for museum curators. It is very usual for the large skirt sections to be reused first, leaving behind many lone bodices.

The report in *La Belle Assemblée* specifically stated that Princess Charlotte wore a court dress for her wedding, and this conjures up images of those lampshade-like draped hoop ensembles which Queen Charlotte so perversely forced upon aristocratic women. The engraving which accompanied the report does not show the bride in a hooped court dress, nor do two sketches of the ceremony, apparently by an eyewitness, now in the Royal Collection (illustration 51).

The ornaments Princess Charlotte wore with the dress were mainly composed of diamonds, those glittering status-giving jewels which, to her regret, ate up so much of the Princess's nuptial purse. As *La Belle Assemblée* relayed to its extensive readership:

> Her fair hair, elegantly yet simply arranged, owed more to natural beautiful wave than to the art of the *friseur*; it was crowned with a most superb wreath of brilliants, forming rosebuds with their leaves … [her] jewellery is most superb; beside the wreath, are a diamond hairpin, ear-rings, and an armlet of great value, with a superb set of pearls.[26]

45 'The Crimson Drawing Room, Carlton House', from W. H. Pyne, *Royal Residences* (1819), vol. II.

This impressive room was specially fitted up for Princess Charlotte's wedding ceremony: a temporary altar with a crimson velvet altarcloth was set up in front of a fireplace, and crimson cushions, prayer-books, plate and massive candlesticks were brought in from the royal chapels in St James's. Princess Charlotte is on record as disliking her father's lavish taste in furnishing and she took a more restrained approach at Claremont.

None of these jewels appears to have survived, none appears in the known portraits of the Princess, and the exact form they took is now entirely speculative. The 'armlet' was possibly that purchased by Leopold out of the 1814 jewels, and this is believed to be shown on his wife's wrist in one portrait (illustration 41). Her biographer Robert Huish described 'a necklace of large brilliants of finest lustre, with large drop earrings to correspond, and a brilliant cestus [ornamental belt] of great value'. His claim that 'the wedding-dress alone cost above £10,000' needs to be interpreted as including the price of the jewels and, perhaps, the whole trousseau.[27]

The glittering figure of the Princess at her marriage, in such contrast to the simplicity she preferred in private life, was the centre-piece of a stunning gathering and it is sad indeed that no detailed permanent visual record of the occasion was made (illustration 51). Prince Leopold was equally resplendent in 'a full British uniform, decorated with the insignia of the new Hanoverian order of the Guelphs, and other emblems of knighthood of Saxony, and of Austria, Russia, the Netherlands, Prussia, Bavaria, Wurtemberg, and Denmark', according to the *Annual Register*: 'His Serene Highness wore a magnificent sword and belt, ornamented with diamonds, and studded with various gems.' The Prince Regent and his brothers also wore military uniforms embellished with insignia, whilst the court dresses of the Queen, Princesses and nobility were, according to *La Belle Assemblée*, 'particularly splendid; we are sorry our limits do not allow us to enter into particulars'. Nevertheless their reporter, perhaps allocated a place in a corridor within Carlton House, could not resist mentioning 'the superb lama dress, so beautifully wrought with silver lilies, of the Marchioness of Cholmondeley'. Needless to

46 Detail: bodice of Princess Charlotte's 'wedding dress'.

Contemporary fashion journals show that lace with scallop shells was generally very fashionable (illustration 55). The rich embroidery on net was formed by wrapping strips of plain or patterned silver or gold 'thread' (*lama*) through the net ground to form the required design. It is typically found on court dresses, and must have been extremely expensive. Nothing seems to be known about the professional embroideresses who carried out such work, but it is assumed that the Princess's dresses were ornamented in London. The silk net ground of the dress is an early example of a machine-made net.

47 Princess Charlotte's 'wedding dress', 1816. (MoL 27.40/1/3, Royal Collection)

This photograph of the 1970s shows the dress as it has always been displayed by the Museum. It is now believed that the dress is an assemblage of pieces from two, or even three, dresses. The 'apron' front is a completely untypical feature on a dress of this period; the padded rouleau which heads the scallops on it is more usually found on contemporary court trains. The borders of the skirt and train are worked with a totally different design: it is inconceivable that this would have been tolerated in a royal wedding dress. A cloth of silver underskirt now associated with the dress shows evidence of being altered from a court dress and is more likely to have belonged to a second, or even third, dress.

48 Back view of Princess Charlotte's 'wedding dress'.

The bodice of the dress, with its elegant dipping neckline, is probably little altered; it seems inconceivable that this would have been covered by a mantle. The present train almost certainly reflects the material and cut of the original bridal 'manteau'.

49 Photograph showing original (yellow tint) and 'wrong' (red tint) parts of Princess Charlotte's 'wedding dress'.

say this, like all the other dresses worn on this occasion, and at all the Queen's Drawing Rooms, has left no trace. Princess Charlotte's dresses are an exceptional survival. [28]

Robert Huish, whose biography of Princess Charlotte was published in 1819, includes an intriguing story about the making of a royal mantle as part of the bridal ensemble. It is a unique account, perhaps gathered from a personal contact in the court circle, and has the ring of authenticity.

> It is the etiquette of the royal princesses to wear a superb mantle at their marriage, which is afterwards the perquisite of the lady in waiting; but, *after* the mantle was made, it was discovered that it is only a King's *daughter* who is entitled to the distinction of the mantle: the Princess Charlotte, however, being only the *grand-daughter*, could not, in strict conformity with etiquette, and without infringing on the privileges of the King's daughters, be married in the royal mantle. This is certainly a distinction not without a difference, but the latter is so slight, that as the expense of the mantle had been incurred, the etiquette might have been waived; … the mantle was carefully laid by …[29]

What he was describing was the mantle of red velvet and ermine worn on state occasions to denote rank. The Princess of Wales, Princess Charlotte's mother, had worn just such a mantle in 1795 at her wedding, and so too had Queen Charlotte when she married George III in 1761 (illustration 21). In her correspondence with the Regent regarding the precedent of the marriage of his aunt Princess Augusta in 1764 Queen Charlotte noted that 'It is only on Public weddings that the Robe & Coronet are worn & that Bride Maids attend'.[30] It is therefore possible that the Queen had put in hand the making of the mantle before the form of the ceremony had been finalised. Given her husband's state of health and the fact that her son, as Regent, was acting in place of the King, she may well have felt that Princess Charlotte was *almost* the daughter of a king. Perhaps the Regent, occasionally more of a stickler for correct form than his mother, was the one to be rigid about court etiquette in this instance. He was possibly unwilling to allow such public acknowledgement of his daughter's proximity to the throne.

The creator of Princess Charlotte's wedding dress, the London dressmaker Mrs Triaud, has not been located in any trade directories and nothing at all is known of her from other sources. Many dressmakers were listed in contemporary trade directories, but many others, like Mrs Triaud, seem to have refrained from subscribing to these valuable publications. Personal recommendation presumably brought them sufficient clients, and in this way they also maintained an exclusivity important to their status. Nothing is known of the size of their workforces, charges for the work they undertook, use of imported silks, laces or embroideries, or their creativeness in introducing novelties. It may be that Queen Charlotte selected Mrs Triaud to make this dress and some of Princess Charlotte's trousseau dresses for the same reasons that in 1794 she chose Madame Beauvais to make the Princess of Wales's wedding dress – as 'the only person capable to command as many hands as we shall want to accomplish it in time'. It seems likely that Mrs Triaud, like Madame Beauvais, had already been supplying Queen Charlotte with dresses.[31] The stuff of Princess Charlotte's wedding dress only rarely survives in museum collections: the very fine silk threads which form the net have a short life and, once the process of disintegration is well advanced, this presents considerable conservation problems. Descriptions of court dresses in fashion journals reveal that these rich embroideries, in gold or silver strip (*lama*), were much in vogue despite what must

The Princess Charlotte of Wales, & Prince Leopold of Cobourg.

50 *Princess Charlotte and Prince Leopold*, 2 May 1816, engraving from *La Belle Assemblée,* June 1816.

The artist responsible for this popular print almost certainly would not have been present at the wedding. Instead he would have relied upon existing engraved portraits and a written description to help him produce a reasonably reliable image. He was obviously not familar with court dress and guessed incorrectly that the train was attached at the shoulders: it seems probable that he was confused by the use of the term 'manteau' for a court train and translated it into the semblance of a state mantle.

51 *The Marriage of Princess Charlotte of Wales and Prince Leopold of Saxe-Coburg, 2 May 1816,* attributed to Richard Westall (1765–1836). (Royal Collection)

The artist appears to have been an eyewitness of the ceremony. His rough sketch is the only record of the occasion and no oil painting seems to have resulted. The bridal couple is shown kneeling at the altar, with the Prince Regent to their left. The sketch is too rough to help with the problems of the Princess's dress. Some figures are reversed in preparation for engraving. The artist later became Princess Victoria's drawing master.

have been their considerable cost. Virtually nothing is known about the workrooms carrying out this work, in London or in Paris, despite the fact that quite surprising quantities of this luxury fabric were absorbed by the fashionable world in London.

We know of a very few suppliers of textiles and other such goods to Princess Charlotte at this time. A number of her shoes survive and some bear the label of Despa, Cordonnier des dames, 32 South Moulton Street, Grosvenor Square (illustration 59). The makers of her shoes in childhood, R. Vandervell, still held her warrant at her death (as Frederick George Vandervell, 16 Cavendish Street), and may well have continued to supply the Princess with footwear. They were to make a pair of tiny black satin shoes for her baby cousin Princess Victoria shortly after her death and the label inside these shows that they supplied other royal ladies at this time (illustration 79). A list of Princess Charlotte's household officers in 1816 ends with the names of William King, silk mercer, and Mary Hillhouse, 'Linen Maker by special appointment' – presumably because they were involved in supplying the Princess's new establishments. William King, of 37 Pall Mall, had long been the Regent's major supplier of furnishing silks for his spectacular interiors at Brighton Pavilion and Carlton House. He had been called in by Queen Charlotte in 1794–5 to supply silks for Princess Caroline's trousseau, and went on to furnish quantities of goods to William IV and the young Queen Victoria. A contemporary account of Princess Charlotte informed readers that her 'body linen was made at Hillhouse's, in Bond Street. The articles are marked with P. C. and a crown, as ordered

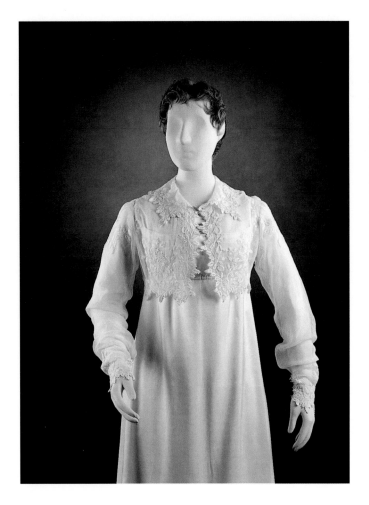

by her majesty. This included her spencers, pocket handkerchiefs, etc. ...' Mary Hillhouse of New Bond Street will also be heard of again as a supplier of baby clothes to Princess Victoria (pp82, 86).[32]

After her wedding ceremony Princess Charlotte changed into a travelling outfit for the journey to Oatlands, the Duke of York's country house near Weybridge, where she would spend her honeymoon. *La Belle Assemblée* was once again privy to many details of this outfit:

> a dress of white corded silk, trimmed with flounces at the bottom of Brussels lace; with ruff and cuff to correspond: over this ... a white satin pelisse, trimmed with ermine; and ... an elegant white satin hat ornamented with blond, and a beautiful plume of white feathers.[33]

No one records whether Prince Leopold changed out of his uniform into something perhaps a little more comfortable.

Two days later the Princess wrote to her friend Mercer:

> I promised you to behave well, ... & everyone complimented me upon the composure & dignity of my manner & the audible manner in wh. I answered the responses ... my last word was with [Princess] Lieven to intreat she would give you a faithful account, & to my maid just as I drove off to go & tell you how I looked.[34]

Not all was well with her trousseau, however, for she was complaining 'Conceive what a <u>bore</u>, hardly a thing of my new clothes fit, so I have been obliged to get a girl from

52 & 53 Embroidered muslin jacket, 1814–17. (MoL 174.100/6)

Naturalistic moss roses are the main element in the fine white embroidery on this jacket or over-bodice. The workmanship is exquisite and there is a matching skirt piece which must originally have been attached at the hem of a coloured silk underdress. So far it has not been possible to find a similar ensemble in contemporary fashion plates. The high quality of the work on these pieces suggests that they may originally have come from one of Princess Charlotte's two trousseaux.

the village to help Louis [Mrs Louis, her dresser] to alter some of them, that I might have something to put on'. Her trousseau, it has to be remembered, had been completed some weeks before, in readiness for an earlier wedding date. In the meantime Princess Charlotte had obviously put on some weight, happy and relaxed about her future. Another unwelcome problem had been 'a very <u>unexpected</u> & <u>undesired</u>' visit from the Prince Regent only two days into the honeymoon!

> He sat some time with us and appeared in good humor ... [discussing] the merits & demerits of such & such a uniform, the cut of such a coat, cape, sleeve, small clothes [breeches], &c. In short for 2 hours & more I think we had a most learned dissertation upon every reqt. under the sun wh. is a <u>great mark</u> of the <u>most perfect good humour</u>. I have since heard ... that he was <u>delighted</u> with his visit & with both of us.

A few days after this parental visitation the couple drove over to Claremont, near Esher, 'wh. is a <u>real paradise</u>. I was [shown] quite over the house & kitchen garden wh. is <u>princely</u>, & I am quite clear it is the <u>most fit royal residence</u> that can be found anywhere'. All in all, although Charlotte admitted not feeling 'much at my ease or quite comfortable yet in his society', with Prince Leopold her life had begun to take a much happier turn.[35]

Married Life and Death, 1816–17

Princess Charlotte and Prince Leopold were to enjoy less than two years of married life together before tragedy struck. For both, the marriage was the happiest period in their lives, and in old age King Leopold looked back with nostalgia upon these months.

The honeymoon at Oatlands was brief. Within eight days the couple was back in London, the focus of numerous formal functions commemorating their marriage. Mourning had meanwhile been adopted at court, on the death of the Empress of Austria, and Princess Charlotte's earliest appearances in London were in sombre black. There is no way of knowing whether her wardrobe always included such mourning attire, as seems to be the case today with royal wardrobes, or whether, and perhaps more likely, an urgent order had been despatched to her dressmaker. New clothes were *de rigeur* for the Princess's first public appearances after her marriage and, whilst previously-worn mourning attire would serve her immediate needs in her private life, the requirement for mourning wear to be included in her trousseau was obviously not foreseen – and may not have been regarded as appropriate. The production of a simply adorned black dress, in a large well-organised London dressmaking establishment, was probably the work of two days, three at the most. Loyal addresses had already been presented to the Queen and the Regent on the occasion of the marriage, and etiquette required that Princess Charlotte and Prince Leopold receive additional deputations on their return to London from, for example, the Lord Mayor, Sheriffs and Common Councilmen of the City of London, and from both Houses of Parliament.

On 10 May 1816 the young couple were the centre of attention at the Queen's Drawing Room, held to allow them to receive the congratulations of the nobility. It was reported that some three thousand spectators flocked to Buckingham House, many arriving in the morning to take up advantageous positions both outside and inside the palace to view the more privileged as they passed through the entrance hall and corridors, into the reception rooms. Drawing Rooms associated with important occasions attracted particularly large attendances of the nobility, anxious to be observed displaying their loyalty, and to mix with their peers. Carriages blocked all the streets in the vicinity and totally choked traffic throughout the West End of London.

Princess Charlotte's appearance at this Drawing Room was said to have been 'unusually superb': her grandmother, the Queen, had presumably devised this magnificence intentionally. Contemporary descriptions of the dress vary, but her biographer Robert Huish described it as consisting of :

54 Dinner or evening dress, 1817. (MoL 74.100/1)

The style of this dress is most distinctive and it clearly absorbed a great deal of hand labour. Dresses shown in contemporary fashion plates are rarely so richly ornamented, and indeed no similarly ornate dress has yet been identified in another museum collection. Fashion plates echo the passing practice of adding a lace frill at the hem: this presumably was a device drawing attention to the widening hemline.

a petticoat of rich silver tissue, and draperies of net, most magnificently embroidered in silver lama, with deep borders, beaded with a costly silver rolio; the draperies elegantly supported with a most brilliant cord of real silver bullion, and very superb silver tassels below the draperies; the dress finished with a most beautiful and elegant garniture in silver lama and tulle, most tastefully designed; mantua of rich silver tissue, with superb border of lama, and the sleeves profusely trimmed with the most beautiful Brussels point-lace, [a] rich silver band, fastened in front with diamonds; head-dress a most superb wreath of the richest and most brilliant diamonds, forming roses and leaves, with a most elegant ostrich plumage.[1]

The diamond wreath sounds very like the Princess's wedding wreath of rosebuds and leaves, but the dress does not match any of those listed in her trousseau and descriptions of it elsewhere do not add materially to our understanding of the appearance of this magnificent confection. The dress is of considerable interest, however, as remnants of it may well form the skirt and 'mantua' (train) of the assemblage now associated with the Princess's wedding (illustrations 47–9). These ornate court dresses, their wide high hoops loaded with rich draperies, had no use outside the court, and none survive in their original form. Princess Charlotte's court dresses were presumably unpicked and remade, either in her own lifetime or, more likely, when they were distributed after her death. We know very little about the fate of her clothing in the period up to the early twentieth century when the first of her dresses entered the London Museum's collections, and we have to guess at the sequence of events.

Another of Princess Charlotte's dresses is likely to belong to this period and like her wedding dress is teamed with an underdress which does not seem to be original to it (illustration 55–6).[2] The addition of an 1840s lace at the neck suggests that the two may have been united some time after this date, possibly for use as fancy dress. Still attractive, the dress must originally have been a very elegant and feminine ensemble for a formal occasion. All the original, and most valuable, lace has been stripped from the dress, but happily the bands of silver-enriched scalloped blonde trimming which run back and forth, up and down the short sleeves, have escaped intact. Similar decoration on sleeves can be found in fashion plates of 1815, when scallop-shaped lace begins to feature in fashion reports: it was a clever device, enlarging sleeves as a counterbalance to the growing emphasis on the hemline. The Princess's dressmakers clearly employed the most fashionable silks, trimmings and embroideries for her dresses and in this way she was naturally in the vanguard of fashion. There is little evidence of the Princess's views

55 White and silver striped dress, 1816–17. (MoL 74.100/2)

An attractive bobbin lace of cream silk and silver thread featuring scallop shells has been used to trim the neck and sleeves of the bodice, to which is attached a very short square-ended train; this is edged with a 'vandyke' bobbin lace.

56 Detail of fabric of striped dress, 1816–17.

The fabric of this dress is believed to have been woven in Spitalfields. Sample books of the products of local firms contain many almost identical examples of this date. As silk designs even then changed from year to year, it seems certain that the dress belongs to the period after the Princess's marriage when she restricted herself to British textiles.

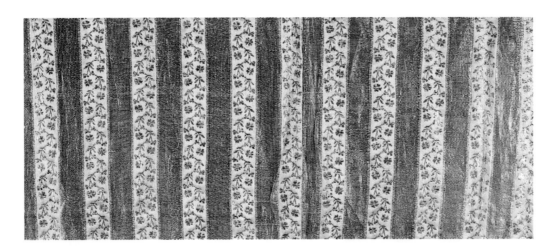

57 Morning cap, 1816–17. (MoL 27.40/7, Royal Collection)

A single piece of fine embroidered cotton forms the basis for this ingenious cap: three horizontal slits with puffs of hand-made net help to shape it over the crown of the head, and it is held in place by ribbon ties under the chin. It is possible that the cap belongs to the last year or two of the Princess's life, reflecting her concern for the plight of the workers in British textile industries. Fine Brussels lace might have been expected, but both lace and net could have been produced in the Midland counties, whilst much fine whitework was made by English embroiderers.

on dress, but she did not inherit her father's enthusiasm and extravagance. She seems to have been more in accord with her grandmother, and all descriptions of her at Claremont stress the simplicity of her dress.

The use of an English silk for this particular dress was not accidental, and can be claimed as a conscious attempt on the part of Princess Charlotte to influence fashion in the capital. The cessation of hostilities with Napoleon Bonaparte in 1815 re-opened the market in French fashion novelties, and London milliners and mercers had flocked back to Paris to acquire quantities of the tempting merchandise which had been blocked by trade embargoes. These goods they then advertised in the columns of the fashion press. In June 1815, for example, fashion plates of evening dresses by Mrs Bean, one of Princess Charlotte's dressmakers, incorporating just such French novelties, appeared in Ackermann's *Repository for the Arts* and readers were directed to her *Magasin des Modes* in Albermarle Street. British textile manufacturers, and London retailers, were outraged by this renewal of competition at a time when they were still suffering from the effects of the recent wars and their workforces were unsettled by radical politics. They complained vociferously. The Prince Regent, more as a public relations exercise than as a serious move to counter these changes, issued instructions that his courtiers and guests, both in London and at Brighton, should appear before him only in garments of British manufacture.

Princess Charlotte, an astute and passionate observer of the political scene, followed this lead, sincerely believing that the example set by the Royal Family might be influential. This small personal act of patronage was naturally represented by her biographers as munificence on a grand scale but it is likely that it cost the Princess little in sartorial pleasure. Although insisting that her trousseau consist entirely of articles 'of British manufacture, and of the richest kind', she excepted Brussels, Mechlin, and Valenciennes laces from her precept.[3] The products of the British lace industry did not match up to their foreign counterparts: royal sacrifices, it has to be deduced, had their limits. Queen Charlotte was a great devotee of fine lace and had a large and choice collection. Like jewellery it played an important role in aristocratic wardrobes for it could be enormously expensive and denoted wealth and status. The elderly Queen's views would have influenced the inclusion in her granddaughter's trousseau of the finest laces available, although Princess Charlotte later seems to have turned her back even on lace of continental manufacture. A decade later, Queen Adelaide was to be criticised for a less than glamorous image, partly the result of her own wholehearted patronage of British textile manufactures, and so too was Queen Victoria.

Princess Charlotte and her spouse had to remain in London for over four months attending court functions, receiving further loyal addresses and the freedom of the City of London, giving their own large dinner parties and receptions, visiting and receiving members of the Royal Family, and generally maintaining a high profile in society. The Prince Regent created Prince Leopold a member of the Order of the Bath at an imposing ceremony at Carlton House, whilst the Fishmongers' Company, in the City of London, bestowed upon him the freedom of their Company. There appears to have been little relief from the remorseless pressures of this existence, apart from carriage rides and visits to the theatre, but even the latter were turned into occasions by their managers and the public. At Drury Lane Theatre, for example, on 20 May 1816 the managers, Dibdin and Rae, appeared in mourning in deference to the continuing sombre hue of the court. Descriptions of the visit provide one of those rare glimpses of the Princess which accords

58 *Princess Charlotte and Prince Leopold in their box at Covent Garden Theatre, 1816*, engraved by W. T. Fry after a pencil drawing by George Dawe (1781–1829). (MoL 93.32)

The artist was much patronised by the royal couple. This portrait was commissioned by Princess Charlotte, but the engraving was not issued until 6 April 1818. She is shown wearing a totally plain dress, but with a magnificent cashmere shawl; none of her costly shawls now survives.

59 Shoes, 1816–17. (MoL 74.100/11)

Princess Charlotte's shoes are identical to any made at the time. Only her satin indoor shoes have survived, although she must have had much stouter shoes for day wear and for her rambles round the Claremont estate. The length of the shoes (9⅜in.; 23.8cm) reveals that her feet were of an average size. Such shoes could have a very short life: those who participated enthusiastically at balls needed several pairs per evening.

with the image portrayed in the extant portraits, wearing 'a chaplet of white roses and lilies round her head', whilst Prince Leopold wore the insignia of his orders. Later, in June, visiting Covent Garden Theatre, the 'Princess was dressed very plain, in a Waterloo green gown, white wreath of roses round her head, and but few diamonds'.[4]

Already, however, the strain of maintaining this high public profile, coupled with the lack of any retreat from the centre of London, seems to have affected the health first of Charlotte and then of her husband, and concern began to be expressed about the Princess. An early absence from public life seems to have been the result of a bronchial infection, but in July she was forced to miss the wedding of her favourite aunt, Princess Mary, to the Duke of Gloucester. The ceremony was performed in the grand saloon at Buckingham House, in an evening ceremony probably much like that for Princess Charlotte two and a half months earlier. Prince Leopold attended the ceremony alone, and it has been suggested that his wife was perhaps already in the early stages of a pregnancy which was to terminate a few weeks later.

By August negotiations for the purchase of Claremont were completed, and the Prince and Princess were at last able to escape from London and their cramped and inconvenient town house (illustration 60). Whilst resident in London Princess Charlotte presumably had often seen her friend Mercer Elphinstone. No letters survive detailing the Princess's busy town life, a disappointment considering the valuable comments and information the previous correspondence contained. However, writing to Mercer was one of the first things the Princess did on taking up residence at

60 (Detail) *Claremont House – The South Front*, 1843, by Caleb R. Stanley (1795–1868). (Royal Collection)

Although this watercolour was painted more than two decades after Princess Charlotte's death, Claremont had probably changed very little. During her pregnancy the Princess loved to drive round the grounds in a small pony cart. Her confinement and death occurred in one of the ground floor rooms. It is easy to see why she and Queen Victoria so loved the place. The Queen had several paintings made by this artist of the house interiors and grounds.

61 Gloves, 1816–17.
   (MoL 74.100/14)

Several pairs of Princess Charlotte's gloves survive. They are all elbow-length or longer gloves of finest kids, suedes and 'chicken skin' (the thin, but still strong, skin of unborn calves) of the type habitually worn with dinner, evening and court dress. They reveal the plumpness of her fingers and arms. All are undecorated.

Claremont. 'With what widely differing feelings to any I ever experienced in my life before, did I quit London this year, and with how little regret', she wrote on 26 August 1816. 'I am so perfectly happy, and every day and hour have I to thank you for being so actively accessory in securing to me that wh. I now enjoy in so great a degree'.[5] She had formed a very affectionate bond with her husband, and together they began to make a life for themselves away from the court, developing their estate, indulging their shared interests in gardening and music, playing host to various members of the Royal Family (including the Regent and Queen Charlotte), and paying return visits to Oatlands and Windsor. They also regularly attended one of the local churches.

According to some of the biographies written within a year of her death in 1817 Princess Charlotte favoured a simple style of dressing which, as one writer has it, 'much resembled that of a respectable tradesman's wife'.[6] This seems very likely, and anecdotes of the Princess's mistaken identity were probably based on fact. Her unadorned straw bonnet and plain velvet pelisse became well known in the locality. Her cloak and bonnet, thrown off after her last walk with Prince Leopold at Claremont, still hung on a screen when her small cousin Princess Victoria visited with her mother a few years later.

The last twelve months of Princess Charlotte's life were spent almost exclusively at Claremont, with occasional brief visits to London to attend formal occasions. She refused to spend either her husband's birthday (16 December 1816) or her own, her twenty-first (7 January 1817), with her father at Brighton; both were celebrated there nevertheless, with British textiles being the order of the day. The Princess's own support of these distressed workers is made much of by her biographers, and Robert Huish in particular relates a number of anecdotes in which she nobly turns away impressive and very valuable Indian shawls, or 'a beautiful cap formed of Brussels point lace, and other costly foreign materials'. [5] Indeed he reports the Princess's comment, about yet another of her glamorous Drawing Room outfits, worn on 20 February 1817:

> 'I should feel no satisfaction whatever in this splendid dress,' said her Royal Highness, 'if the thought did not accompany it that the manufacture of it has perhaps given relief to some distressed workmen; for I know only one court which can impart a pleasant feeling to my heart, and that is the court of Nature . . .' She was heard to say 'that she would have worn the diamonds and pearls which decorated her person with greater pleasure, had they been the produce of her native country.' [8]

> . . .The Princess Charlotte showed herself an Englishwoman in her exterior – no Frenchified gew-gaw was purchased to decorate her person; an Irish tabbinet, a Glasgow muslin, or a Norwich bombazin was the most splendid attire to which the heiress of the British throne aspired.

When smugglers with French goods were detected, 'her Royal Highness clapped her hands, exclaiming, "I am glad of it, I am glad of it; I hope they will be made to pay for their French fashions." '[9] Only three years earlier at Weymouth she had shown herself an eager patron of the local smugglers (p47), and this anecdote, if true, demonstrates the Princess's new sense of responsibility. Her whole-hearted embrace of the principle led her into hot water when it became known that she had presented her friend Lady Susan Ryder with a dress of Brussels lace, worth 300 guineas it was rumoured, for her forthcoming wedding. Following an outcry, it was revealed that the dress was one the Princess had had for some time and which she did not wish to wear now because it was not of British manufacture. [10] That spring of 1817, the Princess and her husband gave proof of their desire to support the Spitalfields silk industry when they placed a large order, said to amount to £1000, for a yellow furnishing silk for use at Claremont; one source suggests that some two thousand yards were involved. The order appears to have been completed by the time Huish's biography was published in 1819. [11]

On 30 April 1817, so Huish asserts, Prince Leopold paid a special visit to the Prince Regent at Carlton House to inform her father of the Princess's certain pregnancy. Thereafter her appearances in London were even less frequent. She was in London in June to attend a Drawing Room, but the heat was so great that the Princess was advised not to attend, and quietly visited friends instead: 'infinitely more gratifying … than sidling about in a hoop in a crowded drawing room on a sultry day in June', Huish thought. [12]

The two last surviving dresses belonging to Princess Charlotte can with assurance be placed in the last few months of her life, that is between May and November 1817. Both are constructed in the same way and it is therefore likely that they came from the workrooms of the same unknown London dressmaker. Almost certainly the earlier of the two dresses, judging by its slightly smaller bodice size, is the one lavishly ornamented with imitation pearls (illustrations 54, 62). All parts of this dress are likely to be of British manufacture, and it was probably worn by the Princess at Claremont in the summer or autumn of 1817 when entertaining guests. [13]

The Princess's so-called 'Russian' dress must be the very last to survive; it is also the

62 Detail of dinner or evening dress shown in illustration 54.

The bold patterning on this dress was achieved by combining a white silk crimped gauze with large imitation pearls. Princess Charlotte was extremely fond of pearls and the idea of a dress thus decorated, albeit with imitations, must have delighted her.

only one she is shown wearing in any of her portraits (illustrations 64–6). In fact the dress bears only a passing likeness to a true Russian sarafan and is of entirely British manufacture. It was a very flattering and appropriate form of dress for pregnancy and may well relate in some way to Prince Leopold's past service with Tsar Alexander I, whose presence in Paris and London in 1814, together with his sister the Duchess of Oldenburg, may have influenced a small fashion trend. The Duchess was a very fashionable woman herself and it seems unlikely that she brought such regional dress in her wardrobe. It is conceivable that she wore something like it in private which later influenced the Princess; or that Prince Leopold may have suggested it. Certainly it shows off perfectly the insignia of the Order of St Catherine, a gift from the Tsar which had highly delighted Princess Charlotte. Already in 1816 she had worn a similar dress, prompting Baron Stockmar, Prince Leopold's personal physician and private secretary, to comment

> I thought her dress particularly becoming; dark roses in her hair, a short light blue dress without sleeves, with a low round collar, a white puffed-out Russian chemisette, the sleeves of lace. I have never seen her in any dress which was not both simple and in good taste.[14]

In August 1817 Prince Leopold reported to his father-in-law on his wife's condition: 'La tranquillité, l'air salutaire de Claremont, ainsi que les accommodations qu'offre la maison, on fait désirer à Charlotte de rester ici pour le temps en question'. He also sought the Regent's instructions on arrangements for the baptism of the child when it arrived, and the Regent in his turn replied fully and helpfully. Public interest, too, was escalating. Cruikshank this month issued one of his famous cruel caricatures, *Progeny in Perspective – Or a Royal Accouchement!!* showing the new-born infant urinating in the direction of the Regent's ministers. There were already bets on the sex of the child: 'a Princess would raise the funds 2½ per cent, whilst a Prince would send them up 6 per cent'.[15]

Obviously a layette, a first set of clothing, must have been prepared for the baby, and it is reasonable to assume that this might have been supplied by Mary Hillhouse of New Bond Street. Two baby shirts now in the Brighton Museum and Art Gallery are traditionally believed to have been preserved from the layette, although there is now no way of proving this (illustration 63).[16] An element of confusion is introduced by the survival of a French bill, presumably Parisian, for a layette and items 'Pour la Princesse' supplied by Mademoiselle Lebeuf and Madame Linère. The bill used to be in Lady Gardiner's possession and must therefore be taken seriously. Was this layette ordered from Paris by Leopold himself, or might it have been a gift from one of his friends, like the Duchess of Oldenburg? What is perplexing is that it does not seem to accord with Princess Charlotte's patronage of British goods. For the time being it must remain a mystery.[17]

Expected in October, the Princess's labour did not commence until 3 November, when it continued for forty-eight hours 'de souffrance' according to Prince Leopold. A 'beautiful fine boy … very large' was born, dead, at nine o'clock on 5 November 1817, a matter of great sadness to the Princess and her husband. There was no reason to fear for the Princess at this point: she was reported to be 'extremely well', almost unnaturally composed and cheerful, and so her household retired to bed. Two hours later, however, she became unwell, and died at half past two on the morning of 6 November. This sudden change in the Princess's condition and her rapid death have long been debated in

63 Two baby shirts, 1817.
(Brighton Museum & Art Gallery)

By tradition these two white cotton baby shirts originally came from the layette prepared for Princess Charlotte's baby in 1817. They bear small crowns embroidered in red silk and descend from a St James's apothecary John Nussey, apparently a supplier to George IV.

64 Embroidered blouse, 1816–17.
   (MoL 74.100/5)

No doubt many Regency women adopted
the practical device of wearing blouses under
sleeveless overdresses during the daytime.
This embroidered blouse of fine linen, rather
like the habit shirt normally worn by women
with riding habits, is believed to have been
worn by Princess Charlotte. It admirably
complements her 'Russian' dress, and in fact
a decorative long-sleeved chemise is what
was usually worn under true sarafans. The
puffs at the top of the sleeve are created by
inner pairs of ties, a clever device to make
laundering easier.

65 *Princess Charlotte Augusta*, 1817, by
   George Dawe (1781–1829). (National
   Portrait Gallery, London)

Several versions of this portrait exist but it is
believed that this was the first that Dawe
painted, and he retained it until his death. It
shows Princess Charlotte wearing her
'Russian' dress together with the star of the
Order St Catherine of Russia. She appears to
wear a lace blouse or bodice under the dress.
It is difficult to know whether this was a
fully constructed garment or simply pieces of
lace pinned in place for the portrait: the two
'sleeves' are rectangles of lace held at
intervals by pearl clips, and would not have
been practical to wear.

66 (Opposite) 'Russian' dress, 1817.
   (MoL 27.40/2, Royal Collection)

Like that in illustration 54, this dress has a
separate front-opening bodice with a
drawstring at the 'waist'. Over it is worn the
slightly flared skirt, which has a drawstring
at the top, a necessary feature in a dress to be
worn during pregnancy. The construction is
somewhat unusual in fashionable dress of
the time, but probably reveals one of the
many small adaptations women made in
their clothing before specially-designed
maternity wear was introduced. The gold
lace is of London manufacture and
incorporates crimson silk.

medical circles and several theories have been proposed. She had been attended by eminent practitioners who kept copious records but could not account for her death; a post-mortem was also inconclusive. Sir Richard Croft, her accoucheur, much criticised in the press and unfairly blamed for the tragedy, was later to commit suicide when in attendance at a similar case. It has recently been suggested that the Princess had inherited porphyria from both her parents, a complaint known to have caused sudden death after a confinement. Current medical opinion is divided and, without the information needed for a more definitive diagnosis, the real reason remains a mystery.[18]

The shock waves produced by the Princess's sudden and unexpected death spread far. Queen Charlotte urged her son to find comfort in

> having had it in your power to make your child completely happy by granting her to marry the man she liked and wished to be united to and who made her happy as also the bestowing upon her a place she did enjoy with every possible gratitude and in which she spent to the very last almost complete felicity.[19]

General mourning was immediately proclaimed: 'It is expected that all persons do put themselves into decent mourning'. Court mourning was set at three months. Arriving in London just before Christmas Richard Rush, the new American ambassador, found that in dress for both men and women 'black predominates. It is universal.' He later noted in his diary the profound effect of the return to colour at court at the Queen's Drawing Room in February 1818: 'It was like the bursting out of spring', after the dismal gloom of this London winter.[20]

The coffins of Princess Charlotte and her baby son were taken from Claremont to Windsor in a discreet procession on the evening of 18 November 1817, lit only by moonlight and with no accompanying flares; here they rested overnight in rooms heavily draped in black cloth. The following evening, after eight o'clock, they were transferred

67 *Princess Charlotte Augusta,* 1817, by Sir Thomas Lawrence (1769–1830). (Royal Castle of Laeken, Collections Royales de Belgique)

This is the last portrait of Princess Charlotte, painted in the autumn of 1817. It shows her as she preferred to be, simply dressed and wearing few jewels. Lawrence was much moved by her subsequent death.

68 *Evening dress,* December 1817, engraved and handcoloured fashion plate, from *The Repository of Arts, Literature, Fashions, Commerce, Manufactures and Politics,* new series, published by Rudolph Ackermann, 101 Strand.

Fashion plates customarily reflected appropriate dress during a period of public mourning. This evening dress of black crape over silk, though sombre, shows no other concession to the national tragedy it marked. A simple expedient for fashion plate publishers was to replace colour-washes with black, but this plate, together with its companion, appear to have been specially engraved. At this time the dressmaker Mrs Bell of St James's Street was supplying the dresses illustrated by Ackermann.

69 *Princess Charlotte's Funeral Ceremony,*
19 November 1817, coloured lithograph
by T. Sutherland after C. Wilde and
J. Stephanoff. (National Portrait Gallery,
London)

to St George's Chapel, draped in black velvet and under a canopy of black velvet, in the midst of a long and sombre procession (illustration 69). Prince Leopold, flanked on both sides by the Princess's uncles in long mourning cloaks, walked immediately behind the coffin, whilst her dresser Mrs Louis was accorded a place at the very end of the procession. A short but moving interment service followed, during which the Princess's style and title were proclaimed by the deputy Garter King of Arms. The two coffins were placed in the Chapel vault, alongside those of several royal ancestors, and in time an impressive white marble memorial designed by Matthew Wyatt was erected at the west end of the Chapel. A flurry of biographies, engravings and commemorative items ensued, but within a generation or two the brief but eventful life of Princess Charlotte of Wales was forgotten. With her died public hope for the future of its monarchy, but within a short space of time that hope was to be rekindled by the birth of several cousins, including the future Queen Victoria.

The Royal Marriage Race, 1818

The unexpected death of Princess Charlotte in 1817, together with her baby, gave rise to a succession crisis of considerable proportions.

George III's very fruitful marriage must have given every expectation that the next generation would be equally productive, but by 1817 the Princess still remained the sole legitimate offspring of the King's nine sons. Two of these sons had died in childhood, whilst the long and disastrous estrangement of the Prince Regent and Princess Charlotte's mother, Princess Caroline of Brunswick, had sealed the fate of this line. The marriage in 1791 of the next brother in line, Frederick, Duke of York, remained childless. Efforts to prise the remaining ageing princes from self-indulgent bachelorhood or from comfortable domestic existences with their mistresses – or even to find suitable wives for them – had all so far failed. Partners for such bridegrooms were severely limited; their brides were more political alliances than personal choices, and therefore held little appeal. Nearly all this generation of royal princes, however, were to marry to alleviate considerable debts. In 1817 there remained four unmarried princes of whom three married in 1818. This sudden spate of alliances has become known as 'the royal marriage race', and eventually a number of possible heirs were produced, including Princess Victoria.

It could be claimed that Princess Charlotte herself played a small part in the genesis of her cousin Princess Victoria. For in 1816 her much-loved uncle Edward, Duke of Kent (now forty-nine years old) was forced to contemplate a politically approved marriage to resolve large debts. Princess Charlotte and Prince Leopold are said to have suggested his sister, Princess Victoire of Leiningen, a widow with a son (Charles) and a daughter (Feodore), as an appropriate consort. Loath to bring to an end his happy twenty-eight year liaison with his mistress Mme de St Laurent, the Duke had been procrastinating, whilst the prospective bride, nineteen years his junior, had also hesitated. Princess Charlotte's sudden death compelled a decision. Their marriage took place on 29 May 1818 at an impressive ceremony at Schloss Ehrenburg in Coburg, the Duke resplendent in his English Field Marshal's uniform, whilst his bride wore an expensive dress of French blonde lace decorated with orange blossoms and white roses. They were remarried according to the rites of the Church of England at Kew Palace on 13 July 1818 in the presence of the very elderly and frail Queen Charlotte. It was a double ceremony, shared with the Duke of Kent's older brother the Duke of Clarence and his bride Princess Adelaide of Saxe-Coburg-Meiningen. The Prince Regent gave both brides away.

70 *Victoria, Duchess of Kent*, 1818, by George Dawe (1781–1829). (Royal Collection)

The Duchess sat for this portrait in July and August 1818, shortly after her marriage. Her black dress indicates that she was in mourning.

71 *Edward, Duke of Kent,* 1818, by George
Dawe (1781–1829). (Royal Collection)

Companion portraits of the Duke and
Duchess were painted at about the time of
their marriage, and in this version the Duke
wears the uniform of a Field Marshal. The
painting was purchased by Queen Victoria
in 1839 and placed in her bedroom at
Buckingham Palace. She always regretted the
father she had barely known.

A SCENE in the New FARCE called the RIVALS or a Visit to the Heir Presumtive.

72 *A Scene in the New Farce called The Rivals – or a Visit to the Heir Presumtive*, engraving by Charles Williams; published by S. W. Fores, 50 Piccadilly, April 1819. (British Museum)

This shows a very pregnant Duchess of Kent, less than two months before the birth of Princess Victoria, with the Duke of Kent, in the company of the Duke and Duchess of Cambridge with their baby Prince George; the Dukes and Duchesses of Clarence and Cumberland, and the Duchess of York look on.

Like his brothers, the Duke of Clarence (the future William IV) was also marrying to alleviate substantial debts. He had separated from his mistress Dorothea Jordan, the actress and mother of his ten illegitimate children, in 1811, and had eventually lighted upon the twenty-six year old Princess Adelaide as a bride. They went on to have several children who did not survive infancy. Thus Princess Victoria, the Duke of Kent's only child, was eventually recognised as heir to the throne following the death of George IV in 1830.

The third marriage of 1818 was that of the Dukes' younger brother, Prince Adolphus, Duke of Cambridge, to Princess Augusta of Hesse-Cassel. Their son George (1819–1904) was the first child born of the 'royal marriage race' in March 1819, just two months before Princess Victoria. He succeeded to his father's title in 1850.

The handful of years following Princess Charlotte's death were to witness great changes within the Royal Family. Queen Charlotte died in November 1818, presumably aware that each of the three brides was pregnant. Just over a year later, in January 1820, her ill and senile husband George III also died, just a few days after Princess Victoria's father, the Duke of Kent. The Prince Regent finally succeeded to the throne, as George IV, and in 1821, not long after his phenomenally ornate coronation (illustration 2), his estranged wife Queen Caroline died.

73 *Queen Adelaide*, 1836, by Sir Martin
   Archer Shee (1769–1850).
   (Royal Collection)

William IV so admired this portrait of his
wife, originally commissioned for the
Goldsmith's Company, that he retained it
for himself and a further version had to be
painted for the Company. The Queen
had too retiring a nature to be a leader of
fashion but she was a loyal patron of British
textiles and insisted upon them being worn
at her courts.

74 *William IV*, 1833, by Sir Martin Archer
   Shee (1769–1850). (Royal Collection)

This flattering large portrait shows the ageing
King in Garter robes, with St Edward's crown
and the sceptre placed by his right hand.
Considered a good likeness by the Queen, it
was hung in the Throne Room at Windsor.
The King wears the heavy Garter collar which
Queen Victoria found too cumbersome when
she came to the throne.

Girlhood, 1819–37

Princess Victoria was born on 24 May 1819 at Kensington Palace. The tensions and disagreements within the Royal Family which were to add misery to the Princess's life until her accession were conspicuous at her christening on 24 June in the Cupola Room at Kensington Palace. Here the Prince Regent, in his most intractable manner, argued over the parents' choice of names for the baby. He grudgingly allowed 'Alexandrina', their compliment to one godfather, Tsar Alexander I, but vetoed their next choice of 'Georgiana', a compliment to himself, the second godparent, and also disallowed 'Charlotte' and 'Augusta'. After some delay the distressed parents were allowed 'Victoria' after the baby's mother. In the early years of her life the little Princess answered to the pet name of 'Drina' before Victoria was finally adopted.

The Duke of Kent, despite his continued financial difficulties, had furnished their apartment at Kensington Palace in some style. The Cupola Room was specially draped for the christening in crimson velvet hangings brought from the Chapel Royal, despite the Regent's injunctions that there be 'no dressing up, no uniforms glittering with gold – "as His Royal Highness considers the Ceremony as Private, the dress best suited to the Occasion will be, Frocks" ' (plain skirted coats).[1] Only a handful of family were present and as a result no descriptions survive of the central character in the proceedings, the baby Princess Victoria herself.

However, it is certain that she was clothed in a befitting manner and an entry in the Duchess's household accounts reveals the princely charge of £103 18s 6d 'for dressmaking for Princess Victoria in 1819' by Mary Hillhouse, of New Bond Street. It seems likely that this sum included a christening robe as well as a suitable layette, and maybe cot-hangings too, just like the preparations for Princess Charlotte's birth. In succeeding years Mrs Hillhouse's charges for providing dresses for the Princess were much more modest.[2]

When the Duke of Kent died unexpectedly of pneumonia in January 1820, just a week before his elderly and by now very senile father George III, he left his wife and baby virtually destitute. Marriage had not produced the solvency he sought; but brief though it was, it had been happy, and the Princess was brought up with good reports of her father. His death left considerable financial problems for his widow and child and it was Prince Leopold who, somewhat unwillingly, took charge. George IV, disliking his late brother and his wife, argued that Leopold, with an allowance of £50,000 from Parliament as Princess Charlotte's widower, could well afford to support his sister and

75 *Princess Victoria Alexandrina*, 1819, by Paul Johann Georg Fischer (1786–1875). (Royal Collection)

The artist apparently prepared this study for the Duke of Kent's birthday on 2 November 1819: the six-month-old Princess wore a Scotch bonnet and a white frock with bows of red and green ribbon. Fragments of these ribbons still survive.

76 Blonde lace dress, 1831–2. (MoL 33.328)

This is the earliest dress of Queen Victoria's known to survive. It was previously dated at 1824, when she was only five years old, but this is patently too early. Although she was a little small for her age, it is estimated that the Princess must have been about twelve when she wore this dress. She holds one of her tiny wooden dolls in her right hand.

her daughter. Realising that the potential heir to the throne might receive a purely German upbringing if his sister returned to Leiningen – something which would not be acceptable to the public – Prince Leopold persuaded her to stay in England and provided her with an allowance of £2000 (later raised to £3000). Meanwhile, the King was persuaded by his sister, Princess Augusta, to allow the Duchess to return to her husband's apartment at Kensington Palace.

Thus Prince Leopold came to play a major part in the Princess's life and to have a second opportunity of influencing an heir to the English throne. His niece often stayed at Claremont, and from her earliest days became familiar with the memorabilia of Princess Charlotte, who had died only eighteen months before her birth. Indeed the second recorded payment for the baby occurs in 1820 when her nurse Mrs Brock paid out £2 5s 0½d 'for Princess Victoria's washing at Claremont'.[3]

First-hand observations of Princess Victoria in early childhood are rare. Most comment on the simplicity of her dress, and her direct and unaffected personality, especially her painful truthfulness. In 1825 the Duchess of Kent's mother, the Dowager Duchess of Coburg, paid her only visit to England, and her letters to her family provide vivid pen-portraits of her small granddaughter, descriptions which reveal her to have been just like any other wilful small child:

77 *Victoria, Duchess of Kent, with Princess Victoria,* by Sir William Beechey (1753–1839). (Royal Collection)

This portrait, painted after May 1821, may have been commissioned by Prince Leopold. The Duchess of Kent is shown in mourning for her late husband, whilst the two-year-old Princess clutches a miniature of her father. In 1822 the painting was exhibited at the Royal Academy, and in the following year an engraving of it was published. Circulation of such prints familiarised the public with the future queen and acted as sources for popular likenesses. In 1867 the portrait was given to Queen Victoria by Prince Leopold's son, King Leopold II of the Belgians.

78 *Queen Victoria, aged Four*, 1823, by Stephen Poyntz Denning (*c*.1787–1864). (Dulwich Picture Gallery, London)

The artist of this charming portrait was Curator of the Dulwich College Picture Gallery between 1821 and 1864. It has always hung in the Gallery, and was for many years the most popular portrait. It seems not to have been a direct commission, but rather a preparation for an engraving. The Princess wears outdoor clothes with an unwieldy hat which echoes the adult fashions of the time.

79 Baby shoes, *c*.1820. (MoL D331, Royal Collection)

The printed paper label in one of these shoes reveals that they were made by Princess Charlotte's shoemaker, G. F. Vandervell. This firm apparently also made shoes for the Duchess of Kent, and it seems likely that this pair was presented to the infant Princess, perhaps in hope of securing a new, and prestigious, royal customer. No payments to this shoemaker are recorded in the Duchess's accounts.

In the morning, she sometimes does not want to get out of bed, preferring to tell all sorts of tales. Lehzen [her governess] takes her gently from her bed, and sits her down on the thick carpet, where she has to put on her stockings.

One has to contain oneself not to burst out laughing, when she says in a tragic tone of voice, 'Poor Vicky! She is an unhappy child! She just doesn't know which is the right stocking and which is the left! I am an unhappy child!'

These stockings were supplied by the Pall Mall haberdashers and hosiers Crook, Son & Besford, who had supplied Princess Charlotte with her childhood socks, and who would supply Victoria with her hose until 1856. In 1826 socks of cotton and of silk were purchased from them for her, whilst other hose or stockings came from the local firm of Breeze & James in Kensington High Street, who would also enjoy a long period as suppliers to the Queen.[4]

The Duchess of Kent seems to have shared the sentimentality of adoring mothers, for the earliest surviving example of Queen Victoria's clothing is a pair of tiny black satin shoes, reputedly those she first wore (illustration 79). These are just under 5in. (12cm) long and possibly date to 1820. They appear to have been little used and it has been suggested that wear marks on the toes and heels indicate that the shoes were already too small when the Princess wore them.[5] The Duchess's accounts reveal that Princess

Victoria's feet were shod from 1824 by Richard Gundry of Soho Square. This firm was to remain her principal footwear supplier until 1898.[6] As with all these accounting entries no details of the quantity and type of goods supplied were provided, whilst the more detailed invoicing bills have all long since perished.

It is fortuitous indeed that this incomplete set of the Duchess's household accounts survives. They include no entries relating to the purchase of the Duchess's own wardrobe but are the sole source of facts about the supply of Princess Victoria's clothing. They cease after 1828 and there is then a gap until her accession in June 1837 when the payment ledgers of the Mistress of the Robes once more provide similar information. It is now possible to see that many of the firms first awarded royal warrants in 1837 had already been suppliers to the Princess for quite some time, and it is probable that many of them had also supplied the Duchess herself. Indeed the billheads of such firms, or occasionally their entries in trade directories, usually proudly proclaim patronage from a number of royal households.

These accounts reveal, for example, that the Princess's hair was cut from the age of five by Stephen Taylor, hairdresser and perfumer. Early portraits show her hair cropped quite short at this age, but by 1830 it was longer and dressed in ringlets (illustration 89). The first entry for stays for the Princess appears in February 1825 when Mrs Elizabeth Fossett, stay and corset maker, was paid £3 12s 0d, the same sum being charged again in March. Both Stephen Taylor and Mrs Fossett were awarded royal warrants in 1837, but neither appears to have worked for the Princess after this. Mrs Fossett's stays would have taken the form of a soft, firm underbodice, probably unboned, but preparing the way for gradually more effective shaping as the Princess matured.[7]

By far the most important information revealed by these accounts is that in August 1824 Mary Bettans of Jermyn Street replaced Mary Hillhouse as the Princess's dressmaker. It seems reasonable to assume that she was already employed upon making dresses for the Duchess and her elder daughter Princess Feodore: in 1826 she was indeed paid £33 13s 6d for making court dresses for the latter.[8] Nothing is known about this dressmaker as an individual, but a book of silk cuttings, apparently from dresses made in her workrooms between 1837 and 1843, includes dresses made for Queen Adelaide, the Duchess of Gloucester and Baroness Lehzen (illustrations 16, 110, 137).[9] Silks for Princess Victoria's dresses were purchased from firms like Harding & Co. (Pall Mall) or D. & P. Cooper (Pall Mall) who had long been patronised by the royal family. An entry in 1827 for Harding's for '½ of a dress 2.12.6.' is less strange than might immediately appear, for all that was needed for the Princess was half of a standard adult dress length. Two muslin pelisses were made for Princess Victoria by Mrs Eliza Whitelaw (Oxford Street) in 1827, whilst her bonnets came from Mme Duchon, milliner, or Arnold & Roxbury, straw bonnetmakers. By 1829, when these accounts cease, an increasing number of tradespeople were involved in providing clothing for the Princess. The annual expenditure had also increased from £407 5s 7d in 1825, for example, to £717 12s 11d in 1829.[10]

The Duchess's difficult financial position meant that she was economical, but these accounts do not suggest that her youngest daughter was in any way deprived materially. Indeed there can be no doubt that the Duchess aimed to maintain a standard for herself and, more particularly, for the future heir to the throne, befitting their rank: gradually she too was incurring debts which she had no way of paying. She led an active social life, but avoided the King, his brothers and other courtiers of whose behaviour she

80 *Self-portrait*, 1832, by Princess Victoria, from Queen Victoria's sketchbook. (Royal Collection)

This rather intense self-portrait was drawn on 10 August 1832 during a stay in Wales. The Princess wears a fashionably-styled day dress with long sleeves puffed at the shoulder like those on many of her dolls. The morning cap and fichu were presumably removed later in the day if there were visitors.

81 *Louisa Lehzen,* 1833, from Queen
Victoria's sketchbook. (Royal
Collection)

Drawing was an early and absorbing
occupation for Princess Victoria, and
Richard Westall was appointed her drawing
master in 1827. The Baroness Lehzen was
one of her earliest regular sitters, captured
here in 1833 with another constant
companion, 'Dash', the Duchess of Kent's
King Charles spaniel. 'Dear Dashy' was
treated as a doll by the Princess, and dressed
'in a scarlet coat and blue trousers'. Louisa
Lehzen was a devoted servant of the
Duchess who in turn commanded the love
and respect of her charge. She probably had
much to do with organising the Princess's
wardrobe and liaising with suppliers even
before Victoria became Queen.

82 Knitted collar, 1825–35. (MoL 63.132)

Collar knitted in white cotton thread in an
undulating wave pattern. It is considered
typical for the period 1810–30 and is of a
type taught in contemporary charity
schools. Baroness Lehzen would have
learned her handiwork skills many years
earlier so they were not fully up to date. She
taught her royal charge to use her spare time
constructively, and embroidery, crochet and
knitting occupied Queen Victoria's leisure
hours throughout the rest of her life.

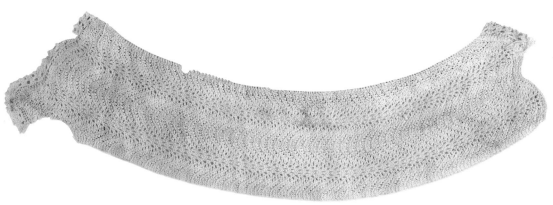

disapproved. Queen Charlotte's authoritative personality, which had guided court
affairs during the Regency, found no successor after her death in 1818. George IV failed
to command respect and loyalty after his accession in 1820, his unseemly and
extravagant lifestyle continuing unabated. When in 1828 he appeared to be much
interested in Princess Victoria's half-sister Feodore, an attractive twenty-one-year-old,
the Duchess rapidly arranged her marriage to Prince Ernest of Hohenlohe-Langenburg.
At the same time the Duchess of Kent introduced her younger daughter to a circle of
acceptable adult contacts, despite her isolation from the immediate court circle, and
exposed Princess Victoria to a rigorous education under stern tutors. The Princess
chafed at the schoolroom discipline and social restrictions, but they formed the
foundation for her remarkable assurance and presence as Queen.

A powerful influence throughout these years was the Princess's governess, the
Baroness Lehzen. She had accompanied the Duchess of Kent to England as governess to
Princess Feodore, and in 1826 became governess to Princess Victoria. The whole of the
Princess's waking day was spent in her company, and she it was who guided her charge's
earliest essays in drawing, sewing and knitting. A knitted collar traditionally claimed to
be the work of the Princess at about this time still survives, but the attribution cannot
now be verified.[11] Its unskilled craftsmanship is rather in its favour, for Princess
Victoria's patience with pencil and paints did not extend to her sewing and knitting
needles. If this collar is in fact her work she would have found the technical intricacies of
creating the undulating wave pattern not a little challenging and irksome.

Kept constantly occupied by her governess, the Princess was surrounded by
industrious needlewomen whose handiwork, like many of the Princess's efforts, was
employed as presents. In her first Christmas Journal entry in 1832 she recorded that

> Mama gave me a little lovely pink bag which she had worked with a little sachet
> likewise done by her ... Aunt Sophia [youngest daughter of George III] gave me a dress
> which she worked herself ... Victoire [youngest child of Sir John Conroy, her mother's
> comptroller] a <u>very</u> pretty white bag worked by herself ... I gave Mama a white bag
> which I had worked ...

Three years later her birthday presents included a pair of slippers worked by her sister
Feodore. The slippers the Queen is believed to have worked for her daughter Princess

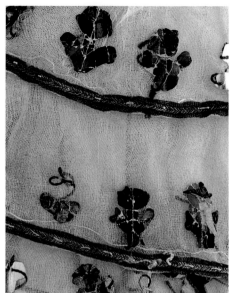

Alice, many years later, were very likely just such a birthday or Christmas present (illustration 135).[12]

The Princess's impatience with her needle is conspicuous in the clothing she made for her army of tiny wooden dolls; her stitching is noticeably more hurried than the extremely neat and unobtrusive work of her governess. These dolls became famous when they were introduced to an inquisitive and admiring public late in the Queen's lifetime in Frances Lowe's book *Queen Victoria's Dolls* (1894). They were amongst the first royal exhibits at the newly established London Museum in 1912. When catalogued by the Princess they numbered 132, but a few have since gone absent without leave. Princess Victoria's catalogue entries show that many of the dolls were dressed between 1831 and 1833, but there is every reason to believe that some of them were created before 1831.[13]

Much has been made of the part these dolls played in the life of Princess Victoria as substitutes for brothers, sisters or other young companions, and towards the end of her life she herself commented on the pleasure and companionship the dolls had given her. In many respects, however, she was like most other girls of her age at the time (and since) in owning and playing with a variety of dolls. When she was fourteen in 1833, all these dolls were packed away. In 1828 she had lost the company of her much loved half-sister Feodore when she married and went to Germany; the imposed friendship of Sir John Conroy's daughters, notably Jane (*b*.1811) and Victoire (*b*.1819), was never any compensation for friends of her choice. The army of small, crudely carved dolls almost certainly started out as occupants of a doll's house in the later 1820s, and indeed in her catalogue of them the Princess divides them into four 'houses'. These were not exactly peer-group companions for the Princess but rather an alternative world of adults whom she admired, a court of her own in embryo. In her Journal, begun in August 1832 when she was thirteen, she mentions playing with the dolls but what form that 'play' took is not known.

The dressing of the dolls was principally an activity shared by Princess Victoria with Baroness Lehzen. The Princess's catalogue shows that the Baroness dressed fifty-six of the dolls herself, whilst Victoria dressed twenty-seven, and they combined forces on a further fourteen. The remaining twenty-nine dolls came either as gifts ('Ernestine' from Berne, 'Lisette' from a Bazaar), often from the Princess's maids. Exceptionally, one was

83 Group of dolls, 1831–3.
(MoL D49/72, 74, 79, 81, 97, 130,
Royal Collection)

Fashionably dressed dolls created by Princess Victoria and Baroness Lehzen in the years 1831–3. Each doll was named by the Princess: from left to right, Miss Arnold; Sir William Arnold; Lady Nina Morton; Héloïse, Duchess of Guiche; the Dowager Countess of Rothsay; Isabella, Lady Poulteney; and (in front) Lady Maria Arnold. It is clear from Princess Victoria's Journal entries that she took a great interest in the dress of fashionable women. These dolls are probably wearing dresses seen and admired on visitors to Kensington Palace, or when the Princess was out for drives or at the theatre. Fashion plates in women's journals must also have been a source of inspiration, whilst other outfits were probably simply imaginary. Paper dolls painted with fashionable dresses were also created and stuck in small exercise books during the Princess's recreational periods.

84 Detail of doll 'Mlle Pauline Duvernay',
1833. (MoL D49/17, Royal Collection)

This doll, dressed to represent the ballerina in *La Bayadère* was wholly Victoria's work as this detail reveals. She cut out and attached coloured foil motifs to represent the embroidery on the original dress.

85 'Catherine, Countess of Claremont', 1831–3. (MoL D49/918, Royal Collection)

The 'Countess of Claremont' is the most glamorous of the dolls. She was created by Lady Catherine Jenkinson and her ensemble was probably intended to represent court dress. The Countess should have feathers in her hair, but instead she has been given a dress cap.

86 'Mlle Sylphide Taglioni'. (MoL D49/10, Royal Collection)

Princess Victoria had probably seen the second London performance of the ballet *La Sylphide* in July 1832. Unwell in Wales on 8 August she described the dressing of this doll by Lehzen, the only time she ever included such detail in her Journal about the making of her dolls. Down to its tiny ballet shoes and painted gauze wings the doll is an accurate representation of the earliest costume for this role.

87 Marie Taglioni in *La Sylphide*, from Queen Victoria's sketchbook. (Royal Collection)

Following one of her theatre visits Princess Victoria drew enthusiastically in her sketchbook. Her quick drawings were very accurate, reflecting her eye for detail; they are usually the earliest representations of the dancers in these important productions.

the workmanship of Lady Catherine Jenkinson, daughter of Lord Liverpool and one of the Duchess of Kent's favourite ladies-in-waiting. Significantly, neither the Duchess herself, nor any of the Princess's aunts, nor either of the Conroy girls contributed to this doll family. The Princess gave each doll a number in her catalogue, recorded its given name, and, in a final column, meticulously noted who had been responsible for dressing it – a corresponding numbered scrap of paper was sewn to the front of the doll's dress. Where dolls were based upon theatrical personalities Princess Victoria noted the character, role, production and date. Thus, for example:

10.	Mlle Sylphide Taglioni married to Count Almaviva	(as Mlle Taglioni appeared in the ballet of La Sylphide in 1832–33 made by Brss. Lehzen.)

The Princess had 'married' this doll (illustration 86) to 'No. 25 Count Almaviva (made by Prss Victoria)' and given them two children (nos 11 and 12), reflecting, perhaps, the dancer's recent marriage in July 1832 to Comte Gilbert de Voisins. This is typical of the intermingling of fact and fiction which runs through the naming of the dolls. The inspiration, for example, for 'No. 131 Leopold, Duke of Plaisance' (no maker given) is obvious, as also is 'No. 91 Catherine, Countess of Claremont' (made by Lady Catherine Jenkinson). The dolls based upon theatrical personalities often combine their name and performing role. Hence those representing Marie Taglioni all bear her surname but are differentiated by Christian names – Henriette, Sophie, Rosalie, Sylphide, and Nathalie – signifying the roles which her young admirer had seen her dance. These theatrical dolls were dressed when the Princess was aged between twelve and fourteen and, together with her well-observed and lively drawings of scenes from ballets and operas she had been taken to see, they reflect personalities who captured her imagination and admiration (illustration 87).[14] They also reflect moments of happy absorption in this fantasy world, so different from her home life of domestic tensions and onerous studies.

The silks, laces and ribbons used for making the dolls' clothes must have come from

the Baroness's bits bag, or may have been remnants charmed out of the dressmaker Mary Bettans. It is tempting to wonder whether any of the pieces might have come from the Princess's own dresses. The fashionably dressed dolls accurately reflect the bold and ornately dressed images of the fashion plates in contemporary women's journals, with their massively-brimmed hats balanced by large puffed or leg o' mutton sleeves and wide skirts. Such journals were certainly available to the Princess at Kensington Palace, for her mother's interest in fashion, and her exalted rank, led to her becoming patroness of such publications as *The New Monthly Belle Assemblée*. Some of the fashionable dolls may also have been miniature representations of the Duchess's guests at her frequent dinner parties and soirées, or ladies of rank and fashion observed by the sharp-eyed Princess during her many theatre visits or at her occasional appearances at court, which brought her a rare contact with an even wider spectrum of elegant society. Occasional references in her Journal reveal that she was capable of assessing the appearance of others, and was not always impressed. But her own sorties into fashion were probably severely limited and her dominant mother may well have made most clothing choices for her.

The Princess's earliest surviving dress was obviously a treasured reminder of an important occasion in her early life, now unknown (illustrations 76, 88).[15] It was a costly indulgence even for a princess. The lace used was one of the most esteemed and expensive textiles of the time, the height of fashion for wedding and ball dresses. Identifying an occasion when the dress might have been worn is difficult since the lace is of French manufacture. Buckingham point lace was used in 1828, for example, for

88 Detail of blonde lace dress.

Much lace, like Queen Victoria's wedding lace (illustrations 123–5), was made using fine white linen thread, but 'blonde' lace was made from natural, unbleached silk (hence its name). This gave a soft, warm and lustrous quality to the finished product and, though expensive, it was very fashionable for evening and wedding dresses. The design of Princess Victoria's lace has been dated to the early 1830s and it is of French manufacture. The main ground, regularly spotted with single flower motifs, is composed of 2⅜in. (6cm) wide vertical strips of lace joined together by invisible stitching. The lower scalloped border (two motifs deep) was worked separately as a continuous horizontal strip and then united with the main section by a cleverly concealed join in the heading of the upper motifs. A heavier silk thread was used to accentuate the main elements of the design.

89 *The Duchess of Kent and Princess Victoria,* 1834, by Sir George Hayter (1792–1871). (Royal Collection)

The artist was introduced to the Duchess by her brother, Prince Leopold, and he made several studies of the Princess before she succeeded to the throne. This painting of 1834, when she was fourteen, shows her hair formally dressed, perhaps in preparation for a small dinner party or theatre outing.

Princess Feodore's wedding dress as well as for Princess Victoria's dress as her bridesmaid. In 1827, £36 17s 6d was paid to 'Clarkson' for Buckingham lace for Princess Victoria, which may have been for this bridesmaid's dress.[16]

With the death of George IV and the accession of William IV in 1830, their niece moved a step nearer to the throne, and her mother began to allow her to make appearances at court. Attending her first Drawing Room on 24 February 1831 she was described as wearing 'a frock of English blonde draped over white satin, and a single row of pearls'. Blonde lace is not known to have been manufactured in England at this date and it seems extremely unlikely that the Duchess of Kent would have flouted Queen Adelaide's ruling that only textiles of British manufacture might be worn at her Drawing Rooms. Changes in fashion, well-designed imports and competition from the increasingly mechanised cotton industry had for some time been eroding the previously successful silk-weaving and lace-making industries. Like Princess Charlotte in 1817, Queen Adelaide had a deep concern for the workers in these industries and was driven to make her own stand on their behalf. In 1831 she had a dress of English blonde made for her in Nottingham; it was of machine-made silk net embroidered by hand, as Princess Victoria's presumably was. The surviving dress of French lace may well have been a present from her Uncle Leopold, now King of the Belgians, or a first gift from his new wife, intended for an important court appearance like this, but perhaps relegated to private occasions.

In 1832 King Leopold had finally remarried. His bride, Princess Louise, daughter of Louis Philippe, King of the French, was only seven years older than Princess Victoria. They met for the first time in 1835 when King Leopold brought his bride to Ramsgate, and Victoria soon wrote in her Journal of her aunt's wardrobe; she was given small gifts from it – cravats, ribbons, a cap and a tippet. Queen Louise's elegant Parisian clothes transported her niece into raptures: this was an aunt quite unlike any of her others. She even sent her own hairdresser to arrange the Princess's hair like hers, with side curls. Princess Victoria was already sickening during this visit, and was quite seriously ill for some weeks after their departure. Already, however, her aunt had set in motion more delights and once Victoria was sufficiently recovered she was able to pore over the boxes of dresses, bonnets and special hairpins which had arrived for her from Paris. The latter were for the moment useless, as quantities of her hair fell out as the result of her illness, but she was probably able to make immediate use of the three dresses, plus bonnets, 'made by Mdlle. Palmyre the 1st Marchande des Modes in Paris'. More delights from this premier house were sent by Queen Louise in the following year: 'a thick pink silk dress, a silk dress couleur de poussière for the morning and a very light figured pink silk for the evening. All these dresses are made by Mdlle Palmyre, the first dressmaker in Paris.' Yet more came later in the year when King Leopold visited Claremont: 'a most lovely light blue silk dress and a light blue satin bonnet', the Princess reported to her Journal in delight. 'They are quite lovely. They are so well made and in so very elegant a manner.' Thus was founded a deep partiality for Parisian fashion luxuries which, when Queen, Victoria found hard to resist. Perhaps, therefore, the charming little lace dress was the first of such temptations, and perhaps it too had to be set aside for patriotic reasons in 1831 or 1832 (illustration 76).[17]

The second of the two dresses surviving from before Queen Victoria's accession is of a fine French silk velvet: once more its origins and the reason for its preservation are elusive (illustration 90). It does not seem to match any of the gifts of Mme Palmyre's creations from the King and Queen of the Belgians as recorded by the Princess, but perfectly exemplifies the qualities which made French goods so attractive.[18]

For several decades this dress has been dated to about 1830, which is far too early. It is only a little smaller than Queen Victoria's accession dress, and therefore should probably be dated between 1835 and 1837. The cut of the bodice, with a waist edge almost reaching the natural waistline and the point at the centre front just beginning seriously to vie with a horizontal waistline, is typical of the mid-1830s, the end of a long transition from the high waisted neo-classical dresses of Princess Charlotte's lifetime. Princess Victoria would probably have worn this dress for an informal dinner party or perhaps even for a theatre visit. Portraits of 1836 show her wearing dresses with similar large puffed sleeves. George IV's impressive state visit to Scotland in 1822 was one of several events which brought tartan, or checked fabrics imitating tartan, into the sphere of the fashionable world. Since 1832 Princess Victoria had seen many performances of the ballet *La Sylphide* which is set in the Highlands, and in January 1836 she had been allowed to read her first novel, Sir Walter Scott's *Bride of Lammermoor*. A general enthusiasm for things Scottish may have been responsible for Princess Victoria's choice of this fabric. Such velvets were particularly fashionable in the years 1825–40, both in England and France. Samples of at least two further 'tartan' dresses almost certainly made for Princess Victoria between 1836 and 1838 are preserved in the books of dress cuttings associated with the dressmaker Mary Bettans.

It is tempting to seek some significance in the dress's preservation, although there could well be none. In May 1836 the Duke of Coburg, older brother of King Leopold and the Duchess of Kent, brought his sons Ernest and Albert to England, and this was the first occasion on which Victoria met her future husband. She was aware of her uncle Leopold's great desire that she should marry this cousin. Could Princess Victoria have worn her tartan velvet dress during this visit? Such an association might well have led to its preservation for sentimental reasons. There may, however, be some other significance – the Princess's eighteenth birthday in May 1837, for example, when she attained her majority, suggests itself as another memorable landmark in her young life.

But already the health of her uncle King William IV was a matter for concern and it was realised that her accession was imminent. The Princess's teenage years should have witnessed her preparation for her future role by attendance at court functions. Instead her over-protective mother kept her away from court as much as possible, disapproving of the presence of the King's illegitimate children and ignoring the sympathetic Queen Adelaide. They were not happy years for Princess Victoria. Nevertheless when she eventually succeeded to the throne in 1837, little known by the court and unfamiliar with its procedures, she astonished the experienced and critical veterans of several reigns by the composure with which she conducted herself.

90 Velvet dress, 1835–7.
   (MoL 33.329, Royal Collection)

The silk velvet of this dress is cleverly woven to imitate tartan, although it does not replicate a recognisable Scottish clan tartan. Vertical stripes of black, blue, green and red are countered by narrow horizontal satin-weave stripes of red, blue and green to produce a checked ground, whilst bold overchecking in narrow white satin stripes completes the impression of a tartan fabric.

Accession, 1837

On Tuesday 20 June 1837 Princess Victoria was woken by her mother at 6am to receive the Archbishop of Canterbury and the Lord Chamberlain, Lord Conyngham, who, as she recorded in her Journal some hours later, 'then acquainted me that my poor Uncle, the King, was no more, and had expired at 12 minutes past 2 this morning and consequently that I am Queen'. By 9am she had dressed and breakfasted, written to her sister and her Uncle Leopold, and was ready to give her first audience to her Prime Minister, Lord Melbourne. At 11am she held her first Privy Council, in the Red Saloon at Kensington Palace (illustration 91).

A once-black dress which Queen Victoria is believed to have worn on the first day of her reign survives (illustrations 92–3).[1] The fact that it was preserved by the Queen herself throughout her reign gives credibility to an association which cannot otherwise be proven. That she was in black was quite unremarkable to herself and to all those who witnessed that historic occasion. Rather than her dress, it was Victoria's calm demeanour which attracted notice. Charles Greville, Clerk of the Privy Council since 1821, recorded in his journal:

91 *The First Council of Queen Victoria,* by Sir David Wilkie (1785–1841). (Royal Collection)

Wishing to capture something of the new Queen's youthfulness and innocence in her interview with her Ministers, the artist requested that she wear a white dress at the first sitting for this painting in October 1837. She wore a 'white satin [dress], covered with gauze embroidered – I think it looks well', he wrote to his sister. Later in her life Queen Victoria seems to have regretted this deviation from the truth, noting tartly: 'He put me in white for effect, I was in black [at the First Council] notwithstanding'. (Millar 1969, p144; Ginsburg, p48).

92 Privy Council dress, 1837. (MoL D330, Royal Collection)

The dress (right) which Queen Victoria reputedly wore on her first day as Queen, 20 June 1837, reflected her cautious attitude to changes in fashion. The attractive sleeves and the asymmetric vertical frill on the skirt had both been featured in fashion plates during the last year, and so were not new to the fashion repertoire: they were still being included in fashion plates of June and July 1837 and had presumably become widely adopted. The straight, almost natural, waistline of this dress also reflects the older line; the pointed waistline had not yet become obligatory in fashionable dresses.

There was never anything like the first impression She produced, or the chorus of praise and admiration which is raised about her manner and behaviour, and certainly not without justice. It was very extraordinary, and something far beyond what was looked for. Her extreme youth and inexperience, and the ignorance of the world concerning her, naturally excited intense curiosity ... She went through the whole ceremony ... with perfect calmness and self-possession, but at the same time with a graceful modesty and propriety particularly interesting and ingratiating ...[2]

This slender, barely adorned dress, much discoloured with age, was originally catalogued as 'blue' (a faded blue-black, a colour-blind curator?) and has further been described in print as

> an old one which the economical Duchess of Kent had had dipped at home when King William's mother-in-law died [in March 1837]. The dye was not fast but was no doubt considered good enough to the Duchess who, as well as being economical, disliked the King and Queen intensely. [3]

Nothing could be further from the truth. That the dress was not an economical dipping is readily demonstrated by the original fine white silk linings, still intact and virtually pristine. These are not later additions, and the dress shows no evidence of the misleading later alterations which afflict many dresses. The blotched discoloration of the

93 Detail of dress shown in illustration 92.

Sleeves like these were given several names in contemporary fashion journals. They were an attractive means of restraining the fullness of the sleeves of the 1820s and early 1830s and bringing about the fitted line of the 1840s. This sleeve is cut in a single piece, with the fullness held in pleats at the shoulder and by bands down the arm. The lace-trimmed embroidered cuff seems to be original to the dress and may have matched a fichu, covering the neck and shoulders, which would have been added to the dress for morning wear.

94 'General Mourning for His Late Majesty
King William the Fourth', *The World of
Fashion*, July 1837. (Gallery of English
Costume, Manchester)

The Lord Chamberlain's Office was
responsible for announcing court and public
mourning on the death of a member of the
Royal Family. Their formal instructions
were published in newspapers and women's
journals. As the Earl Marshal's notice makes
clear, it was expected that everyone who
could possibly afford it would adopt black
out of respect for their late monarch, and
those who did not were very noticeable. It
was customary to comply.

95 Fashion plate, *The World of Fashion*
July 1837. (Gallery of English
Costume, Manchester)

When a royal death suddenly put the
country into mourning, black washes simply
replaced the planned colour washes in
fashion plates, and small changes would be
made to the prepared text just prior to
printing. If time or finances allowed plates
showing specially-devised mourning
fashions might be used. See illustration 68.

finely ribbed silk is a familiar phenomenon since in past centuries the fixatives used for
black dyes made them unstable, liable to discolour like this or, worse, to destroy the host
silk. Numerous examples of seventeenth-century blackwork embroideries lacking their
black thread demonstrate the problems inherent in black dyes.

It is anyway inconceivable that the Duchess of Kent, previously so ambitious for and
protective of her daughter, would stoop to a petty economy of this kind for her first
appearance as Queen. The cost of such a new dress was insignificant compared to the
enormity of the occasion, and the Duchess's earlier household accounts amply
demonstrate the nature of her expenditure on Princess Victoria's dresses in childhood. It
could be said that she was excessively conscious of her daughter's position as heir to the
throne, and her debts of £70,000, uncovered by Queen Victoria on her accession,
witness her anxiety to maintain this status. It is equally inconceivable that either
Baroness Lehzen or the Princess herself would have tolerated such a pointless economy.
On her eighteenth birthday only four weeks earlier the Princess had been granted her
own income by the King (though it had perhaps not yet been received), and less than two
months after her accession she was clearing quite large debts out of her Privy Purse
allocation to some of her major suppliers – Mrs Bettans, her dressmaker, and Richard
Gundry her shoemaker, for example.[4]

It is possible that the dress had been made and worn earlier in the year as mourning for
Queen Adelaide's mother. However, as the Princess's own Journal entries for June 1837
reveal, William IV's death had been expected for some weeks and there was plenty of
time for new mourning clothes to be made for the future Queen. There was indeed an
increasing tension as the days slipped by and the King's condition worsened. By 15 June
Victoria recorded in her Journal: 'The news of the King are so very bad that all my lessons

save the Dean's are put off, including Lablache's … I regret rather my singing lesson … the Doctors think my poor uncle the King cannot last more than 48 hours!'[5]

To have to forego her singing lessons with the famous bass Luigi Lablache was a considerable loss to the Princess, who was reported to have a pleasant voice and had found these lessons a great release from her daily routine. They were presumably not thought seemly in view of the King's serious condition. The Princess did not record in her Journal more practical preparations for what was clearly viewed as inevitable. When the news of her uncle's death reached her, it is likely that pre-arranged plans were set in motion. The world outside the palace also had to change gear suddenly: court mourning was decreed, and fashion plates had to take on sombre hues, whilst the accompanying text provided readers with suggestions for appropriate dress during official mourning (illustration 94).

Overnight the Princess's life had changed abruptly: her schoolroom books were replaced by documents of State, her tutors by Ministers of State, and her modest and obscure day-to-day existence gave way to the succession of ceremonies and public appearances which are the lot of any modern monarch. She also took charge of her own life and was able to refute by her actions the charge made to Lord Liverpool just before her accession, by Sir John Conroy (the Duchess of Kent's Comptroller, who aspired to be the new Queen's Private Secretary), that

> she was totally unfit by nature for the consideration of business, and was younger in intellect by some years than she was in age – that her tastes were light and frivolous and that she was easily caught by fashion and appearances; as a proof of which he said that she was much taken with the manners, dress, etc. of the young Duchess of Sutherland …[6]

That same Duchess of Sutherland, Harriet Leveson-Gower (1806–68) was in fact one of the Queen's very first official appointments, as Mistress of the Robes, a choice much approved by Victoria's fashion-conscious Prime Minister Lord Melbourne, as she noted in her Journal entry for 26 June 1837: 'I forgot to say that Lord Melbourne told me [yesterday] that the Duchess of Sutherland has accepted the office of Mistress of the Robes… At ½ past 2 came the Duchess… whom I am delighted to have… she was looking so handsome and nice' (illustration 96).[7]

Who did select the Queen's dresses? Whatever the system had been before her accession, she now required a much larger, well-organised team to deal with this aspect of her busy new life, and what must have been suddenly a much extended wardrobe. Parliament had voted the Queen a toilette allowance of £4000 (soon proved inadequate and raised to £5000) and Baroness Lehzen emerges from the Office of Robes records as the Palace contact who, in the first months of the reign at least, handled the contacts with the Queen's suppliers. Because of the gap in the Duchess of Kent's household accounts from 1829–37 it is not possible to know what staff Princess Victoria brought with her. Her senior dresser Marianne Skerrett, as the Queen herself recorded some years later:

> entered the Queen's service almost immediately after her accession … being recommended … by the late Marchioness of Lansdowne [Principal Lady of the Bedchamber]. She was the niece of a Mr Mathias, who had been sub-treasurer to Queen Charlotte … She is a person of immense literary knowledge and sound understanding, of the greatest discretion and straightforwardness.[8]

She was already, it would seem, about fifty-two or fifty-three years old, and must have

96 *Harriet, Duchess of Sutherland, c.*1839, by Charles Robert Leslie (1794–1859). (Wolverhampton Museum & Art Gallery)

Harriet Leveson-Gower was the wife of the second Duke of Sutherland. She served four terms of office as Mistress of the Robes to Queen Victoria and is here shown in her coronation robes. She became one of the Queen's closest friends, and it was her company which the Queen sought in the first weeks after the death of Prince Albert.

97 Office of Robes Accounts Ledger, March
1838. (Public Record Office, London)

The brief records of payments were kept in
an orderly fashion, from dressmakers
(Bettans, Vouillon & Laure, Palmyre) and
mercers (Howell & James) to suppliers of
accessories and perfumes; it was a pattern
that would be adhered to throughout the
reign. The royal hairdresser (Isidore
Marchand) presumably charged for fresh or
silk flowers used by him when dressing the
Queen's hair for formal occasions.

brought experience as well as maturity to her new post; she remained until 1862. On
Baroness Lehzen's departure in 1842 Marianne Skerrett seems to have taken over her
administrative duties, and a third dresser was appointed.

Shortly after the Queen's accession a second dresser and two wardrobe maids were
appointed to work under Miss Skerrett's direction, all paid out of the Queen's toilette
allocation. The duties of these most intimate of the Queen's staff were written down
some thirty years later and from them we are able to gain a greater understanding of the
technicalities of caring for the Queen's clothes, as well as the process of dressing her (see
Appendix 3). Essentially the dressers were responsible for the care of the Queen's clothes,

having everything ready when she needed to change, seeing that all was cleaned or mended before being put away, packing and accompanying the clothing trunks on the Queen's many travels, and overseeing the wardrobe maids. Recently the published letters of one of the later dressers, Frieda Arnold (1854–9), have given greater insight into the day-to-day lives of these hardworked royal servants, who although privileged had few friends and little time of their own. [9]

In the summer of 1837 the late King's Office of Robes at St James's Palace had to be disbanded and a new Office established with the Queen's own appointments: this was a separate entity within the Lord Chamberlain's department, and was manned by a Groom of the Robes, a Clerk of the Robes, and a Messenger. Like the Mistress's post, that of the Groom was essentially ceremonial, and the burden of running the Office was borne by the Clerk. As well as caring for the monarch's robes, the Office saw to the quarterly payments to the Queen's clothing suppliers, obtaining the finance necessary from the Treasury. The Queen's toilette allowance was also required to cover the salaries of the Office staff, the Queen's dressers, wardrobe maids and hairdresser, plus a furrier's retainer fee for maintenance of the ermine-trimmed robes. The Clerk of the Robes was also responsible for issuing royal warrants to the tradespeople who supplied the Queen's clothing needs.

Three large leather-bound letter books of the Office of Robes are now the sole source of information about the provision of clothing for Queen Victoria (illustrations 97, 108, 109). [10] They cover all sixty-four years of her reign, providing information about her suppliers – over 450 individuals, firms or institutions – and her personal staff. The Queen objected to being required to submit her suppliers' detailed bills to the Office, as a letter from Baroness Lehzen to the Duchess of Sutherland in December 1837 reveals:

> as Her Majesty does not wish to send some of the Bills (like those of the Dressmakers', etc) to the Office, She has commanded her Dresser to make Abstracts of them, and enclose them with the other Bills for Mr Browell [the Clerk of the Robes] … [via] Your Grace. [11]

Thus all the details which today would have provided a much more complete picture of the Queen's wardrobe, and particularly the making of those garments which have

98 Design for Queen Victoria's Garter collar, 1837, by Rundell, Bridge & Rundell. (Royal Collection)

The royal jewellers submitted these modified designs when new insignia were found necessary for Queen Victoria. William IV's Garter collar, for example, was very heavy and was normally worn over uniform. In contrast the Queen's décolleté demanded a much lighter and longer collar, and her new one contained seventy-two sections as opposed to the normal forty-eight. The collar is of enamelled gold and still survives. She is often shown wearing it in portraits (illustrations 15, 128), and the bodices of her dresses had to be designed to be compatible with the collar and sash. New, smaller, Stars of the Orders were also made at this time, and these continue to be worn by royal consorts.

99 *Queen Victoria Riding Out,* 1839, by Sir Francis Grant (1803–78). (Royal Collection)

Queen Victoria enjoyed many 'ridings out' at Windsor with her Prime Minister Lord Melbourne (on her left) and presumably commissioned this painting set in Windsor Great Park to commemmorate them. When she saw the completed painting she expressed disappointment in the likeness of Lord Melbourne – 'not flattering, rather caricatured'. The artist was also dissatified with the likeness, explaining that he had found the Prime Minister's face very changeable.

survived, were retained by the Queen and subsequently destroyed. Nevertheless a great deal can still be gleaned from the briefer records, such as who supplied the Queen at any one time, what the changing pattern of supply was, what monies were expended in each quarter of each year of her reign, the appointments and retirements and salaries of her most personal staff. Information drawn from them is used throughout the text.

It took a little time for the Office to adjust to the new, strongly female regime at Buckingham Palace – previous kings had not required the daily attendance of a hairdresser, for example, and many memoranda were exchanged before the source of his salary was established. Least comfortable with the Queen's approach to the privacy of her clothing bills was the Treasury, always on tenter-hooks about the possibility of overspending after its experiences with her extravagant uncles. At the beginning of the reign Baroness Lehzen, responding to one of these Treasury queries, agreed 'that should the expenses exceed that sum [ie the official toilette allocation], the Queen must make up the deficiency out of Her Privy Purse'.[12] The Privy Purse accounts reveal that occasionally this was done. The least overspending triggered alarms. When it happened in 1840, just after the Queen's wedding, the Treasury refused to advance the necessary £700 from the next quarter's allocation. The sum was eventually paid out of the Privy Purse, but only after the Clerk had managed to negotiate with some of the major suppliers to put the debts on account, and to hold some bills over to the next quarter. Such accounting slip-ups rarely recurred in the Queen's long reign, but each occasion elicited sharp rebukes from lesser Treasury officials. The Clerk of the Robes, however, learnt his lesson in 1840 and thereafter shrewdly hoarded occasional surplus income in the Office's Drummond's Bank account for future emergencies.

The most pressured of the Queen's suppliers in the first month of her reign was the robemaker John Hunter.[13] In the space of just three weeks he had the task of providing robes of the Orders of the Garter and Bath (for Chapters held on 12 and 14 July 1837), and a crimson velvet Parliament robe for the Proroguing (ie dismissing at end of session) of Parliament on 17 July 1837. Precedents for the correct form of robe (ie kirtle and mantle) for a Queen regnant had to be researched: Queen Anne (1702–14) had been the last queen to reign in her own right. The workrooms of John Hunter in Great Maddox

100 Presentation shoes, 1837–8.
    (MoL 33.77/1)

The embroidered motifs and inscriptions have led to the mistaken assumption that these attractive shoes were worn by Queen Victoria at her coronation on 20 June 1837. They are of a deep purple silk velvet embroidered in coloured silks and gilt thread, mainly in satin stitch. The gilt-thread embroidery on the lining and innersole is incompatible with comfortable wear, particularly for a lengthy ceremonial on a warm summer's day.

101 Detail: inside of shoes.

Embroidered on the innersoles of the shoes is the inscription 'Ll & N makers', which seems to confirm that they were made by Llewellyn & Naish of Bristol. The Queen never became a customer, but the firm was issued with a royal warrant on 3 February 1838 – a consolation prize perhaps. Bristol trade directories reveal that the firm had held warrants under George IV and William IV.

Street, as well as those of the furrier Robert Drake at 25 Piccadilly, must have been very busy in these weeks. There was probably little time for consultation with the Queen, who as yet had only limited experience of court ceremonials, or for fittings. On 17 July 1837, scrutinised by Ministers, Members of Parliament and officials of all kinds, she had to process to the throne in this exceedingly heavy ermine-lined garment.[14] This she achieved without rehearsal or mishap, and with the quiet assurance which had so impressed her Privy Council. According to the usually well-informed *The World of Fashion* she wore a 'white satin petticoat, embroidered with gold' under the kirtle.[15] On other occasions, such as her first Drawing Room on the previous day, she continued to wear mourning for her uncle:

> a black crape dress, richly embroidered in jet, over black silk; a train of black crape over black silk, tastefully ornamented with jet flowers. Head-dress: feathers, jet ornaments, and crape lappets. Her Majesty wore the ensigns of the Order of the Garter, the badge and star of diamonds.[16]

This popular fashion journal, which in the previous reign had contained more restrained reporting of royal occasions, now blossomed with enthusiastic accounts of the young Queen, coupled with such discreet gossip as it could muster. Its numerous eyewitness reports of royal ceremonies or of details of the Queen's private life suggest the pen of a patrician fallen on hard times or of an indiscreet member of the royal household staff. The October 1837 issue furnished readers with an account of the Queen's Parliament robe, from an unrevealed source naturally, which included the information so beloved of the press, that the eight-yard train (ie the mantle) weighed 20lbs.[17] 'The back of the body [ie of the kirtle] is beautifully embroidered in gold (oak) leaves; the sleeve in particular is curious, being cut in the same fashion as that worn by Queen Anna Boleyn' (illustration 165). *The World of Fashion* was able to disclose at the same time that the 'orders [collars] and medals worn at the end of the ribbons belonging to the Orders of the Bath and of the Garter, are now being made smaller, as the weight of the former ones was found inconvenient to her Majesty at the late Prorogation of Parliament' (illustration 98).[18]

The Office of Robes records show that this first hasty robe apparently did not please the Queen, for the following May a note from Baroness Lehzen, copied into the ledgers, transmitted a request from the Queen for new Parliament robes. It is now difficult to disentangle the exact course of events from the brief ledger entries. Charges held over by John Hunter from 1837 until the following year, when he presented his bill after the Queen's coronation, suggest that a new robe was made for the Prorogation of Parliament in July 1837, and then a second new robe was made for her coronation a year later. [19] The bills of the robemaker and furrier for these two robes, amounting to £640 8s 9d and £643 8s 9d respectively, seem to confirm that a completely new making occurred and that none of the previous velvet or costly ermine was reused. Moreover, the two robes were still in the keeping of the Office in 1851 when a third kirtle was made for the Queen, and the Duchess of Sutherland claimed the 1838 kirtle as a perquisite of her office. Neither of the two 1830s kirtles has survived. [20]

Once the exhausting series of inaugural ceremonials in July was successfully accomplished Queen Victoria retired to Windsor where she enjoyed frequent horseback excursions, accompanied by members of her family or household or by ministers. The sum of £62 11s 6d paid to her habitmaker Peter Thompson of Frith Street in Soho in September must represent several elegant habits made for these rides. One of the early images of the new Queen to be circulated in popular prints showed her on horseback, representing a youth and vigour which had been lacking from the monarchy since her cousin Princess Charlotte had likewise captivated the public imagination. Unfortunately, none of the Queen's riding habits now survives. However, the jacket of one ensemble of this date was preserved by the Queen herself and through it can be sensed the young Victoria relishing her freedom and status (illustrations 102–4). [21]

It appears that a decision had been made to hold the sovereign's customary review of her troops during the Queen's stay at Windsor. Whether by design or chance the location of the review at Windsor on 28 September 1837 provided a neat solution for those, the Queen included, not eligible to wear military uniform. This was the adoption of a form of the Windsor uniform, devised by George III in the 1770s when he made Windsor his principal residence (pp26–8). Female versions of this private uniform had been worn by his wife and daughters in the earliest days of its use but it appears to have been exclusively male wear in the nineteenth century. However, Queen Victoria saw to it that many of her entourage and family did wear it, and in her Journal there are admiring references to Lord Melbourne and later to Prince Albert in their uniforms.

For the Queen the day was a triumph. When the regiments saluted her, she confided to her Journal, 'I saluted them by putting my hand to my cap like the officers do, and was much admired for my manner of doing so … The whole went off beautifully; and I felt for the first time like a man, as if I could fight myself at the head of my Troops.' Exhilarated by the day's events she added one of her infrequent descriptions of her attire:

> Dressed in a habit of dark blue with red collar and cuffs (the Windsor uniform which
> all my gentlemen wear), a military cap, and my Order of the Garter as I was going to
> review the Troops … [who] consisted of the 1st Regiment of Life Guards who are
> beautiful, of the Grenadier Guards, and of some of the Lancers.

She rode her horse Leopold and was accompanied by her gentlemen either in military or Windsor uniform. The exact form of the Queen's military cap is uncertain and two popular prints show quite different styles. [22]

102 Detail: cuff with buttons.

Nineteenth-century tailors frequently used buttons marked with their own names, but on Queen Victoria's Windsor jacket the gilt metal buttons bearing her cypher are marked 'JENNENS. LONDON' (for Joseph Jennens & Co., Buttons, Military & Naval Ornament Manufacturers to her Majesty, & the Royal Family, 134 Regent Street). Fine cloth frayed little and to avoid bulky hems the edges were frequently left raw on men's coats and uniforms, as they are here.

103 Detail: lining of Windsor uniform jacket.

English tailoring was at its peak at the time this jacket was made. This view reveals a little of the labour which went into such garments. Much hand-stitching and manipulation of the fine wool cloth, hidden within the padded and quilted lining, was used to mould the garment and to make discreet 'improvements', whilst layers of tailor's canvas were wad-stitched within the shapely masculine collar.

A further relic of the Queen's first year on the throne is a pair of slim shoes of embroidered silk velvet, which have always been associated with the Queen's coronation (illustrations 100–1). [23] Research for this book has fortunately uncovered an entry in the 1 February 1838 issue of *The World of Fashion* which exactly describes these shoes:

> Her Majesty's Slippers. – Her Majesty has perhaps the most beautifully formed foot in the world; it is a pattern of grace and symmetry; as those who have been so fortunate as to obtain a sight of a splendid pair of dress slippers recently made for the Queen at Bristol, may have been able to conceive. These shoes almost rival the famous glass slipper of Cinderella. They absolutely seem the manufacture of Robin Goodfellow, Queen Mab, and her band of fairies, rather than the work of the fingers and thumbs of mere mortals. They are of purple velvet, the Royal Arms and the Initials V.R., being embroidered in gold upon the front. The figures are admirably delineated, well relieved, and the whole executed with great art and exquisite delicacy. Around the sides are entwined wreaths of oak leaves, interspersed with acorns and roses, of gold thread and silk. The inside is of white satin, and exhibits, also in gold, the rose, the thistle, and the shamrock, twining around the words 'All hail to Victoria'. These exquisite productions are enclosed in a box of sandal wood, with a golden lock and key, the cover being ornamented with the Royal Arms, superbly carved in ivory.[24]

On this occasion it seems likely that the makers of the shoes, bursting with pride, may have engineered their own 'leak'. It is an invaluable passage as it establishes that the shoes were made and presented long before the coronation. From time to time such presentations were made to the Queen by firms hoping to elicit her custom and thereby to be eligible for a royal warrant. They were usually returned. A single fine silk stocking, worked with an elaborate lace design on the instep, which has been further enriched with embroidery in gold purl thread, had likewise been believed to have been worn at her

104 Windsor uniform jacket, 1837. (MoL D327, Royal Collection)

All that now remains of Queen Victoria's dashing review uniform is the superbly tailored jacket, whose sculpted lines (right hand page) reflect the slender form of its owner. It can be attributed with assurance to the Soho establishment of her habitmaker Peter Thompson, who received a royal warrant in August 1837 and had probably supplied riding habits to the Duchess of Kent and her daughter for some years.

coronation by Queen Victoria. There is nothing to support this assumption and this is again likely to have been a special presentation piece sent to Buckingham Palace in the months following the Queen's accession. The woven inscription 'VICTORIA 1ER REINE D'ANGLETERRE' indicates a French manufacturer, but no payments to a French hosier are recorded in the Office of Robes payment ledgers.[25]

It is generally believed that Queen Victoria was not interested in fashion and did not dress fashionably. Neither is true, and only with the death of Prince Albert did her interest in her own appearance wane dramatically. Her mother's predilection for fussy and ornate fashions, coupled perhaps with Baroness Lehzen's rather modest and bourgeois taste, must initially have been formative influences. Her early Journal entries reveal that Princess Victoria had decided views on what she liked or disliked in the dress of those she met, and no doubt as she grew older these opinions were more openly expressed. Her aunt, the elegant French-born Queen Louise of the Belgians, did not have a high opinion of the Duchess of Kent's taste and had attempted to counter it with her frequent gifts of Parisian dresses and accessories to Princess Victoria. With days filled only with lessons from a succession of stern visiting masters – and the liberating release of riding denied by her own choice (her mother had insisted that the hated Sir John Conroy accompany Victoria when out riding) – it is not surprising that the teenage Princess sought relief in fashion and the theatre. Her accession to the throne released her from restrictions and thenceforward she was free to wear what she liked. However, her Journal entries soon show how engrossed she became in the business of monarchy, a diversion which far surpassed the transient novelties of fashion. Portraits of her at this time suggest that she retained a simple hairstyle and uncluttered approach to her dress, and by no means allowed her elevation and liberation to lead her into extravagant ways.

The Queen's approach to fashion was that held to be appropriate for all gentlewomen of her generation. She later outlined her views in a letter to her son the Prince of Wales (the future Edward VII) when he was given his own establishment in 1858:

> Dress is a trifling matter … But it gives also the one outward sign from which people in general can and often do judge upon the <u>inward</u> state of mind and feeling of a person … we do not wish to control your own tastes and fancies … but we do <u>expect</u>, that you will never wear anything extravagant or slang.[26]

Her views are those to be found in the increasing number of etiquette books which were aimed at the rising middle classes. For example *The Ladies' Pocket Book of Etiquette*, already in its seventh edition in 1840, advised 'Affect not the extreme mode – it is the most certain index of a little mind; but let elegance and simplicity ever be the prominent character of your dress'. In 1849 *The English Gentlewoman* cited the Queen herself as an ideal: she 'dresses like a gentlewoman, on all ordinary occasions; and, both in her own costume and in that of her royal children, is said to prove her true good taste by preferring the simplicity so truly becoming to youth'.

It was natural that the fashion press should look eagerly to the Queen to endorse new fashions and generally to become an icon for women of her age. As had been the practice in previous decades several articles were named after her, for example, 'The Victoria Bonnet', although they were not necessarily copies of anything she had herself worn. Images of her proliferated rapidly too, aimed at the loyal and curious, who had little idea of the appearance of their new monarch. Some of the prints were crude and inaccurate and certainly cannot be relied upon for modern research purposes. However, they

105 *Queen Victoria*, 1838, by Alfred Edward Chalon (1781–1860). (Scottish National Portrait Gallery, Edinburgh)

This attractive watercolour study shows the Queen apparently on a terrace at Windsor with St George's Chapel in the distance. An embroidered black apron, perhaps of her own making or a gift, protects her fashionably-styled watered silk dress. Chalon was made Portrait Painter in Watercolours to the Queen in 1837 and was the first artist to whom she sat after her accession.

provided a generally recognisable image to the Queen's scattered subjects. In time this would be supplemented by a succession of engravings after more accurate portraits and, of course, by the profile head of the Queen which appeared on coinage and then stamps. The lengthy descriptions, to be found in most women's journals of the time, of both royal and society women attending major events in the social calendar, also served to endorse the fashions extolled in accompanying columns and fashion plates. Whilst enjoying the pleasures of dress, of selecting fine silks and lace for her dresses, Queen Victoria almost certainly saw herself more as a follower of fashion, cautious of novelties and conforming with those about her, than as one of fashion's leaders. Conversely, her subjects were inclined expectantly to view her as a fashion leader, and thereby in time became disappointed.

Accession had propelled Queen Victoria from a studious secluded life with only occasional social contacts, to the very centre of London society. It must have been a daunting and difficult experience but she appears to have chosen her mentors well. Of these it was her fashion-conscious Prime Minister Lord Melbourne whose comments on fashion were to appear most frequently in the Queen's Journal before her marriage.

> I asked Lord Melbourne how he liked my dress. He said he thought it 'very pretty' and that 'it did very well'. He is so natural and funny and nice about toilette and has a very good taste I think …

So good Lord M. was asked repeatedly by his young sovereign for his comments on her toilette. Lord M. thought 'my diadem … very handsome', 'my dress … beautiful'; of 'a cherry-coloured silk with a magnificent old lace flounce, "It's very pretty", he said, "I like those bright colours; it's very handsome". The dress I had on the day before, a striped one, he didn't think ugly, but said it was like the pattern of a sofa'. Worse was to come:

> I couldn't get my gloves on … Lord M. said, 'It's those consumed rings; I never could bear them.' I said I was fond of them, and that it improved an ugly hand. 'Makes it worse,' he replied; I said I didn't wear them of a morning. 'Much better,' he said, 'and if you didn't wear them, nobody else would'. Ear-rings he thinks barbarous.[27]

It was a considerable novelty for the Queen to have the company of such a sympathetic and tactful male counsellor. Apart from the occasional visits of her beloved Uncle Leopold she had daily had to run the gauntlet of Sir John Conroy's acerbic tongue. Her fashion advisors had been solely women; now her tastes and attitudes could be tested more reassuringly through her Prime Minister. Their discussions otherwise were extremely wide ranging and he was responsible for helping to form her political tenets. But although his opinion of the royal wardrobe was sought – and sometimes offered gratuitously – the Queen was by no means dominated by it. She disregarded his views on her rings and earrings, and also his dislike of blue: 'It's an unlucky colour; no girl ever marries who wears a blue gown'.[28] She continued to wear blue and in a short time was married. The opinions of the new man in her life, Prince Albert, were to be much more influential.

Coronation, 1838

106 Frame of Imperial State Crown, 1838.
(MoL 58.74, 36.112/1, 2)

Finding George IV's massive new crown too heavy, Queen Victoria had a new State Crown made by Rundell, Bridge & Rundell for her own coronation. This continued to be used until 1937 when a copy was made, and it is this copy which George VI and HM The Queen have used. The Imperial State Crown was worn for the procession from the Abbey at the end of the coronation ceremonial; it is also used for the opening of Parliament. Queen Victoria obviously preferred the lighter George IV circlet (illustration 119) and is less frequently portrayed in her State Crown.

107 The *supertunica*. (MoL 48.14/10)

It is not certain what form the cloth of gold *supertunica* took in 1821 and 1831 (right hand page). In 1838 this flattering and dignified version was evolved for Queen Victoria. The original medieval form had already disappeared by 1685 when the form of the *supertunica* provided for James II reflected the fashionable cut of men's coats (illustration 113). The rather neat solution was a garment which owed much to legal and academic robes. The Queen's *supertunica*, therefore, whilst innovative, cleverly combined a seemingly ancient form with an outline in accord with contemporary fashion. In 1902 Edward VII reverted to the 1685 form, rather lengthened, and this has been retained in all subsequent coronations.

The English coronation ritual is of very ancient origin, now more than one thousand years old, and over the centuries it has evolved gradually into an imposing and lengthy ceremonial. In the middle ages it was necessary to confirm the new king, by anointing and crowning, within days of his predecessor's death. Once the urgency to establish the new monarch via these symbolic rituals abated, a more relaxed approach began to be taken about the period between accession and coronation, which enabled much more elaborate preparations to be made. George III allowed an interval of eleven months, and this practice has continued to the present day.

It is not certain when practical preparations for Victoria's coronation commenced but it was certainly not until April 1838 that the Mistress of the Robes received an enquiry from the Treasury about the cost of the robes the Queen would require; they needed to compare these with the last coronation and then include them in the overall coronation expenses, which were to be presented to Parliament for official approval. The stern tone of the Treasury communications reminds us that the extravagance of George IV's coronation was not forgotten and that strict control over the monarch's spending was now maintained by the government's servants.[1] After a flurry of memoranda – for neither the Mistress of the Robes nor her office staff had yet quite grasped what was needed – an estimate of £1458 for all but the cloth of gold robe was submitted. It was now May and at this point the Queen made her formal request for new Parliament robes, whilst John Hunter, the robemaker, submitted a further estimate of £1033 to cover the cost of the cloth of gold robe and the accessories relevant to it – the *armilla*, the *colobium sindonis* and the special coronation gloves (illustrations 112, 117). John Hunter appears to have handled the arrangements for the making of all the Queen's robes, and his bills did not mention who supplied him with the velvet or the specially-woven cloth of gold. His final bill, coupled with that of the royal furrier Robert Drake, amounted to £2467 18s 6d; the cost of the new Parliament robe was £643 8s 9d.[2]

The coronation took place at Westminster Abbey on 28 June 1838, just over a year after the Queen's accession, and she wrote a long description of it in her Journal, a unique record of the event from the viewpoint of the central figure; this has frequently been quoted.[3] The form of service and ceremonies followed almost exactly that devised for her uncle William IV in 1831, while Queen Anne's coronation in 1702 was also looked to as the precedent for a coronation of a Queen Regnant. Like the 1831 coronation, that of Queen Victoria was considerably less flamboyant and less expensive

An Account of Expenses incurred within the Department of The Mistress of Her Majesty's Robes, for the Coronation of Her Majesty.

	Hunter Robe Maker	Drake Furrier		
The Parliament Robes				
The Kirtle	120 . . .	8 . 8 . 9	128 . 8 . 9	
The Mantle	150 . . .	350 . . .	500 . . .	643 . 8 . 9
A Bag to contain them	15 . . .	„ „ „	15 . . .	
The Coronation Robes				
The Dalmatic Mantle	380 . . .	„ „ „	380 . . .	
The Supertunica	410 . . .	„ „ „	410 . . .	
The Armilla	75 . . .	„ „ „	75 . . .	975 . . .
The Collobium	80 . . .	„ „ „	80 . . .	
Wrappers and Bag	30 . . .	„ „ „	30 . . .	
The Robes of Estate				
The Kirtle	120 . . .	8 . 8 . 9	128 . 8 . 9	
The Mantle	150 . . .	350 . . .	500 . . .	643 . 8 . 9
A Bag to contain them	15 . . .	„ „ „	15 . . .	
A Crimson Mantle or Cloak	50 . . .	17 . 13 . 6	67 . 13 . 6	
A Purple Do.	50 . . .	17 . 13 . 6	67 . 13 . 6	165 . 7 . .
A Star of the Garter for Do.	30 . . .	„ „ „	30 . . .	
A Cap of Estate	3 . 10 . .	1 . 10 . .	„ „ „	5 . . .
A Cap of Maintenance	12 . 1 . 6	5 . . .	„ „ „	17 . 1 . 6
A Pair of Gloves	6 . 6 . .	„ „ „	„ „ „	6 . 6 . .
A Handkerchief and Bag	12 . 6 . 6	„ „ „	„ „ „	12 . 6 . 6
	1,709 . 4 . .	758 . 14 . 6	£ 2,467 . 18 . 6	
Parliament Robes made July 1837 on Her Majesty's Accession				
The Kirtle	120 . . .	8 . 8 . 9	128 . 8 . 9	
The Mantle	150 . . .	350 . . .	500 . . .	640 . 8 . 9
Remaking, Loss of Lace, &c.	12 . . .	„ „ „	12 . . .	
	1991 . 4 . .	1117 . 3 . 3	£ 3,108 . 7 . 3	

This Account to
the Treasury
July 23d 1838

(signed) H. Sutherland
Mistress of the Robes

108 & 109
Office of Robes Accounts
Ledgers, 1838. (Public Record
Office, London)

Accounting break-down of robemaker's and furrier's charges for Queen Victoria's robes in 1837 and 1838; these charges include the cost of the velvet, cloth of gold and ermine. The clerk also copied into the ledger the detailed descriptions supplied by the robemaker with his invoice. These are now the sole source of information about the materials which made up the robes.

Coronation Bills

Her Most Gracious Majesty

To John Hunter, 16 Maddox Street
Hanover Square

The Coronation Robes

To a rich Cloth of Gold Dalmatic Robe brocaded with Silver and Coloured Silks in devices emblematical of Sovereignty and the United Kingdoms, the whole bor= =dered with rich dead and bright Gold bullion Fringe, and lined with very rich Crimson Satin, also a rich chased Gold Clasp with frosted Eagle &c. to fas= =ten the Robe on the Breast. — — — — — — — — 380: — : —

To a rich frosted Cloth of Gold Supertunica brocaded with Gold and coloured Silks in devices of Palm and the Badges of the United Kingdoms, the whole bordered with rich gold Pillow Lace, lined throughout with rich Crimson Satin, also a very rich Gold Girdle with Tassels. — — — — — — — — — — — — — 410: — : —

To a very rich Gold Tissue Armilla embroidered in Silver and Silks, viz. Eagles, Crowns, Roses, Thistles and Shamrocks, and at either end Saint George's Cross proper, trimmed with Gold bullion Fringe and lined with very rich Crimson Satin. — — — — — — — — — — 75: — : —

To a very fine Cambric Colobium Sindonis trimmed round the edges and flounced on the bottom with very fine Honiton Lace. — — — — — — — — — — 80: — : —

To a pair of fine white kid long Gloves richly embroider= =ed on the backs of the Hands and up the Arms with Gold, faced with rich white Satin, & trimmed with fine Buck= =ingham Lace & finished on the tops with Gold Pillow Lace Gold Cords and Tassels. — — — — — — — — — 6:6: —

Carried forward — 951:6: —

A piece of Queen Victoria's Coronation dress. June 28th 1838.

A piece of Queen Victoria's Coronation Robe, 28th June 1838.

110 Dress-cuttings books, 1837–44 (MoL 80.424/1; Private Collection)

In paintings of Queen Victoria's coronation her dress is consistently obscured by her robes and only recently has it become possible to gain an idea of this rich silk dress. The ledgers of the Office of Robes contain an unusually specific entry for the purchase of '18 yds Richest White Ground Gold Flowered Brocade, 63/- [per yard (1.14 m)] £56 14.0.' from the royal mercer, William King. The silk is possibly of Spitalfields manufacture. On the white satin ground a design of cartouches and flowers is worked in silver-gilt strip. This appears to have been an 'off the shelf' fabric rather than one specially woven: its width of 20in. (51cm) explains why such a large quantity was acquired. It seems likely that the dress was made by the Queen's long-serving dressmaker Mary Bettans.

111 The *dalmatica*. (MoL 48.14/11)

Unlike the *supertunica*, the Queen's *dalmatica* (right hand page) closely follows the 1685 precedent (illustration 113). This ceremonial vestment has been variously – and confusingly – termed *dalmatica, pallium,* and imperial mantle by past antiquarians. In its present form reminiscent of a cope, it is not thought to derive from ecclesiastical vestments but rather from a much older royal ceremonial garment. The front edges of Queen Victoria's *dalmatica* were cut away so that her hands were not obstructed when holding the orb and sceptre. This *dalmatica* has not been used at any coronation since 1838. See also illustration 120.

than George IV's in 1821, but it nevertheless retained some of his introductions: the form of the cloth of gold robes is a notable example. The ancient procession of the peerage on foot from Westminster Hall to the Abbey before the service, and the return procession and banquet afterwards had both been abandoned in 1831. In 1838 the impressive carriage processions between Buckingham Palace and the Abbey were introduced with the specific aim of involving more of the populace and allowing them to see their new Queen.

On 28 June 1838 the Queen set off from Buckingham Palace at 10am wearing the kirtle of her Parliament robe over her dress of gold-brocaded white satin (illustrations 110, 165). When she arrived at the Abbey the heavy velvet and ermine mantle, with its eight-foot-long train, was added for the procession down the nave to the prepared 'theatre' at the crossing of the nave and transepts; here the several chairs and thrones used during the service were placed on a raised dais. The nave and transepts were lined with additional seating for the large congregation of politicians, clergy and aristocracy entitled to witness the ceremony. The great procession down the nave included the regalia and other ritual objects. The Queen was at the end of the procession.[4]

Following the formal rituals of the recognition and oath the Queen was divested of her Parliament robe (ie kirtle and mantle) in St Edward's Chapel. Normally a king was disrobed in full view of the congregation – this practical necessity had over the centuries become a ritual symbolising the divesting of his secular status – and he was then invested with his next set of robes in the course of the post-anointing ceremonial. However, from motives of delicacy, anointing on the breast was omitted at Queen Victoria's coronation and she therefore re-entered the 'theatre' already wearing the cloth of gold *supertunica*

112 The *colobium sindonis*, 1838.
     (The Archaeological Journal, LI,
     1894, plate II)

The *colobium sindonis* was a coronation garment of such antiquity that its original significance and form are unknown. The Queen herself described it as 'a singular sort of little gown of linen trimmed with lace' when she wrote up her Journal at the end of her coronation day. This surplice-like garment was made of a very fine and translucent linen, and trimmed with deep borders of specially-made Honiton lace. It seems to have been derived from the engravings published to record the coronation of 1685 (illustration 113). This photograph, published in the 1894, is the only other known illustration of this ancient form of garment. The Queen's *colobium* must have been preserved with her other coronation robes by the Office of Robes, but it seems to have disappeared at her death.

114 Detail of shoe in illustration 115.

The printed paper labels stuck to the inner soles of shoes provide useful information about the makers and their customers. The firm of Gundry & Son made the Queen's shoes throughout her lifetime.

115 Shoes and silk stockings, 1838–40.
     (MoL 32.61/1, 32.61/2;
     54.121/16)

These shoes, and the top stocking, are traditionally believed to have been worn by the Queen at her coronation, and she is indeed shown wearing very similar shoes in her coronation portrait (illustration 116). They were made by the Queen's shoemaker Richard Gundry, who very likely made her coronation shoes. The shoes do not come from a royal source and there is now no way of confirming the association. The lower stocking comes from the group preserved by Lydia Greatorex (p127) and is likely to be authentic, but later in date.

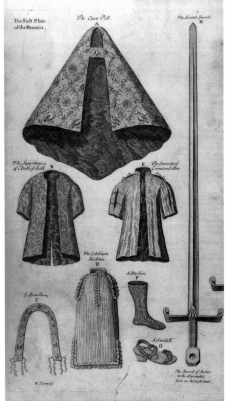

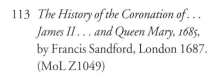

113 *The History of the Coronation of . . . James II . . . and Queen Mary, 1685,* by Francis Sandford, London 1687. (MoL Z1049)

In 1820 George IV turned to this authoritative study when he sought precedents on which to model his own coronation, and the form of his cloth of gold robes owed much to Sandford's images. This source must have been used again in 1837, although different forms of the *colobium sindonis* and *supertunica* were devised for Queen Victoria. The engraving records the seventeenth-century form of the medieval tunic (or surcoat), the first garment the king put on prior to his coronation. This had a number of slits to allow anointing on various parts of the body, a practice later abandoned.

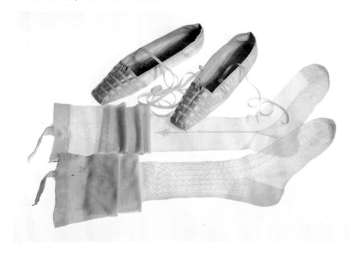

116 *Queen Victoria*, 1838,
    by Sir George Hayter (1792–1871).
    (Royal Collection)

Hayter painted this portrait for the Queen
shortly after her coronation. She at first sat to
him in her robe, but later he used a lay-figure
or his daughter Mimi dressed in the robe. He
noted how, at the first sitting, the Queen
tripped ascending her little throne and
accidentally put her foot through the lace of
her *colobium sindonis*. The portrait shows
clearly the *colobium* and *armilla* worn under
the *dalmatica*, and the morse fastening it.

117 *Armilla*, 1838–1902.
    (Historic Royal Palaces)

The *armilla* (below) is of very ancient origin
and was originally associated in the
coronation regalia with two ceremonial
bracelets, perhaps attached to each of them.
Over the centuries it has gradually taken on
the form of an ecclesiastical stole. This
armilla is now associated with Edward VII's
coronation vestments of 1902. However,
Queen Victoria's *armilla* was photographed
in 1894 and it now seems likely that the
embroidered elements were reused in 1902.

over her *colobium sindonis* (illustrations 107, 116). Seated on St Edward's chair, beneath a
cloth of gold canopy held by four knights of the Garter she was anointed, on her forehead
only, by the Archbishop of Canterbury. This is the most solemn part of a coronation
ceremony. The Queen was then robed in her *dalmatica* and returned to St Edward's Chair
for the crowning and investiture with regalia (illustration 116).[5]

When the homage and remainder of the service were completed the Queen retired to
St Edward's Chapel to be divested of her cloth of gold robes, which by tradition were left
at Westminster. She was now arrayed in a purple velvet robe (ie kirtle and mantle) in
which, wearing the Imperial State Crown and carrying her sceptre and orb, she processed
back down the nave and out of the Abbey to the state coach, which took her back, in a
long impressive procession along a crowded route, to Buckingham Palace. Having
become a little more accustomed to the weight of her ceremonial robes Queen Victoria
experienced for the first time the discomfort of her state crown and of the orb, which she
carried with the sceptre, in this coach procession. There were no rehearsals of the
ceremonial, and Greville, the Minister and diarist, noted 'there was a continual difficulty
and embarrassment, and the Queen never knew what to do next'.[6] Lord Melbourne
saved the Queen from some difficulties when, accompanying her to view preparations at

118 The morse, 1838, actual size 4½in.
(11.50cm) × 1⅝in. (4cm).
(MoL 52.141)

The fastening for the *dalmatica*, made of silver-gilt and gilded copper alloy, bears an imperial eagle. It was originally attached at the front on the chest, and imitated cope fastenings. This morse was removed early in the twentieth century and used to form the central motif on a belt for Queen Victoria's daughter-in-law, Queen Alexandra. A modern replica now replaces the original on the *dalmatica*.

119 Diamond circlet of George IV, 1821.
(Royal Collection)

The narrow circlet of diamonds and pearls is surmounted by crosses-pattée alternating with sprays formed of a rose, shamrock and thistle. It was originally designed in 1821 to be worn by the King on a black Spanish hat during the preliminary coronation ceremonials (illustration 2); he abandoned the idea at the last moment, and the hired diamonds with which it had been set by the jewellers Rundell & Co. were returned. In 1838 Queen Victoria had it reset with diamonds and pearls from the royal collection and wore it constantly until the death of Prince Albert. It is one of the most familiar pieces of royal jewellery following its appearance on postage stamps from 1840, and its continued use by queen consorts since 1902 and by H.M. The Queen.

120 Detail of fabric in illustration 111.

The gold tissue relates to that of George IV's *dalmatica* and was woven by the Jacquard method. It is possible that the design, warp pattern drafts and pierced cards were retained; in 1821 and 1831 both kings were elderly and further coronations could be foreseen. There is no known documentation of the weaving of this fabric or that of the *supertunica*, but the silk-enriched cloths of gold are believed to have been made in Spitalfields. Both the 1821 and 1838 fabrics are derived from the Sandford engravings but include thistles and shamrocks, and foliage to the Tudor rose. The medieval fleurs-de-lis and imperial eagle also appeared on the pre-Commonwealth *dalmatica*.

the Abbey on the eve of the coronation, he suggested that she try her several thrones – which indeed were found to be too low. As a result of various other mishaps rehearsals became standard practice for twentieth-century coronations.[7]

After dinner the events of the long day were discussed with Lord Melbourne who 'thought the robes and particularly the Dalmatica, "looked remarkably well"', the Queen recorded in her Journal. These impressive symbolic vestments, perhaps the most costly and little-worn garments ever made for her, were presumably carefully preserved by the Office of the Robes. They have never been used at any subsequent coronation.[8]

Her purple velvet robe must have closely resembled her Parliament robe. It seems never to have been drawn or painted and in August 1838 the Duchess of Sutherland wrote formally to the Clerk of the Robes:

> Understanding from precedent that I have a right to claim the Robes used at H.M.'s Coronation I do claim as my privilege the purple Robes of Estate – a purple Cloak, – a Cap of Estate and a pair of Gloves, and I beg of you to take charge of the same for me.

These were delivered a year later, together with a crimson cap of estate, to the Duchess's London home at Stafford House: the gloves she had no right to claim and she was not allowed them. None of these items can now be traced.[9]

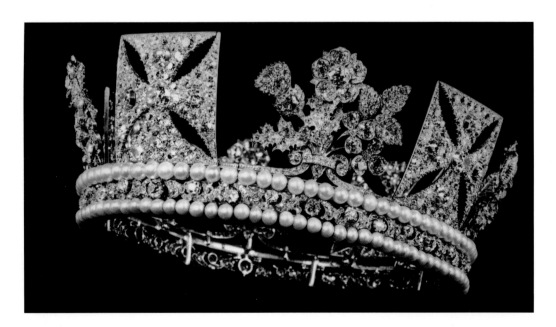

Marriage, 1840

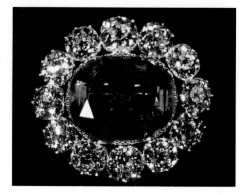

121 *Prince Albert,* 1840, by Sir George Hayter
   (1792–1871). (Royal Collection)

The artist made this copy from his wedding
painting (illustration 128). It hung in Queen
Victoria's bedroom at Buckingham Palace and
conveys something of what had so captivated
the Queen in her twenty-year-old bridegroom.
She frequently eulogised his good looks – his
blue eyes, his beautiful figure, his fine waist – in
her Journal. For the ceremony he wore the
uniform of a British Field Marshal with the
insignia of the Order of the Garter.

122 Prince Albert's sapphire brooch, 1840.
   (H.M. The Queen)

Prince Albert gave this brooch, with its
immense sapphire surrounded by diamonds,
to his bride on the eve of their wedding; next
day she wore it pinned to the front of her
dress (illustration 126). She was to wear it
constantly during the Prince's lifetime, but
rarely after his death. In her will she left it
to the Crown, for use by future queens of
Great Britain.

123 Queen Victoria's wedding dress, 1840
   (MoL D325 a & b, Royal Collection)

Shown here without its lace flounce
(illustration 124), the dress is made of light,
finely woven Spitalfields silk satin. Originally
a creamy white, it has aged to a distinct cream
colour. Its style is classically simple, allowing
the fine lace to provide a discreetly sumptuous
effect amongst the colourful congregation in
the Chapel Royal. Engravings of the dress in
fashion journals of the time were not always
accurate, but its uncluttered line, compared to
the often very ornate wedding dresses shown
in fashion plates, must have found many
imitators amongst contemporary brides.

Apart from her accession and coronation, Queen Victoria's marriage on 10 February
1840 to her cousin Prince Albert of Saxe-Coburg-Gotha was the most important and
memorable occasion in her life (illustration 128). It brought her immense personal
happiness and support for the next twenty years.[1] The match had been engineered by
King Leopold, the uncle of both bride and groom. Once it had become clear that his
niece seemed likely to succeed to the British throne and might face difficulties similar to
those of Princess Charlotte in finding a suitable husband, he had devised his own plan.
This was to groom Albert, the younger son of his brother the Duke of Saxe-Coburg-
Gotha, as a potential suitor: he was of a similar age to Victoria, came from a similar
background, and had no local responsibilities. Both had been brought up with the idea
of the match and had liked each other when brought together in 1836, but Queen
Victoria nevertheless carefully discussed all her options with Lord Melbourne. Once she
was established on the throne her marriage and, more especially, the production of a
further heir to the throne had become topics at court. When Albert now returned to
London in 1839 the Queen rapidly fell in love with him and, as her status required her to
do, soon proposed marriage to her cousin.

Naturally the Queen was concerned to appear appropriately dressed for the ceremony
in the Chapel Royal, St James's, and occasional brief references in her Journal reveal that
she did indeed give careful thought to all aspects of it, especially in discussions with Lord
Melbourne, her Prime Minister. They looked to various eighteenth-century marriages,
particularly that of George III in 1761, as precedents before the Queen decided – with
Melbourne's wholehearted encouragement – against wearing her crimson velvet robe of
state. Her role on her wedding day was primarily that of a bride. To adopt a robe of state,
appropriate to her status as a reigning queen, would only emphasise her seniority, and
overshadow the role of her future husband. Correctly she realised that this would not
be a happy move. As paintings – but not her Journal – reveal she devised her own
compromise: a court train, attached at the waist and ornamented with sprays of orange
blossom, flowing from the waist of her otherwise utterly conventional white bridal dress.
Gone, too, was the use of cloth of gold or cloth of silver which English princesses of lesser
rank, including Princess Charlotte, had adopted as of right for their weddings. Nor did
Queen Victoria choose to wear, for example, George IV's glittering diamond circlet
(illustration 119). Instead she adorned herself simply with a wreath of artificial orange
blossom, a relatively recent introduction for brides. As she had already invested Prince

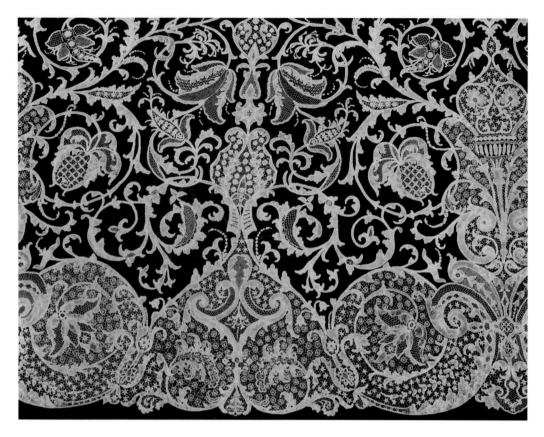

Albert with the Order of the Garter, she could in conscience wear her own collar of the Order, a colourful and unique jewel for a bride (illustrations 98, 128).

Today it seems rather surprising that Queen Victoria included so few of these practical considerations in her Journal. Even more difficult to explain is the silence about the creation of her wedding lace, a commission of some magnitude for the waning lace industry in Honiton, Devon, which was almost completely overshadowed at this time by the fashion for Brussels lace. The Queen was simply following a well-established royal precedent of support of British textile manufactures, and it is possible that the dress lace had already been commissioned before the Queen's engagement, as a political gesture. In the summer of 1838 Lord Melbourne had relayed to his sovereign criticisms of her patronage of the French textile and dressmaking industries.[2] Her best counter, he advised, was a well-emphasised policy of patriotic spending.

The design of Queen Victoria's wedding lace was considerably in advance of its time. Recent research has revealed that the Pre-Raphaelite artist William Dyce (1806–64) became involved in the project at the Government School of Design at Somerset House (illustration 124).[3] The quality of this design is still evident, and indeed the same lace was to grace the Queen's dresses on numerous occasions throughout her life (illustration 209). It also gave a tremendous boost to the Honiton industry, reinstating its products in the world of fashion and demonstrating that it was the quality of the design rather than any lack of technical expertise which impeded its success on the international market. This early collaboration between the arts and industry was a harbinger of the developments which eventually resulted in the Great Exhibition of 1851, again involving the Queen and her husband. The Queen continued to use Honiton lace on her own and her children's clothes, and also insisted that the wedding dresses of her daughters-in-law were trimmed with it.[4]

124 Detail of skirt flounce from Queen Victoria's wedding dress. (Royal Collection)

Honiton lace is a bobbin lace in which the separately worked motifs are joined together by hand or applied to machine-made net. The deep skirt flounce was an ideal vehicle for the striking and densely patterned design of scrolling stems with exotic leaves and flowers, which was embellished with a variety of decorative fillings. Elements of the design were incorporated into the bodice ornaments and the veil. The flounce is 25½in. (65cm) deep and 4 yards (3.66m) in circumference.

125 Detail: bodice.

The falling collar and shaped sleeve frills are now frail, having been moved from dress to dress throughout the Queen's lifetime. As was usual with Queen Victoria her short double puffed sleeves had been safely in fashion for a year or two, and the waistline was back at its natural level. The orange blossom wreath is a modern replica.

126 *Queen Victoria,* 1847, by Franz Xaver
Winterhalter (1805–73). (Royal
Collection)

This study was painted for the Queen as a
present to Prince Albert on their seventh
wedding anniversary. She had given
Winterhalter 'a very long sitting as a surprise
[for Prince Albert] . . . I wearing my dear
wedding veil'. She also wore her wreath of
orange blossom, the sapphire brooch given
to her by Prince Albert, and her small collar
of the Garter. The earrings and necklace
were those she wore with her wedding dress,
made for her from Turkish diamonds given
by the Sultan Mahmud II in 1838. (Millar
1992, p294.)

127 *Sketch by VR for the dress of the Queen's
12 Brides Maids,* 1839–40. (Royal
Collection)

Queen Victoria 'designed' the dresses of white
silk trimmed with white roses for her
bridesmaids, giving this sketch to the Mistress
of the Robes, the Duchess of Sutherland, to
ensure that her wishes were clearly
understood. Like her own dress, they
represent a very straightforward and
uncluttered fashion preference. The dresses
were perhaps made by another of Queen
Victoria's dressmakers.

Fashion journals and newspapers carried generalised descriptions of the Queen's appearance. Some claimed that the lace had cost the then considerable sum of £1000. It is difficult to prove this claim. Certainly no single payments of this magnitude were recorded. Work on the lace was superintended by Jane Bidney, a native of the area, who had premises in St James's Street, Pall Mall; she must already have been supplying the Queen before her accession, for she received a warrant in August 1837.[5] The press reported Miss Bidney's connection with the Queen's wedding lace but no mention was made of the dressmaker responsible for the dress itself. It may be reasonable to attribute the dress to Mrs Bettans of Jermyn Street, the longest-serving of the Queen's dressmakers, and one who did not court press attention.[6]

The Queen received no additional funding for her wedding toilette (ie her trousseau), and as might be expected her bills exceeded the quarterly allocation from the Treasury, a temporary embarrassment eventually covered out of her Privy Purse (p101). As well as the sum of £250 paid to Jane Bidney – presumably for or towards the cost of the wedding lace – large bills had also come in from her two principal dressmakers (Mary Bettans and Vouillon & Laure) and there were lesser debts to several other London dressmakers and milliners, and to the Paris house of Palmyre Chartier Legrand. The bills of her regular suppliers – for silks, laces, stockings, shoes, gloves, etc – were also inflated by the needs of assembling the royal trousseau. That of Harriet Moon, maker of dressing gowns and

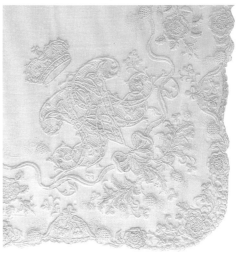

128 *The Marriage of Queen Victoria, 10 February 1840,* by Sir George Hayter (1792–1871). (Royal Collection)

The figure of the Queen shows her dress complete with its original court train (no longer extant). The Chapel Royal was crowded with family and ministers. Lord Melbourne and the Duchess of Kent stand to the Queen's left. On the Prince's right are the Dowager Queen Adelaide, and Prince Albert's father and brother.

129 Embroidered handkerchief, *c.*1840. (MoL 70.189)

The elaborate and symbolic embroidery, worked in cotton thread on a very fine muslin ground, suggests that this was a commemorative piece, perhaps presented to the Queen by one of her embroidery suppliers. The design incorporates roses, thistles and shamrocks, the Queen's coat of arms and her initials intertwined with those of Prince Albert. The embroidery, carried out in satin and stem stitch, with decorative infillings of french knots and drawn threadwork, is typical English work of the 1840s.

130 Going-away bonnet, 1840. (MoL D325c, Royal Collection)

Queen Victoria preserved the bonnet she wore during her carriage ride to Windsor for her honeymoon. It is a deeply brimmed bonnet covered with ribbed silk, and ornamented with orange blossom. The veil now attached to the bonnet is incomplete and may not have belonged to it originally.

other linen goods, of Green Street, Grosvenor Square, came to £317 5s 0d and must represent a generous quantity of dressing gowns, caps, and nightgowns, and possibly chemises and petticoats too.[7]

On 10 February 1840, her wedding morning, Queen Victoria recorded in her Journal: 'Had my hair dressed and the wreath of orange flowers put on' (in between breakfast and receiving various visitors, including Prince Albert). Only after all this did she briefly record: 'Dressed … I wore a white satin gown with a very deep flounce of Honiton, imitation of old. I wore my Turkish diamond necklace and earrings, and Albert's beautiful sapphire brooch.'[8] She was accompanied in her carriage from Buckingham Palace to St James's Palace by her mother and the Duchess of Sutherland. Here processions formed which then moved to the Chapel Royal (illustration 128). The Queen thought 'the Ceremony was very imposing, and fine and simple, and I think OUGHT to make an everlasting impression on everyone who promises at the Altar to <u>keep</u> what he or she promises.[9] Dearest Albert repeated everything distinctly. I felt so happy when the ring was put on and by Albert'. Afterwards the procession made its way to the Throne Room so that the register could be signed, and then everyone returned to Buckingham Palace for the wedding breakfast. Then, the Queen noted, 'I went upstairs and undressed and put on a white silk gown trimmed with swansdown, and a bonnet with orange flowers. Albert went downstairs and undressed.' What he put on is not known, but the Queen preserved her bonnet (illustration 130). Then '… we took leave of Mamma and drove off at near 4; I and Albert alone'.[10] The brief honeymoon was to be spent at Windsor Castle. Here both changed again, Prince Albert into his Windsor coat. Next morning he breakfasted in a black velvet jacket without any neckcloth so that his throat could be seen 'and looked more beautiful than it is possible for me to say'. They both took a great interest in each other's clothes thereafter: one of the Prince's first acts, she having watched him shave, was to help her put on her stockings. It was, the Queen noted in her Journal, the 'happiest time of my life'.[11]

Married Life and Family, 1840–50

Very little indeed of Queen Victoria's clothing from the first ten years of her marriage has been preserved and it is impossible to explain why this should be. Although pregnant much of that time – she gave birth to the first seven of her nine children in that decade, in 1840, 1841, 1843, 1844, 1846, 1848 and 1850 – it was precisely the period of her youthful prominence in the world of fashion. Not only was she recorded as having worn attractive and expensive dresses, but there were many happy occasions which, with their associations, might have led to the preservation of a few more items of clothing.

Was it, perhaps, that the Queen saw her happiness at this time symbolised by ephemera of her offspring? Like any doting parent she preserved examples of her children's first or early footwear, carefully embroidered baby shoes or tiny leather miniatures of adult slippers or boots, and fine silk socks. There also remain a few baby robes, dresses and caps, and the ermine-trimmed velvet christening capes used for her two eldest children; small silver boxes even preserve samples of their christening cakes. Like most of the Queen's clothes those of her children were usually passed on, via their maids and nurses, and quite a number of dresses and accessories, carefully preserved by the recipients and their descendants, have survived.

131 *Queen Victoria with Victoria, Princess Royal, and Albert Edward, Prince of Wales*, 1842, by Sir Frances Grant (1803–78). (Royal Collection)

The Queen commissioned this very personal portrait with their two eldest children – and the pet dogs Eos and Dandie – as a Christmas present for Prince Albert in 1842.

132 Circlet, earrings and brooches designed by Prince Albert, 1839–46. (Royal Collection)

Prince Albert started presenting this orange blossom set to Queen Victoria in November 1839, before their marriage, when he sent the first of the brooches from Germany. He went on to give her the earrings and a second brooch as a Christmas present in 1845, and the circlet on their wedding anniversary in 1846. 'My beloved one gave me such a lovely unexpected present', she noted in her Journal on that occasion: '. . . the leaves are of frosted gold, the orange blossoms of white porcelaine & 4 little green enamel oranges, meant to represent our children.' (Bury, p303.)

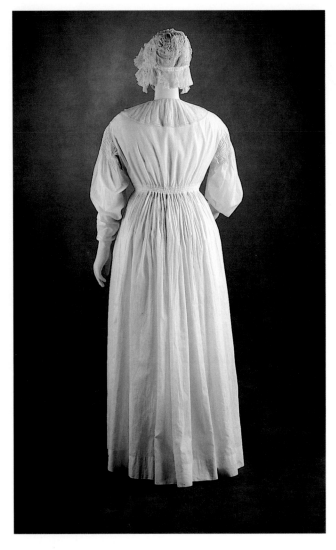

133 Dressing gown, 1840–50. (MoL 54.121/1)

This garment is made of an extremely fine cotton, with a narrow bobbin lace edging. It is handstitched with the tiny and beautifully regular sewing which is always associated with the Queen's personal linen. The robe is completely open at the front, while the fullness at the back waist is cleverly controlled by two pairs of gauging tapes so that it can be adjusted to fit the wearer. This may have been a common feature in contemporary women's dressing gowns, but it is tempting to associate this garment with the Queen's pregnancies. The front edges may have been overlapped during wear and held in place by a silk sash round the waist.

134 Morning cap, 1840–50.
(MoL 66.79/21)

Like all aristocratic ladies of the time Queen Victoria habitually wore caps of this kind in the morning before she was fully dressed for formal occasions in the afternoon and evening. This very fine linen cap is ornamented with whitework embroidery known as Ayrshire work (distinguished by the decorative needle-lace fillings), and frills of Valenciennes lace; it was a gift to the Museum from Princess Marina and there is no reason to doubt its authenticity. The Queen devoted much of her morning to work on official documents; it is very likely she had fittings and selected dress materials submitted by her dressmakers and other suppliers at this time too.

135 Shoes of Princess Alice, 1850–1.
(MoL 46.16/8 a & b)

Traditionally these shoes are believed to be the handiwork of Queen Victoria, for her second daughter Princess Alice: they passed into the possession of the Queen's wardrobe maid Lydia Greatorex, so the association seems likely. The embroidered design of roses and rosebuds is worked in half-cross stitch on a fine white twilled wool, and the shoes certainly seem to have been worn. Queen Victoria liked always to be occupied with some sort of needlework or knitting in her leisure hours and must, throughout her lifetime, have worked a great many such pieces. It seems likely that the shoe uppers were supplied with the design already drawn or printed on them, for they are apparently adapted from an adult size.

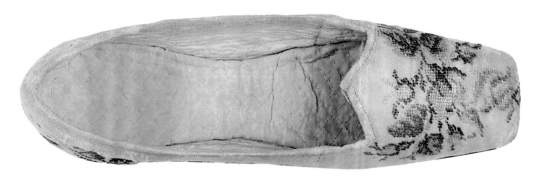

136 *The Queen's Dressing Room, Windsor Castle,* 1847, by Joseph Nash (1809–78). (Royal Collection)

This watercolour of the Queen's orderly dressing room reflects none of the bustle and, presumably, temporary untidiness which must have prevailed during her dressing sessions. A maid usually slept in the room at night in case the Queen needed anything. Adjoining rooms provided facilities for bathing, for storing clothes, and for workrooms and accommodation for the dressers and wardrobe maids.

137 Dress-cuttings books, 1837–44. (MoL 80.424/1, Private Collection)

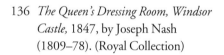

The cuttings associated with Mary Bettans's workshop include this small piece of poplin (a silk and wool mixture), probably manufactured in Ireland, with the note 'Worn at the Birthday Drawing room after the Christening of H.R.H. The Prince of Wales'. It is impossible to know whether this textile had been commissioned by the Queen or was a gift from one of her regular suppliers, possibly W. F. Fry of Dublin. The Prince of Wales was christened in St George's Chapel, on 25 January 1842. A fragment of the white and silver dress the Queen wore on that occasion, with her Garter robes, is shown in illustration 16.

One particularly interesting group was accumulated by Lydia Greatorex, wardrobe maid to Queen Victoria between 1848 and 1857. During this period she acquired a number of items from the early childhood of the Prince of Wales (*b.*1841), as well as accessories and underwear from her mistress. Much may have passed through her hands and been altered and worn out by recipients. What remains reveals the private family life of the Queen. Although from necessity and custom she could not participate fully in the day-to-day life and upbringing of her children she nevertheless made time to visit them each day in the royal nursery. One of the few relics of these intimate occasions is a small double apron, with her monogram in red thread under a crown, said to have been used by the Queen during such visits. The apron is constructed like a large pocket and possibly held a towel to give better protection to the Queen's dresses.[1] Both she and Prince Albert cared much for their children and closely supervised their upbringing. Her sketchbooks are full of drawings of them – in the arms of their nurses, crawling, playing with toys, being bathed or taking first steps – whilst her letters and Journal proudly record their childish sayings and accomplishments.

Also in this group of royal relics is an early dressing gown almost certainly used by Queen Victoria during the 1840s (illustration 133). Since few examples of its type survive it is of considerable interest. Dressing gowns were commonly worn as part of the dressing, and probably undressing, ritual by a lady of fashion. With the assistance of her maid she put on all her underwear – chemise, stockings, corset and petticoats – and over this went her dressing gown. At this stage her hair was well-brushed by her maid, a lengthy process in the nineteenth century. Before her accession Queen Victoria often recorded that she was read to by Baroness Lehzen while her hair was brushed: this was primarily intended to prevent idle chatter in front of the maids, but also extended the Princess's familiarity with biography and literature. It was a practice which the Queen

maintained throughout her life. It is likely that her hair was first dressed into a simple style by her maid under a morning cap, and then dressed later in the day by her official hairdresser. From 1837 to 1867 two hairdressers (Isidore Marchand from 1837 to 1846, and his son-in-law Jean Nestor Tirard from 1846 to 1867) were employed to dress the Queen's hair wherever she was, travelling with her to Balmoral and Osborne. They were well remunerated for what must have been a very disruptive element in their businesses.

This dressing robe or gown has mistakenly been associated with the Queen's accession, when she was roused early in the morning to be told of her uncle's death (p94). There is no evidence to support such a claim. At this distance in time it is difficult to be certain how much it follows the normal form of a dressing gown. It certainly seems eminently suited for a pregnant woman. In his *Hints to Mothers* (1841) Dr Thomas Bull advised:

> A loose dressing-gown is best in the earlier part of the labour. This must be exchanged when the patient lies down for good, for a chemise and bedgown folded up smoothly to the waist, and a flannel petticoat, without shoulder straps, that it may afterwards be readily removed.

Pregnancy was what the Queen most dreaded from marriage, although in time she became used to the process. She experienced some uncomfortable pregnancies, needing to take periods of rest on her sofa. This gown would seem ideal for such occasions, when Prince Albert read or sang to her.

In 1858 the Queen explained her own pregnancy practices to her eldest daughter the Princess Royal, now Princess Frederick William of Prussia. It seems she did not attend drawing rooms and levées (where she would have to stand for long periods), but did receive diplomats and dignitaries, visit the theatre, and continue with her usual business. She believed in maintaining her usual standards, and always 'dressed properly of an evening', having her hair 'just twisted' in the morning, and then properly dressed later in the day. She disapproved of tight lacing during pregnancy: she put aside her usual stays until the pregnancy was over, and wore a series of larger stays, carefully dated by her dresser as she expanded. She also wore the same night shift for her confinements, and this was lent to her second daughter Princess Alice in 1863: 'I wish you could have worn it too', the Queen commented to the Princess Royal.[2]

The Office of Robes' accounts are discreet about the sources of the Queen's underwear and nightwear but it seems likely from these records of payments that much was acquired from Harriet Moon's child-bed linen warehouse off Grosvenor Street. Harriet Moon was one of those who received a warrant early in the Queen's reign and frequent payments are recorded to her or her successors until 1877.[3] This kind of establishment dealt not only with babies' first clothing and wear for small children, but also with such items of ladies' clothing as 'muslin morning wrappers', night caps and night gowns, chemises, petticoats and drawers. An embroidered cap dating from this time may also have come from Harriet Moon's shop, but could equally well have been purchased from other suppliers: the milliner Mrs Amelia Wilkinson of Lower Grosvenor Street, for example, or Mme Julie Adèle Métayer, a dressmaker and milliner in Conduit Street, off Bond Street, both of whom were paid for goods supplied at this time (illustration 134).[4]

Little is known about the many firms or individuals who supplied clothing and accessories to the Queen, but the high quality of craftsmanship and finish to be seen – in dresses, underwear and shoes in particular – confirms that all were leading specialists in

138 (Previous page) *The Royal Family in 1846*, by Franz Xaver Winterhalter (1805–73). (Royal Collection)

Winterhalter painted a great many portraits of the Queen and her family between 1842 and his death; he was said to catch a good likeness. This portrait shows the Queen in evening dress wearing a sapphire and diamond coronet probably designed by her husband. Prince Albert, in court dress, wears the Garter (below his left knee) and the ribbon and star of the Order and the badge of the Golden Fleece. Their children are (from left to right) Prince Alfred, the Prince of Wales, Princess Alice, Princess Helena and the Princess Royal.

139 Nightdress, 1845–55. (MoL 36.19/1)

A number of nightdresses from late in the Queen's life still survive (illustration 198), but underwear and nightwear from earlier years are exceptionally rare. This early nightdress was once in the possession of a woman employed at Osborne and, although now crudely altered at the neck, seems to be genuine. It is made of a very fine linen, which through much washing now almost feels like silk.

140 Fashion plate, 1843. (MoL Z331)

From the time of her accession, English fashion journals frequently featured Queen Victoria, a device to attract more readers. How accurately such plates portrayed the Queen's dresses is hard to judge. The source of this detached plate of 1843 (from a spring or autumn edition – the Duchess of Kent carries a muff and Prince Albert has a second waistcoat) is unknown, but the journal would also have carried detailed descriptions of fabrics and trimmings used.

141 Slippers, 1858. (MoL 55.74 a & b)

An inscription on these slippers records 'Given by H.R.H. The Duchess of Kent Xmas 1858', whilst the nineteenth-century shoe box in which they reside gives the additional information that they passed to a lady-in-waiting in April 1901. It seems likely that the elderly Duchess embroidered these slippers herself for her daughter. They are worked in tent stitch in coloured wools with a design of strawberries, probably from a design on squared paper obtained from a woman's journal or an embroidery supplies shop; the shoes would then have been made up professionally.

their field. The Queen maintained a stout loyalty to her suppliers, refusing to be lured from them by ambitious entrepreneurs. She was, however, ready to try new suppliers from time to time when attracted by the fashions of her court ladies.

The name of Mary Bettans has already been mentioned and it is fortunate that two sets of dress samples can now be fairly positively associated with her workrooms in Jermyn Street (illustrations 16, 110, 137). She is otherwise a rather shadowy character, never referred to in the fashion press. She must already have been well established when she began making Victoria's dresses in 1824, and may well have worked for the Duchess of Kent since 1818. She was clearly no longer young and was probably conservative.[5] Queen Victoria's second principal dressmaker at the beginning of her reign was the firm of Vouillon & Laure in Prince's Street, off Hanover Square. How the Queen divided her patronage between such firms is impossible to know, but it seems likely that this very fashionable firm had also supplied goods before her accession.[6] In 1837 Vouillon's sister Mlle Laure appears to have taken over the dressmaking side of the business, possibly bringing fresh contacts with the French suppliers of the luxury fashion goods so admired in London. This is merely speculation, of course, but Lord Melbourne 'spoke of Mdlle Laure' one evening after dinner, immediately after commenting upon 'an amazing cargo of bonnets and things come from Paris' in February 1838. He had to explain his knowledge of such trifles to his amused young Queen: ' "They tell me of her", he said, "And I fancy she has beautiful things" '. This is an unique entry in the Queen's Journal, for she never otherwise mentions her suppliers there or in letters. Lord Melbourne's source may well have been his sister Lady Fanny Cowper, a noted beauty of her day, whose dress the Queen had admired for several years.[7]

François Vouillon was listed as a mercer in trade directories, and the association of a mercer with a dressmaker is interesting and merits further investigation. Past practice had been that customers obtained material from a mercer, draper or linen draper and then took it to the dressmaker of their choice. Obviously for someone in Queen

Queen Victoria sat to the artist in May and June 1842 and thought the picture 'is becoming quite beautiful'. It was eventually hung at Osborne. Over two thousand attended the *bal* in the Throne Room at Buckingham Palace; this was appropriately decorated for the occasion and Landseer has included these 'medieval' embellishments in his background. Nothing is left of these two elaborate and expensive costumes, but one of the pages' tunics survives.

143 Bonnets, 1845–55.
     (MoL 66.79/16, 17, 18)

These are the only known examples of Queen Victoria's bonnets from before 1861. A gift to the Museum from Princess Marina, their authenticity seems reasonably assured. They are typical for their period. Two have been built up by sewing together braids – first in a coil and then in parallel rows – of horsehair (left) and a machine-woven cotton (centre). The third is in the form of a small calash or hood, raised above the head by wires inserted into casings in the silk. The flowered ribbons may be a product of the Coventry ribbon weavers.

144 Slippers, 1850–60. (MoL 63.20 a & b)

The leather soles of these slippers bear the stamp of the shoemaker 'Gundry', but it is possible that the fine linen uppers, embroidered with narrow coloured ribbon, were the handiwork of the Queen herself or, more likely, a gift. The slippers are for a broader foot, suggesting a date late in the 1850s. The Duchess of Kent may again have been the donor, or perhaps the Princess Royal or Princess Alice.

Victoria's position this was not practicable and it seems likely that her dressmakers obtained samples from mercers which were then submitted to the Queen, so that a selection could be made. *Blackwood's Lady's Magazine and Gazette*, under the patronage of the Duchess of Kent and Princess Victoria by 1836–7, revealed that just such an arrangement existed between Mrs Bettans and Griffiths & Crick, of Chandos Street, Covent Garden, for the supply of silks woven in Spitalfields. These mercers, the magazine stated, supplied the silks for the dresses the Queen wore in November 1837 for the Opening of Parliament and for the Guildhall Banquet given for her by the City of London. They received a royal warrant that November but were never paid directly through the Office of Robes: payment must have been made via the dressmaker's quarterly invoices. This arrangement perhaps explains other warrants to manufacturers who were also not paid directly. For example, the same fashion journal reported that 'Queen Victoria has been pleased to honor [*sic*] Mrs Geary (stay and corset maker) of St James's, with an appointment, the notice of which arrived too late to insert with the advertisement'. Mrs Geary received a royal warrant in November 1837, but was also never paid directly by the Office of Robes for any goods she provided for the Queen: she probably worked in association with one of the royal dressmakers who included charges for corsets in her bills. This is a natural partnership, although nothing is known of it as a practice. Then, as now, subtle or even radical changes could be wrought on the human form by different corsets, and it would have been vital to the Queen's dressmakers that they construct her dresses to fit properly over her corseted frame.[8]

From the pages of the press we learn also of the involvement of Vouillon & Laure in the creation of one of Queen Victoria's most elaborate ensembles (illustration 142). The launch edition of the *Illustrated London News* (drawing upon reports already published

in the *Morning Post*) devoted two pages to an illustrated report of the Queen's first *bal costumé*, on 12 May 1842 at Buckingham Palace. Ostensibly this lavish spectacle was intended to boost the declining London silk industry by requesting the two thousand invited guests to wear accurate historical costume of any period or country, or national dress, made of Spitalfields silk. The costume historian James Robinson Planché was drawn in to advise the Queen and Prince Albert.[9] They had elected to appear as Queen Philippa and Edward III, noted supporters of the English medieval weaving industry (although it is not clear whether the Queen knew of this connection), as they were portrayed in their tomb effigies in Westminster Abbey. The unflatteringly corpulent image of Queen Philippa was modified with details taken from the small figure of Blanche de la Tour on Edward III's tomb (thus undermining the plan that the representations were to be accurate); Prince Albert's costume was also a somewhat 'improved' version of the original. Members of the royal household dressed to represent members of the fourteenth-century court.[10]

The administration of the making and fitting of the many royal dresses had presumably been refined to a smooth and trouble free process by Lehzen and Skerrett, but now the Queen found herself 'quite bewildered with all the arrangements for our <u>Bal Costumé</u>', as she lamented to King Leopold on 19 April 1842: '. . . there is such asking, and so many silks & Drawings and Crowns, & God knows what, to look at, that I , who hate being troubled about dress, am quite <u>confuse</u>'.[11] Much of the 'asking' must have come from Planché and from Vouillon & Laure, and indeed it was 'the genius and skill' of the latter that the *Illustrated London News* credited: Vouillon, 'an amateur of the pictorial art', had worked with Sir Thomas Lawrence (*d.*1829) upon a previous magnificent *bal costumé*. On 9 May the Queen had tried the completed costume on, finding it 'handsome', and evidently on 11 May Vouillon & Laure had been allowed to exhibit it (minus jewels), when '250 carriages of the élite of the aristocracy and *beau monde*' crowded to see it.[12]

It is not surprising that the dress has not survived for, as can be seen from Sir Edwin Landseer's double portrait, it was composed of rich and costly furs, velvets, brocades and jewels, all of which must have been recycled after the ball.[13] Something of the colour and glamour of the *bal* comes over in the albums published shortly afterwards showing the costumes of the principal personalities.[14] Commenting on the effect on the struggling weaving industry *The Times* acknowledged that there had been 'an extraordinary improvement': two hundred looms had been employed and a new style of silk-weaving developed. However, as with the foundering lace industry, poor design was seen as the weak element in English silks, affecting their ability to compete with European – particularly French – silks. 'If the taste in pattern and the elegance in design had been at all equal to the Costliness of the material or the excellence of the workmanship, the Spitalfields weavers would have needed no ball to assist them for they would command the market of the world', opined *The Times* on 25 May. The dilemma which faced the Queen was that if she overtly supported the English textile industries she inevitably fell short of what was perceived as a fashionable image. Combined with her own less than whole-hearted interest in fashion and the tremendous distractions of her office and family life, this gradually moved her from centre stage as a fashion icon.

In the early 1840s the quantity of work carried out for the Queen by Mary Bettans waned and her workroom appears to have closed down completely in about 1844.[15] Perhaps already anticipating the loss of this long-serving dressmaker the Queen had begun patronising Mme Elise Papon of Brook Street, and later Grosvenor Street (off

145 Queen Victoria and the Princess
      Royal, *c.*1845, calotype, probably by
      Henry Collen. (Royal Archives)

The earliest photographs of Queen Victoria
were taken by her painter of miniatures
Henry Collen, who had recently become
interested in the calotype process. The stark
realism of these early photographs is
something of a shock after the flattering
images of court painters. They are, however,
of immense value as records not only of the
Queen's appearance, but also of her dresses
and hairstyles over the next half century.
These first photographs were for private use
and it was not until *cartes de visite* began to
be published in about 1860 that such
images of the Royal Family began to
circulate widely in Britain. This coincided
with the Queen's descent into black in
1861 and her subsequent loss of interest in
her appearance.

Bond Street), in 1842. The attractive products of this dressmaker were to be seen on the
person of the Queen's pretty and fashion-conscious maid of honour, the Hon. Eleanor
Stanley (*b.*1821) who often recorded the Queen's interest in and admiration of her dresses
in the letters she wrote to her parents. Both also patronised the Portman Street
establishment of Mrs Mary Murray. Eleanor Stanley's letters show that at this time Queen
Victoria was usually very fashionably dressed: black lace over pink silk, in 1842, she
judged 'very smart'; in 1843 she described the Queen wearing 'cerise crêpe de Chine,
trimmed … with three rows of lace … a very handsome gown … [which] sets off her
jewels and blue ribbon very well, but it looks very hot …'[16] Courtiers like Eleanor Stanley
not only offered the Queen practical examples and detailed knowledge of fashion houses,
but some youthful competition too. One cannot miss Eleanor's note of triumph in 1848
(writing from Osborne to her father):

> We all appeared in pink yesterday, except Lady Charlemont, with green leaves in our
> hair, only mine were sham, and the Queen's and Duchess's [of Nemours?] were real
> ivy. Their gowns were pink barège with white flounces; mine was pink and black, and I
> am happy to say it was considered the prettiest …[17]

These flower and foliage wreaths were much worn with dinner and evening dresses

146 Dressing gown, 1854–6. (MoL 66.79/11)

Queen Victoria's pleasure in feminine clothes is evident in the dressing gowns from the last years of her married life. This example has lilac ribbons slotted behind some of the fine whitework embroidery which is a feature of this attractive piece of lingerie. It would have been necessary to remove the ribbons each time it was washed. Originally it would have been starched crisply, but this is now contrary to conservation practice.

147 Detail of dressing gown.

and Lady Charlotte Canning, Lady-in-waiting to the Queen since 1842, recorded an amusing incident in 1844 at Blair Castle in Perthshire:

> The Queen sent me a bundle of heather & I found she had been enquiring for me. When I went to her it was to beg me to make her a wreath of heather. She told me Isidore [Marchand, the Queen's hairdresser] was rather jealous of my performances & said 'je ne sais pas si cela tiendra', and abused my wires; but she says he does not make natural wreaths half as well as I do, which I am proud to hear.[18]

Such family letters, and indeed the Queen's own Journal, from time to time record gifts made to her ladies, very often shawls from Paisley or India. Nowhere, however, is there any mention of the distribution of the Queen's discarded clothing, a process which must have been carried out discreetly through personal contacts. If earlier precedents were still in operation, this process commenced with the Queen's ladies and maids of honour, and her personal staff. Most garments seem to have been worn, as the Queen intended they should be, and have not survived. With only two exceptions all her dresses and outerwear surviving from before 1861 were preserved by the Queen herself, and it is small accessories like stockings, shoes and nightdresses which, together with some of her children's clothing, seem to have been given to household staff like Lydia Greatorex (illustrations 135, 168).

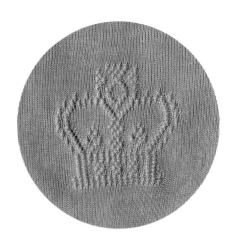

148 Detail of silk stocking, c.1837. (MoL 32.61/2)

149 Detail of dressing gown.

150 Dressing gown, 1858–62.
     (MoL 38.167/1, 36.42/2)

This broderie anglaise dressing gown is cut
with sufficient fullness to cover the very wide
petticoats, or even crinoline, which the
Queen was wearing at the end of the 1850s.
The mid-nineteenth-century branch coral
tiara has no royal association.

Lace was second only to jewellery as a prized possession. It would have been removed
from the Queen's dresses by the wardrobe maids, to be used again on another royal dress.
The only record of such reuse is of the Queen's wedding lace which she frequently wore
on her wedding anniversaries and children's christenings. Payments throughout the
Queen's reign to lace dealers and manufacturers show that Victoria bought a great deal of
lace, most of which has now been dispersed. She not only bought newly-made lace and
perhaps continued to commission pieces when she could, but seems to have acquired
fine examples of old laces when the opportunity arose.

When removed from her dresses the lace was sent to a specialist firm of lace cleaners,
Curling & Co., who served the Queen throughout her reign. An advertisement which
Jane Curling inserted in a directory in 1835 reveals that the firm also undertook to clean
embroideries, muslins and shawls, and offered a dyeing service, together with 'French
Fluting, Gauffering, Crimping, and Pinking'.[19]

No other payments record cleaning or dry-cleaning the Queen's clothes. It has to be
assumed that the care lavished on them by her wardrobe maids – careful brushing and
spot-cleaning together with proper storage – sufficed while the Queen needed these
garments, and that when they were too soiled or creased they were discarded. New outerwear was bought for the Queen each year, including stout capes and raincoats for her

expeditions at Balmoral. Some of this clothing was purchased, apparently readymade, from established clothiers and suppliers of waterproofed garments.

The advent of domestic washing machines has minimised the importance of underwear as a protection for clothing from soiling by bodily substances. In earlier days amply cut linen and cotton underwear almost completely covered the body and, as far as we know, any lady of standing washed carefully daily. Who washed the Queen's personal linen is not absolutely clear. There appears to have been a body-linen laundress, who was presumably stationed at Buckingham Palace, and she must have dealt with the underwear of the royal family, and possibly other residents in the royal household.[20] A laundry also existed there to deal with table and bedlinen, but this is altogether an aspect of life in royal palaces which has left few records behind. It was usual for women to own quantities of underwear which, in the middle classes at least, were washed on a monthly basis when the necessary hot water was specially heated up.[21] It is impossible to determine whether this was the system in the royal household, but the Queen possessed numerous sets of underwear and nightwear which were marked with her cypher and a sequence of numbers (illustrations 148, 200).

Apart from Windsor Castle and Brighton Pavilion Queen Victoria at first owned no property which could offer her and her family a pleasant and secluded retreat from public life. In the earliest years of their marriage she and Prince Albert stayed at Claremont and other country houses lent to them by ministers or nobility, and eventually their search for a property of their own led to the acquisition of Osborne House, on the Isle of Wight. The original house was soon found to be too cramped and, as later at Balmoral, Prince Albert initiated an ambitious building project. Here they were able to come each year to enjoy a relaxed normal family atmosphere. With them, of course, they brought all their household staff, and a large assortment of personal luggage. The letters of Frieda Arnold, one of the Queen's dressers from 1854–9, describe the trials endured in transit with this luggage, its packing and unpacking. At Osborne there was a large purpose-built wardrobe room, next to the Queen's bedroom, which was furnished with three vast mahogany wardrobes. One of the maids slept here at night to be on hand should the Queen need her, and a duty maid was present all day. The Queen's daily pattern of changing her clothes required a dresser always to be on duty too. The same pattern was followed in the migration each autumn to the distant Balmoral and there are glimpses here, either in Frieda's letters or in the Queen's Journal, of outings in pony carriages with the Queen's hairdresser, Nestor Tirard, in off-duty hours. Nothing is said of the extra work necessitated by the often inclement weather at Balmoral where the Queen rode or tramped over the dusty or muddy estate, and sometimes ventured further afield.

By the time Frieda Arnold joined the Queen's personal staff in 1854, well-tried and tested routines were in place to accommodate the Queen's visits to her various properties. Excursions beyond this, including her state visits abroad, brought new hazards and excitements for all in the entourage: luggage might not arrive in time for dressing for dinner parties, instructions might be imperfectly relayed by host domestics, but still the Queen's routine must continue and she must be presented to her public with her bodice well laced and her jewels all in place. Prince Albert, who lavished much attention on his wife's appearance, noticed the least thing amiss and would reprimand her staff accordingly.[22]

151 Cape, 1855–65. (MoL 33.200)

The origin of this very ornate velvet cape (right) has not yet been identified. It is believed to have been presented to Queen Victoria and has until recently been recorded as 'Indian work'. It is now thought to be European work of the late 1850s or early 1860s, probably French, though this is not confirmed. Its elaborate nature strongly suggests that it was a specially-commissioned gift to the Queen, or worked for exhibition purposes. A further possibility is that it was presented to the Queen during her state visit to Paris in 1855.

Public Life, 1851–61

Queen Victoria's clothes surviving from the 1850s are mostly associated with public or court events and they illustrate the public and ceremonial aspects of the Queen's life.

Prince Albert's position as consort of a reigning queen initially had presented both himself and Queen Victoria with unexpected problems of adjustment. Brought up to take an active and dominant role in manhood he was frustrated by the limitations at first imposed upon him after marriage. However, he established a role for himself in the royal household, directing his energies into reforming the wasteful and bureaucratic system which surrounded the Queen, kept a watchful eye on the upbringing of his growing family, took a keen and orderly interest in the royal library and art collections, and designed new homes at Osborne and Balmoral. At first distrusted by the Queen's ministers and the public he gradually created a public role for himself quite separate from that of royal consort. Of all the ventures the Prince lent his support to, it was the Great Exhibition of 1851 for which he will be best remembered.

The Great Exhibition was first conceived in 1849, following the success of a number of small exhibitions promoting art and industry with which the Prince had been associated. Prince Albert entered into the project wholeheartedly, raising the necessary funds, arguing for the large central site in Hyde Park, supporting Paxton's revolutionary design for the building and working indefatigably to bring the exhibition, the first of its kind, to fruition. It was divided into four sections: raw materials, machinery and mechanical inventions, manufactures, and sculpture and the plastic arts. The emphasis was on modernity, invention and discovery, a policy largely responsible for the exhibition's great success. Queen Victoria opened the exhibition formally on 1 May 1851 in the presence of a crowd of 86,000 guests and spectators. The Queen's long Journal entry, detailing the events of the day, bears witness to her pride in Prince Albert's achievement. No wonder, then, that she should preserve the dress worn on that day (illustrations 10, 154, 155).

The Queen had visited the exhibition frequently with Prince Albert before the official opening and after the opening she made thirty-four visits, getting up early in the morning so that she could arrive before 10am. She worked her way systematically through each section, carefully noting her preferences – the Indian pearls were one – and her dislikes. The Koh-i-Nûr diamond, set in an Indian armlet, was an exhibit which attracted a lot of public interest. Payments made later in the year show that the Queen made a number of clothing purchases at the exhibition: Genoese velvets, French silks,

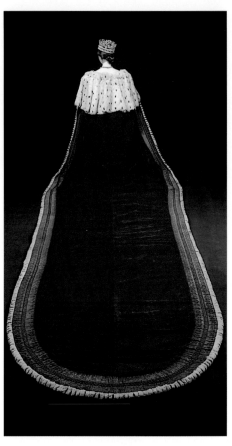

152 Back view of mantle.

The mantle is of a silk velvet almost certainly woven in the Spitalfields area of London; it is 16ft 5in. long by 47in. wide (5.08m x 1.20m) and still retains its ermine lining. The original ermine cape is missing and the present cape of rabbit fur is probably an early-twentieth-century replacement.

153 Parliament robe, 1838–51. (MoL 48.14/12, Castle Howard Estates Ltd)

In its present state Queen Victoria's Parliament robe seems to be composed of the mantle made in 1838 for her coronation, and the 1851 kirtle. Queen Victoria refused to wear the robe after Prince Albert's death. The replica of George IV's circlet shows it as altered for Queen Alexandra.

154 (Detail) *The Great Exhibition in Hyde Park, London; the Opening by H.M. Queen Victoria on 1st May 1851,* by Henry Courtney Selous (1811–90). (Victoria & Albert Museum, London)

Queen Victoria was accompanied at the opening of the exhibition by the Prince Consort and her two eldest children. The nine-year-old Prince of Wales wore full Highland dress whilst the Princess Royal's dress was 'lace over satin, with a wreath of pink wild roses in her hair', as the Queen recorded in her long Journal entry describing the momentous day. She is flanked by her ministers (left), and by foreign ambassadors (right).

155 Silk dresses, 1851.
     (MoL 33.133, 38.91)

For the opening of the Great Exhibition Queen Victoria wore, in her own words, 'a dress of pink and silver, with a diamond ray Diadem and [Queen Charlotte's] little crown at the back, with two feathers, all the rest of my jewels being diamonds' (Journal, 1 May 1851). The silk of the dress, a deep pink with vertical bands of interlocking silver circles, is believed to have been of Spitalfields manufacture (illustration 10). The dress has perhaps been altered for later wear: the plump bows which now ornament it are not shown in contemporary paintings of the occasion, and would have spoilt the lie of the Queen's broad Garter ribbon. The 'tartan' dress is believed to have belonged to one of Queen Victoria's daughters, probably the Princess Royal, and dates from about 1850–2. It is made of a silk satin imitating Royal Stuart tartan which was probably woven in Spitalfields. The figure holds the parasol shown in illustrations 156–8.

The handle is elaborately ornamented with an
enamelled Garter ribbon winding down to a
knob set with semi-precious stones. An
enamelled hand is ingeniously employed as an
opening mechanism.

158 Parasols, 1845–55. (MoL D169, D168,
D431, Royal Collection)

The green silk parasol (bottom) is the earliest
of Queen Victoria's parasols, and is thought
to date from the 1840s. The 'Royal Victoria'
parasol (left) was advertised in the *Illustrated
London News* in March 1851 by Cheek &
Marsh of the Golden Perch in Oxford Street;
this example is thought to have been
presented to Queen Victoria at the Great
Exhibition opening ceremony. The metal
slide on the braid-ornamented folding parasol
(right) is inscribed 'Lewis & Allenby' for the
Regent Street firm which supplied Queen
Victoria for most of her reign with rich silks;
the parasol probably dates from about 1850.

159 Detail of green silk parasol
(illustration 158, bottom)

Queen Victoria experienced several
assassination attempts, the first being in June
1840. Some unknown person – presumably
Prince Albert or a parasol manufacturer –
devised this parasol incorporating a layer of
mail between cover and lining as a protection
for the Queen. However, the weight of the
mail made it impossible for the parasol to be
held normally – it weighs 3.237lb (1468g) –
and it was probably never used by the Queen.

a Turkish dress and accessories, a Spanish mantilla, a Leghorn bonnet and Tunisian
jewellery. She is not known to have visited shops since her childhood and the
exhibition's impressive displays, stand after stand generously draped with silks, laces,
shawls, and cloths or crammed with all manner of exquisite accessories and novelties,
would have struck her just as forcibly as they did the humblest of her subjects. Indeed the
quarterly totals of her clothing bills were high at this time, and it is a wonder that she did
not spend much more extravagantly.

A further royal *bal costumé* took place just six weeks after the opening of the Great
Exhibition, and happily the dress she wore on this occasion has survived, probably the
most glamorous of all the Queen's existing dresses (illustrations 160–3).[1] The theme
selected, 'The Court of Charles II', once more allowed for sumptuous dress, particularly
this time for the men. Prince Albert's outfit was entirely of British manufacture, the
orange and gold brocade for his coat, so *The Times* revealed, 'of Spitalfields manufacture,
completed in twelve days from the order being given'. Queen Victoria thought the coat
brocade 'did the greatest honour to Spitalfields'. Albert, she noted in her Journal:

> looked very handsome in his [costume]… Mine was of grey moiré antique,
> ornamented with gold lace, – a very long waist with a berthe of guipure & sleeves
> trimmed with old lace. The petticoat showing under the dress, which was all open in
> front, was of rich gold and silver brocade (Indian manufacture) richly trimmed with
> silver lace… In my hair I wore an arrangement of pearls, and a large emerald, – my
> small diamond crown & pearls… in the back of my hair. The shoes and gloves were
> embroidered to match the dress.

She added to her Journal description a small coloured sketch of herself, Albert and her
half-brother Charles in their costumes.[2]

It is not certain which of the Queen's dressmakers was responsible for making this
fancy dress. The thirteen-year association with Vouillon & Laure, makers of the 1842
fancy dress, had ceased in 1850, and in 1851 the Queen was just commencing business
with two new dressmakers – Elizabeth Gieve (28 Davies Street, Berkeley Square) and
Sarah Ann Unitt (21 Lower Grosvenor Street). Nothing is known of the workrooms or

160 Detail: lace collar.

The collar lace was cut from a larger piece rather than worked specially to this shape. It is a copy of seventeenth-century Venetian raised point needle lace of a type made in Ireland around this time. Examples of such work, including a very similar piece by Jane Clark, the Regent Street lace-dealer, were shown in the Great Exhibition. Queen Victoria is known to have bought lace from Jane Clark between 1848 and 1852, but it cannot be established whether this piece was amongst those purchases.

161 Detail: brocade petticoat.

The rich gold and silver brocade of the Queen's Stuart fancy dress was woven in Benares in India. It may have come as a gift from an Indian potentate, or have been acquired from the Great Exhibition. It is possible that the fabric was supplied by Howell & James of Regent Street, whose bill in 1851 was considerable.

162 Fancy dress, 1851. (MoL 33.199)

The dress (right) worn by Queen Victoria at the Restoration ball, at Buckingham Palace on 13 June 1851, was designed by the French painter and costume designer Eugène Lami (1800–90). He was temporarily in London in the train of Louis Philippe after the 1848 Paris uprising and the Queen had long been familiar with his work. The dress he designed was a masterly interpretation of the stiff-bodied fashions of the seventeenth century. Twenty years earlier Lami had been responsible for the costumes for the original production of *La Sylphide* which Queen Victoria had so admired, and some credit him with 'inventing' the plain white tutu of the Romantic ballet – still worn in classical ballet – for Marie Taglioni (illustrations 86–7). Did Queen Victoria perhaps remember this in 1851?

output of these two dressmakers. It is possible that the dress was made by one of several Parisian dressmakers whose bills were presented at this time. The French designer of the dress, Eugène Lami, is likely to have favoured one of his countrywomen, with whom he may already have worked on theatrical productions. It may be no coincidence that the moiré of the Queen's dress is thought to be of French manufacture. In the capable hands of this experienced designer the Queen seems to have been spared the fuss which so unsettled her in 1842.

Although fashion journals in the late 1830s and through the 1840s were advocating all manner of frills, bows and novel trimmings, it does seem from her portraits that Queen Victoria stuck to simple, lightly adorned styles, relying much on fine laces, and probably embroidery also, to enrich the plain satins or highly patterned silks which appear to have been the mainstay of her formal wardrobe. Judging from her comments in 1842 about her Plantagenet fancy dress (p134) it seems likely that she accorded a rather

163 *Queen Victoria and Prince Albert in Costume of the Time of Charles II*, by Franz Xaver Winterhalter (1805–73). (Royal Collection)

This oil study was started by the artist two days before the ball, when the couple may have been trying on their costumes.

low priority to the minutiae of fashion novelties, perhaps being guided by her several dressmakers in the more general changes as the decade progressed. Her steadfast refusal to adopt and appear publicly in short-lived fashions meant that the fashion press eventually lost its original enthusiasm for reporting everything she wore. However, her dress naturally always attracted attention and must have been imitated by those with social pretensions or indeed by those who shared her conservative approach; her views were after all wholly typical of a large section of British society.

Charlotte Brontë had noted her sovereign's plain dress in 1843 when the royal carriage passed her in a Brussels street, a comment which perhaps reveals more about the novelist's expectations than the Queen's taste in dress. During the Queen's subsequent State visit to France the French fashion press had found much to praise in her demeanour and dress. Her wardrobe was doubtless well calculated to flatter French fashionable taste; she was still patronising Vouillon & Laure and had more recently added Mme Elise Papon (presumably another expatriate) to her small circle of dressmakers.

However, when Queen Victoria paid her next state visit to Paris in 1855 much had changed. Not only was she older and of a more mature frame, but she had largely abandoned the simple dress which had been so effective earlier in her reign. The fashions of the later 1840s and 1850s were far less flattering: the expanding multi-tiered skirts of the 1850s and larger, bolder prints only served to underline her thicker waistline and

164 *Queen Victoria,* 1859, by Franz Xaver Winterhalter (1805–73). (Royal Collection)

The Queen is wearing George IV's circlet, with the new collet necklace and earrings made for her in 1858 from large diamonds removed from George III's Garter badge and a ceremonial sword. On her right wrist is one of the portrait bracelets of Prince Albert which she was fond of wearing. On the stomacher of her dress she wears a fringed corsage ornament. This was the last portrait to be painted of Queen Victoria in her Parliament robes.

165 Back view of kirtle (illustration 153).

By 1851 Queen Victoria had borne seven children and it is likely that her first kirtle could no longer accommodate her expanding figure. A new kirtle was therefore made by the robemaker John Hunter, at a cost of £118. Its form seems to have closely followed that devised in 1837–8. If originally embroidered golden oak leaves had ornamented the bodice (p102), they were replaced in 1851 by gold lace, a more traditional ornament on ceremonial robes.

short stature. Furthermore she now had to contend with the beauty and the stylish Parisian dresses of the Empress Eugénie, the new young wife of Napoleon III. During their visit to London in April 1855 Victoria had noted the Empress's wardrobe with care and with her own special brand of honest admiration. It is doubtful that she really felt threatened by Eugénie and their subsequent friendship and affection only serve to demonstrate the older woman's self-assurance and readiness to be influenced in matters of fashion by fresh young practitioners. Indeed, she had again attempted to flatter her visitors by acquiring part of her wardrobe for the visit from the Paris dress houses of Palmyre Legrand and, to a lesser extent, Deschamps Sellier. As far as the Queen seems to have been concerned such a compliment to her hosts took precedence over her own support for British textiles.

For her return visit later in the summer Queen Victoria again selected her wardrobe with great care, including dresses from the Paris houses of Deschamps Sellier, Chardon & Lagache and Camille. No doubt as a compliment to the Empress's Spanish origins she went to some trouble to acquire a mantilla. Despite all the fuss and worry occasioned by this gathering together of an impressive array of dresses, there can be little doubt that Queen Victoria enjoyed this further excuse to indulge openly in the forbidden fruits of Parisian dresses. Exceptionally she noted in her Journal what both she and the Empress wore for most of the formal occasions, and even described the Empress's informal dress

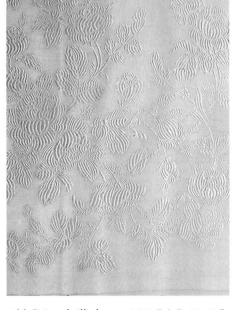

166 Printed silk dress, 1855. (MoL 33.136)

Queen Victoria is traditionally believed to have worn this dress during her state visit to Paris in August 1855. Although she kept a well-detailed account of the visit, in which she usually described her own dresses and jewellery as well as those of her hostess, there is no reference which seems to match this dress. It is certainly of a French silk, which suggests that it was indeed worn for this visit or, alternatively, was made up from a length of silk purchased in Paris.

167 Detail: skirt silk.

The ornate design of spring and summer flowers includes peonies, lilies of the valley, narcissi, etc. It is a chiné silk, in which the blurred cloudy effect was achieved by pre-printing the pattern on the stretched warp threads before the piece was woven. The silk was subsequently processed through rollers so that the ribbed ground developed the moiré (watered silk) effect. Ingres' 1856 portrait of the fashionable Mme Moitessier in the National Gallery, London, shows a very similar flowered silk dress.

168 Scarf, 1855. (MoL 46.16/7)

It is claimed that Queen Victoria wore this long silk scarf at the opening of the Paris exhibition in 1855, but this cannot be proved. The scarf found its way into the possession of the Queen's wardrobe maid Lydia Greatorex.

when it caught her eye. Prince Albert was not blind to the beauty of his hostess and he rather touchingly recorded the Empress's outfits which he most admired. Victoria was well aware of her husband's admiring eye: was she perhaps storing away his impressions with a view to following them up in the future? Eugénie is said to have introduced the crinoline during this visit, but if she did the Queen did not comment on the fact in her extensive Journal entries.[3] Florence Nightingale, that heroine of the Crimea, later described Eugénie tartly as 'the Empress who was born to be a dressmaker' because of her predilection for very fashionable dress.[4] The Queen greatly admired the simplicity of the Empress's appearance, but failed to emulate it herself.

The more conservative stately wardrobe she took with her to Paris in 1855 received its share of opprobrium from the court and French fashion press. General Canrobert privately mocked the crude green of her mantle and parasol, her massive best bonnet with its tuft of marabout feathers on top, and the gold poodle embroidered on her enormous white satin reticule (the work of the Princess Royal?). Canrobert also carped about the Queen's white dress ornamented with red geraniums, 'which would have done credit to Paxton's conservatory'.[5] In her Journal the Queen describes this particular dress, of white net embroidered with gold, 'very full', which, she continued, 'was very much admired by the Emperor and the ladies. The Emperor asked if it was English I said, No, it had been made on purpose in Paris!'

170 Uniform jacket: back view.

As no uniforms for women existed, it was necessary for an appropriate modification to be devised for the Queen: the solution was a variant on a riding habit. The jacket was probably the work of the military tailor Frederick Mortimer of Conduit Street, to whom several payments were made at about the appropriate time. It cleverly incorporates the essential details of a military tunic, lending it an air of authenticity and authority, whilst at the same time retaining an element of femininity.

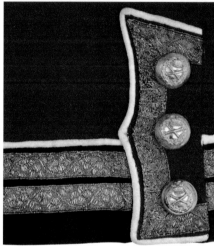

171 Detail: cuff of uniform jacket.

169 Military uniforms of Queen Victoria and Prince Albert, 1856–61. (MoL D328, D329, D231, Royal Collection; MoL A1907; The Guards Museum)

Two of Queen Victoria's military jackets survive from the 1850s but she was only ever portrayed wearing the version with the V-neckline. It is uncertain whether the high-necked jacket (on stand) was a rejected first version or was a new design made for the Queen just before Prince Albert's death: it is larger round the waist, which seems to indicate the later date. The V-necked version was acquired by a private collector from a Red Cross sale in 1917 and its previous history is not known; presumably it had either been dispersed from the Queen's possessions in 1901, or had been lent to G. H. Thomas for his painting. The habit skirt originally belonged to Queen Victoria, but is thought to be from a riding habit.

The Emperor had provided his wife with some magnificent parures of precious stones to complete her ensembles but the young Empress could not compete with the Koh-i-Nûr diamond which sparkled in the Queen's diamond diadem on this occasion (illustration 178). Jewels probably excited the Queen's interest far more than dress. She clearly much enjoyed wearing them and very carefully recorded which jewels both she and the Empress wore. She had by now accumulated a large and enviable collection and during this visit her jewels must have been the most admired aspects of the Queen's evening ensembles.[6]

As head of state Queen Victoria was also commander-in-chief of the army. At the beginning of her reign her Windsor uniform had provided a suitably pseudo-martial image, but her numerous pregnancies inevitably ruled out horseback appearances in successive years. In 1856, however, the return of the troops from the Crimea prompted a succession of reviews to welcome them home. Where possible she tried to appear on horseback, at first wearing a dark green riding habit with a round black hat trimmed with red and white feathers. 'Over her shoulder Her Majesty wore a belt of gold and tissue work, which added greatly to the effect of a most elegant costume', the *Morning Post* reported on 19 April 1856. The feathers and 'belt' (a sash?) suggest a preliminary attempt to create an appropriate military appearance for the Queen. By 16 June, no doubt at Prince Albert's prompting and probably to his design, Queen Victoria appeared for the first time in her scarlet military tunic, a modified version of a British general's tunic

Queen Victoria commissioned a number of paintings showing her reviewing her troops in the 1850s, and G. H. Thomas's canvas is believed to depict the review on 9 July 1859. The Queen is wearing her V-necked tunic (illustration 169) with a General's sash and a General's plume in her hat.

173 & 174 Military hats. (MoL D328, Royal Collection; MoL A19071)

The wide-brimmed felt hat which completed the Queen's military outfit was also drawn from ladies' riding wear. Such hats had recently become fashionable, and several photographs of the Queen from 1854 onward show her wearing silk or straw versions. The hatter W. C. Brown had been supplying the Queen for some time and, as had been the practice since the later years of the eighteenth century, inserted his label in the hats' lining.

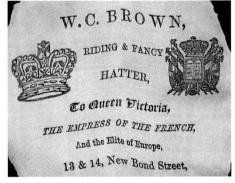

(illustrations 169–71). In her Journal the Queen recorded that she was 'not a little proud' of the tunic, whilst *The Times* described her outfit as 'a piquant and graceful costume'.[7] In November 1856 the Queen's final pregnancy forced her temporarily to relinquish horseback reviews until after the birth of Princess Beatrice in April 1857. By July 1857, however, she was back in uniform to distribute the first Victoria Crosses to Crimean veterans and she continued to wear this striking martial outfit in succeeding years. A second tunic which buttoned to the throat and had a standing collar imitating that on men's tunics is slightly larger in size and is thought to be a later version (illustration 169). These superbly tailored tunics, like the Queen's much earlier Windsor jacket, demonstrate how much more flattering tailor-made garments were to the Queen, especially in these middle years of her life, than the soft and frilly dresses customary for day and evening wear. The vogue for tailored outfits was just about to dawn but it was the next generation who would benefit from this swing in fashion, the Princess of Wales and the Empress Eugénie: in the 1860s Queen Victoria had lost all interest in her clothes and only paid lip service to the new simplicity of line.

The last dress surviving from the period before the Queen plunged into irrevocable black was one she wore for the confirmation of her eldest child, the Princess Royal, in March 1856. Now exceedingly brittle and faded, this is yet another example of the elaborate fashions of the 1850s which the Queen adopted, apparently with enthusiasm:

175 Circlet, 1853. (MoL 58.74/2)

The frame of the Grand or Regal circlet made for Queen Victoria by Garrard's in 1853 followed the form of a similar circlet owned by Queen Adelaide in 1831. The detachable crosses and fleurs-de-lis enabled Queen Victoria to substitute another cresting with a special setting for the Koh-i-Nûr diamond. In 1858 many of the stones used for the circlet had to be returned to Hanover. It was altered and reset for Queen Alexandra, but the stones have since been set in other royal jewellery.

176 Fan, 1858. (Royal Collection)

Queen Victoria's crown and cypher and the date 24 May 1858 suggest that this may have been a present to the Queen on her thirty-ninth birthday. There is no mention of the gift in her Journal. It is a large fan, and the leaf of silk 'petals' has been specially painted with a design incorporating roses, thistles and shamrocks. The sticks and guards are of intricately pierced and carved mother-of-pearl.

177 Queen Victoria, 14 November 1861, photograph by Charles Clifford. (Royal Archives)

Commissioned by the Queen of Spain, this is one of the last photographs taken of Queen Victoria before Prince Albert's death; it is also one of the few showing her formally dressed. She may still be in mourning for her mother, and seems to be wearing a crinoline under her full-skirted moiré silk dress.

178 Queen Victoria, 1856, by Franz Xaver Winterhalter. (Royal Collection)

Winterhalter's portrait is an important record of the Queen's jewellery just before she was forced to relinquish Queen Charlotte's jewels to the elector of Hanover. She had inherited the jewels in 1837 and had been resisting having to return them ever since. Round her neck is a rivière of diamonds which had belonged to Queen Charlotte, and on her head is her new circlet (illustration 175), which incorporated many of her grandmother's diamonds. The brooch has as its centrepiece the famous Koh-i-Nûr diamond, which had been cleverly mounted so that it could slot into the circlet.

'we ladies, all, wore smart morning dresses', she noted in her Journal. This dress was originally a delicate lilac silk taffeta patterned in a velvet pile to imitate seventeenth-century Italian needlepoint lace.[8] The high-necked bodice has long trumpet-shaped sleeves and flows jacket-like over the wide many-tiered skirt. The Queen was now having to wear many stiffened petticoats to hold out these voluminous textile dome-like skirts, and in July 1858, afflicted by enormous heat which made her summer muslin petticoats go limp, she succumbed to a 'cage' or crinoline. Who supplied this novelty is not apparent from the quarterly payments. It may have been one of her dressmakers.[9]

The Princess Royal was already privately engaged to Prince Frederick William of Prussia. When they were married in January 1858 the bride, as had become traditional, wore specially commissioned Honiton lace on her dress and veil while her mother wore her own wedding lace for the last time, as it transpired, before the death of Prince Albert. The Queen had always taken care that her children were suitably dressed and often noted their appearance in her Journal entries, overlooking her own. Now all this maternal concern concentrated upon her eldest daughter and great were the energies poured into Vicky's trousseau to ensure that her new family in Berlin were suitably impressed. When nothing was said in Vicky's first letters home, the Queen impatiently wrote demanding details: 'I am anxious to know how all my toilettes succeeded'.[10]

Widowhood, 1861–1901

The unexpected death of Prince Albert on 14 December 1861 introduced considerable changes in the lives of the Queen, her household and court, and also temporarily affected the world of fashion. Worn out by years of overwork and strain Prince Albert had succumbed to typhoid fever, dying at Windsor Castle after an illness of only three weeks. Queen Victoria had not realised the seriousness of his condition and therefore found his death, coming less than a year after her mother's, all the more devastating. 'My life as a happy one is ended! The world is gone for me!' she wrote to her uncle King Leopold of the Belgians.[1]

Until this time the Queen's adoption of the sombre black of mourning had been a social convention, in keeping with traditions current among her subjects, though naturally often reflecting her genuine grief for an esteemed relative or public figure (illustrations 92, 177). In contrast the deep mourning that she adopted in December 1861 held a powerful emotional significance, one so integral with her loss that she never relinquished it fully for the rest of her life.

Of the numerous dresses which have survived from the Queen's long widowhood only one belongs to this earliest phase (illustrations 180, 182).[2] Epitomising the deepest stage of mourning, in which a dress was almost entirely covered by black crape, the style of this dress nevertheless remained discreetly fashionable. It reveals the transition currently taking place as a result of the adoption of the crinoline: that is, the raising of the bodice waistline to the natural line coupled with the increasing spread of the hemline. Photographs of Queen Victoria earlier in 1861 show that she had begun to adopt this new style, especially in her formal evening dresses, but had maintained the longer pointed bodice line on her day dresses (illustration 177).

Retreating totally from public life in the first years of her widowhood the Queen needed fewer clothes, and it is not surprising to discover that expenditure on her dress decreased noticeably at this time. In fact it had already dropped earlier in 1861 when she went into mourning on the death of her mother, the Duchess of Kent, on 16 March, and it is possible that she reused some of this mourning at the time of Prince Albert's death in December.[3] Considerable purchases were made at Caley's in Windsor whenever the Queen was in residence at the Castle, and the payment to them of £155 at the end of this particular quarter must surely reflect acquisition of mourning for the Queen and her family: the Prince's illness, death and funeral took place at Windsor, where the Queen remained for some time before burying herself at Osborne.

179 Queen Victoria, 1862–3, photograph by Ghémar Frères. (Royal Archives)

The Queen, still in deep mourning, is dressed for outdoors in a short loose jacket and her special widow's hood edged with a thick white frill.

180 Mourning clothes of Queen Victoria, Princess Beatrice and Prince Leopold, 1862–3. (MoL 54.137/1–4)

Through good fortune these three early royal mourning outfits have been preserved. The Queen's dress is cut on comfortable lines with a button fastening from neck to hem, an unusual feature on a dress of this date; the collar is original, but the cap is a modern replica. Princess Beatrice's poplin (wool and silk) dress has bands of crape on the skirt. The boy's Highland outfit is believed to have belonged to Prince Leopold, then nine years old. It is of a fine black cloth and could possibly have been made by the uniform makers Meyer & Mortimer of Conduit Street.

181 Princess Beatrice, 1862–3.
(MoL 54.137/4 over 54.137/3)

With Princess Beatrice's dress there has
survived this hooded cape of black twilled
wool, unlined, with the edges bound with
twilled braid. Inside it is a rare early survival
of a maker's label, a piece of white silk
ribbon printed in black 'Her Royal Highness
The Princess Beatrice, Scott Adie
Waterproof'. This firm had opened its
Scotch warehouse at 115 Regent Street,
specialising in goods from northern
England, tartans, shawls and waterproofs, in
1854. It was patronised by Queen Victoria
from 1855 and by 1860 had received a royal
warrant, as Waterproof Cloak and Jacket
Maker to Her Majesty.

182 Detail of crape on Queen Victoria's
dress in illustration 180.

183 *In Memoriam,* by Sir Joseph Noel
Paton (1821–1901). (Royal
Collection)

This painting was commissioned by the
Queen in 1863 but, although always
meaning to, the artist failed to complete it.
He was lent the Queen's dress and the outfits
of Princess Beatrice and one of the younger
princes and these continued in family
possession until they were presented to the
Museum in 1954.

Little of the emotional drama which had engulfed the Queen is revealed by the
prosaic records of the Office of Robes. Payments in January 1862 for extra mourning
allowances of £10 to Marianne Skerrett and the two dressers, and of £6 each to the two
wardrobe maids 'being immediately about the person of the Queen' were possibly to
enable them to maintain the extended mourning which the Queen decided was
appropriate in her household.[4] On 15 December 1861, the day following the Prince's
death, the Lord Chamberlain's Office had issued its customary orders for court
mourning:

> The Ladies attending Court to wear black woollen stuffs, trimmed with crape, plain
> linen, black shoes and gloves and Crape Fans.
> The Gentlemen attending Court to wear black cloth, plain linen, Crape Hatbands and
> black swords and Buckles.

By the end of the month the Lord Chamberlain was informing his Comptroller that:

> The Queen desires that the mourning for the Prince Consort shall be ordered for the
> longest term in modern times. It would therefore be for 3 months … The Queen
> further wishes that none of the Household, should appear in Public out of mourning
> for a year. [5]

At this time the Queen was still patronising the dressmakers Sarah Ann Unitt and
Elizabeth Gieve (both appointed in 1851), and she continued to do so until 1876 and
1887 respectively. It is impossible to know for certain which was responsible for making
the surviving early mourning dress, but as Miss Unitt presented a bill for £109 16s 4d in

184 Queen Victoria spinning, 1863–5,
photograph by J. E. Mayall.
(Royal Archives)

Little appears to be known about this new hobby of the Queen's. She referred to it fleetingly in her Journal on 26 January 1865: 'Css. Blucher came to my room & showed me how to spin. I am getting on, in spite of a bad wheel & bad flax' (Fulford, *Dearest Child*, pp199–200). It is an occupation which requires much concentration and patience, and apparently the Queen spun sufficient linen thread for several damask napkins. These were shown at the 1888 Glasgow International Exhibition but have not been located. Queen Victoria had now adopted the peaked widow's cap, a style which she wore for the rest of her life.

March 1862 (Mrs Gieve's was only £17 5s 0d) there seems a strong possibility that it came from her workshops. The Privy Purse accounts reveal that Miss Unitt supplied goods for the younger Princesses in the later 1850s, so she may have made Princess Beatrice's dress too.

In fact Queen Victoria continued to patronise the majority of her previous suppliers and the regular quarterly statements of payments continue much as before. What was different, a difference these payments rarely reveal, was that these firms were now supplying black, rather than coloured or patterned, goods: the materials and workmanship remained of the highest quality. It is also not possible to deduce from these records who was responsible for the Queen's ubiquitous tulle widow's caps – 'Ma's sad caps', as the small Princess Beatrice called them – but they were probably supplied by one of the two dressmakers.[6]

Modern historians present Queen Victoria as the epitome of nineteenth-century widowhood, frequently maintaining that she was responsible for initiating the widespread adoption of mourning wear during her reign. The abiding image of her in people's minds is of an unsmiling, diminutive and plump elderly figure in black, an image widely disseminated through official portraits and photographs and, on a more popular level, through commemorative items and even advertisements. Few today, it seems, make a ready link with the Queen's happier years, with her youthful accession image, or her domestic contentment as wife and mother.

It is true that the last half of her life – four long and lonely decades – was spent almost entirely in black, often in deep mourning, but at other times in black relieved by white. The conventions of mourning had been deeply instilled into her and, though she found the laying aside of colourful clothing irksome, before the deaths of her mother and husband, she nevertheless conformed. In 1858, shocked by the Prussian court's more relaxed approach to mourning, she commented to her daughter, the new Crown Princess of Prussia:

> About the mourning. I wish to say a word as I feel strongly upon the subject … Court mournings are short and worn here for all Crowned Heads and Sovereigns, etc., who are no relations – but private mourning we wear as long as we like; and this private mourning no earthly being can prevent you from wearing in your own home and when you do not appear at Fêtes.[7]

In adopting black for the rest of her life Queen Victoria was conforming with a practice customary amongst her subjects, but it was an extreme measure for one of her years and position. It reflected the total loss she had experienced: 'our pure, happy, quiet, domestic life, which alone enabled me to bear my much disliked position, cut off at forty-two', she lamented to King Leopold. So much that she had shared and enjoyed with her husband – his interest and involvement in her appearance, his advice on silks, dress styles and accessories, the jewellery he designed for her, his admiration for her shoulders – *en décolleté* – were suddenly things of the past, gone forever. 'My poor sad face and garb must tell its tale.'[8]

Trade in the elaborate trimmings of death and mourning had been gathering momentum since the time of Queen Victoria's accession. The extraordinarily rapid increase in Courtauld's manufacture of black crape in the 1830s and 1840s, the result of the introduction of a secret process, reflected an industrial response to social change.[9] In turn, however, this increased mechanisation and large-scale production was to have a

185 *The Marriage of the Prince of Wales, 10 March 1863,* by William Powell Frith (1819–1909). (Royal Collection)

The marriage took place in St George's Chapel, Windsor, at 12.30pm and the artist was present in the Household Gallery to sketch the ceremony; he later also used photographs taken at the time. He borrowed uniforms, dresses, jewels and Orders so that his ambitious painting was as accurate as possible, and was allowed to keep the 'Scotch dress' worn by Prince Arthur and Prince Leopold. The bride's dress had already been cut up by the summer of 1863 and Frith had to be content with using the remnants and photographs to achieve his likeness.

186 Queen Victoria with Princess Beatrice and Prince Arthur, 1878, photograph by G. W. Wilson & Co. (Royal Archives)

During the 1870s Queen Victoria emerged from her deep mourning and, when not in mourning for other members of the family, appears in photographs in a muted form of fashionable dress. This photograph reveals that she had discarded much of the earlier skirt fullness in favour of a narrower skirt with pleats emphasising the vertical lines. She wears an elaborately braided mantle with a small silk scarf. Her flower-trimmed hat foreshadows many variants on the same theme over the next two decades.

powerful impact on social habits. Quantities of crape, at affordable prices, enabled increasing numbers to adopt formal mourning. Commerce similarly played an influential role by promoting these products through newly-established mourning warehouses selling the requisite textiles, trimmings and garments to the middle classes, who were now borrowing many such practices from their social superiors to validate their status.

It has been claimed that the mourning following the Prince Consort's death, and particularly the Queen's adoption of black, considerably influenced the fashions of the 1860s. There is only a small element of truth in this claim: fashion was anyway moving towards a major transformation. The seeds of that change were already apparent before December 1861 and fashion continued its remorseless transition unaffected by the royal tragedy at Windsor. Paris was the centre of fashion. Here Charles Frederick Worth, his fellow couturiers and their rich clients – especially the Empress Eugénie – ruled fashion absolutely. The adoption of the new silhouette and diminution of ornament were a reaction to the 1850s.

Also traceable to the 1850s was an increasing preference for a muted palette. This can be seen in fashion reports of the time, and although the half-mourning colours of lilac, grey and white may, for a short period, have predominated, there were changes in the dyeing industry, particularly William Perkin's invention of aniline dyes in 1856, which were enormously influential in exactly these years. Thus mauve (the new aniline dye mauveine) and its various tints suddenly became very popular at the end of the 1850s.[10]

On 1 July 1862, just six months after the Prince's death, his second daughter Princess Alice was married to Prince Louis of Hesse privately at Buckingham Palace. The Queen insisted that her nineteen-year-old daughter have an all-black trousseau, but allowed her

187 Fan, 1880–1900.
(MoL D416, Royal Collection)

Fan with a fine silk leaf painted with a view of Balmoral within a cartouche of stems of heather and signed 'E. Sydney'. The intertwined initials 'VR' are painted on the reverse, and the mother-of-pearl sticks are marked 'DUVELLEROY, LONDON' for the important Regent Street fan dealers. It is likely that this was a gift to the Queen.

188 Fan, 1877.
(MoL D418, Royal Collection)

Fan with a fine silk leaf painted with a view of Windsor Castle within a cartouche, signed 'Cte Nils'. The fan is believed to have been given to Queen Victoria in 1877 by the Prince of Wales.

a white wedding dress and bridesmaids in white. In deepest mourning herself, she dominated the mute ceremony.

Even when official mourning came to an end in 1863 the Queen continued to dictate the outward appearance of women at court, a trait she would never wholly relinquish. Thus, for the first Drawing Room held since the Prince's death, the Lord Chamberlain was informed 'that Her Majesty wishes the ladies of the Corps Diplomatique, the wives of the Cabinet Ministers and the Ladies of Her Household to be in black, with black feathers and gloves … all other ladies may be in colours'. For the second Drawing Room of the season, presided over for the Queen by the new Princess of Wales, these ladies were allowed 'black with white feathers and gloves and diamonds'.

The marriage of the Prince of Wales on 10 March 1863 could in no way be a private affair like that of his younger sister (illustration 185). It was celebrated in St George's Chapel, Windsor, and for this the Queen conceded, via the Lord Chamberlain, that 'everyone may be in colours – excepting the Ladies of Her Majesty's Household who must be in grey, lilac or mauve'.[11]

Out of respect for her future mother-in-law, Princess Alexandra of Denmark had worn half-mourning on her arrival in England at Gravesend on 7 March 1863. In the midst of the continuing royal gloom she presented an attractive youthful image to all those who gathered to welcome her, and enchanted her future mother-in-law: 'this sweet bright being whose soul seems very like the lovely robe which envelopes it'.[12] The fashion world's enthusiasm for a new royal bride is perennial and it was not to be disappointed by this Princess's elegance in succeeding years: she was to have a far greater influence upon the world of fashion than her mother-in-law ever did. At this time, however, the Queen continued to dictate what those in her presence should wear, explaining to her eldest daughter, now Crown Princess of Prussia:

> decidedly none of you ought to be in colours at the wedding [of the Prince of Wales] but in grey or silver or lilac and gold and so on but not merely gold and white: it is the first occasion of any of you children appearing in public and as all when in England will not wear colours … I think it ought not to be.[13]

She herself remained unable to compromise in any way. Dressed in her usual deep crape mourning she observed the ceremony alone, from Catherine of Aragon's closet high above the altar, too entrapped by her own powerful emotions to realise the impact she made on the congregation below. There, a much happier image was presented by the bridal couple, the Prince resplendent in his scarlet Guards uniform under his sweeping blue velvet robe of the Order of the Garter, and his beautiful bride traditionally dressed in products of British manufacture: white satin and cloth of silver from Spitalfields, and cornucopia-strewn Honiton lace from Devon, whilst the myrtle in her bouquet was from the bush grown from a sprig of the Queen's own wedding bouquet.

In July 1862 Marianne Skerrett, the Queen's Principal Dresser for twenty-five years, retired aged seventy-nine, 'anxious to pass the remainder of her active life with her sister'.[14] When Baroness Lehzen retired in 1842 Skerrett must have taken over many personal administrative duties for the Queen and Prince Albert, such as liaising with artists and tradespeople. So far as we know she already liaised with all the Queen's clothing suppliers, compiling the quarterly list of dressmaking bills for the Office of Robes, and she must therefore have been in a strong position to influence her mistress's

choice of silks, dress styles, and accessories. She was not replaced immediately, and eventually Sophie Weiss, a dresser since 1852, took charge. She herself retired four years later, and thereafter these most intimate of the Queen's daily companions, together with her wardrobe maids, slowly came and went.

Now that the Queen wore her hair plainly drawn back and mostly hidden under her widow's cap she had far less need of her official hairdresser Monsieur Nestor Tirard, and so he retired on a pension charged to the Office of Robes account in 1867. Presumably the Queen's hair was now dealt with entirely by her dressers or maids.

The responsibility for selecting and ordering the Queen's clothes probably now rested even more heavily upon her most senior dresser, for it seems that the Queen lost interest in her appearance. Her regular suppliers must have continued to try to influence her choice through the materials and trimmings submitted to her, but her innate conservatism and protracted deep mourning left them with little leeway. Interestingly enough she seems almost never to have patronised the specialist mourning suppliers and their proliferation of black goods in Regent Street. Judging from photographs, her dresses in the first three or four years of her widowhood were all very similar in design but, as previously noted, her widow's cap was modified by 1864 (illustration 184).

For outdoor wear the Queen was provided with a variety of loose jackets, capes and mantles of wool or silk according to the season. With them, in the earliest years of her widowhood, she is always seen in a specially-constructed hood-like headcovering of black crape. This had a stiffened upstanding section round her face lined with a white frilling (illustration 179). Some photographs of the Queen at Balmoral and Osborne at this time even show her wearing this head-dress on horseback, but there are others which show a more stylish deep-brimmed hat similar to that of her military uniform. Clearly, however, the exercise she now allowed herself to take in no way matched the joyous gallops of her teenage years.

The Queen's continued refusal to make public appearances antagonised her subjects and there was talk of abdication. Her place in the public eye was taken by the young Prince

189 Queen Victoria, 1889, photograph by Byrne & Co. (Royal Archives)

Paintings or photographs showing the Queen occupied with knitting or crochet are rare. Here she seems to be posing rather stiffly with what looks like crochet work. She wears one of the fine patterned shawls in which she was fond of enveloping herself, though the cold did not normally trouble her. Her widow's caps had by now developed into elaborate constructions of tulle or silk frills rising high on her head. They seem to have had wired net-covered bases, and sometimes had streamers ornamented with tulle frillings.

190 Cot cover, 1883. (MoL 82.60/44)

Queen Victoria liked to have some handiwork with which to occupy herself, and once grandchildren and great grandchildren began to appear she busied herself with working cot covers for them. This bright cover was made for Princess Alice, the daughter of Prince Leopold, Duke of Albany, who was born in 1883 and died in 1981. The Queen was very proud of her cot covers and embroidered her cypher on each one to ensure that her handiwork was recognised.

191 Queen Victoria with Princess Beatrice and grandchildren, September 1887, photograph by W. Watson. (Royal Archives)

The fossilisation of the Queen's dress style is evident in this photograph showing her with her stylish young granddaughters, although it is fair to point out that she did have many smart, but not ultra-fashionable, hats. The young Princesses Alix and Irene of Hesse were the daughters of the Queen's second daughter Princess Alice. Prince Albert Victor of Wales, eldest son of the Prince of Wales, died four years after this whilst engaged to Princess Mary of Teck.

and Princess of Wales, who naturally attracted increasing popularity. However, in June 1864 the Queen was persuaded to make her first public appearance, a ride in an open carriage. She of course appeared totally in black. Then at the beginning of 1866 she surprised her household by announcing that she herself would open Parliament in February. She utterly refused, however, to resume her regal image by donning her crimson velvet and ermine Parliament robe, and a compromise had to be devised. The Office of Robes was therefore informed that 'the Mantle will be placed upon the Throne by the Groom of the Robes, so that Her Majesty may sit upon it, and it can be wrapped round Her Majesty by the Princesses'. The Queen again appeared in black, but a black enriched by some of her fabulous diamonds: a diamond aigrette in front of her widow's cap, the necklace with its massive diamonds, and the Koh-i-Nûr diamond set as a brooch. The blue ribbon of the Order of the Garter was the only note of colour in the sombre ensemble.[15]

As Queen Victoria gradually increased her public or court appearances, so her expenditure on dress naturally rose. A single bill of £508 paid to the fashionable Regent Street mercers Howell & James in March 1866, together with often high payments to such other silk and cloth suppliers as Caley's (Windsor), Romanes & Patterson (Edinburgh), Halling & Pearce (Pall Mall), or Swan & Edgar (Piccadilly Circus), reflect the renewed activity within the Queen's wardrobe. These bills are matched by higher bills from the dressmakers Miss Unitt and Mrs Gieves.[16]

Photographs of the later 1860s show the Queen wearing lighter crape trimmings on her black dresses and, eventually, jet-ornamented braids or even pleated frillings on her skirts; for outdoors she began to don lightly trimmed bonnets. But, conservative as she had always been, the Queen at this period applied her brakes steadfastly, allowing herself to look much older than her years and at times presenting a quite frumpy appearance. This is especially noticeable in group photographs with her younger daughters, daughters-in-law, or older grandchildren. She had always preferred her clothing to be comfortable, and now, lacking the discipline imposed by wearing fashionable dresses on public occasions and the controlling influence of Prince Albert, she gradually eschewed the increasingly rigid corsetry required to create a fashionable outline. Photographs frequently show her diminutive but expanding frame enveloped in shawls and mantles. On occasion, however, they also reveal smart, almost chic, outfits, especially mantles and bonnets (illustration 186). From time to time she must have been influenced by her daughters, and especially by the gentle and fashion-loving Princess of Wales. Although no longer an active participant in fashion Queen Victoria maintained a robustly critical view of the dress she observed around her and her sharp eye was quick to spot innovations which went beyond her approval.

The year 1876 witnessed the ending of another twenty-five year association when the dressmaker Sarah Ann Unitt ceased working for the Queen. Between 1876 and 1877 Elizabeth Gieve was the Queen's sole regular dressmaker, although from time to time small payments to other dressmaking and millinery establishments were recorded. In 1876 the Queen adopted new milliners (apparently to replace Sarah Ann Unitt), Perryman & Parsons of Brook Street, Grosvenor Square, an association that would last until the end of 1891. Both had worked for Miss Unitt, whose probable retirement had no doubt prompted them to set up in business for themselves.[17] To judge from the evidence of photographs the Queen's headwear definitely improved at this time: she is shown wearing a variety of bonnets trimmed with black or white flowers, feathers, lace and ribbons (illustrations 186, 191, 207).

192 Jacket, 1890–1900. (MoL 33.277)

Queen Victoria continued to wear short black wool jackets when out of doors and these changed little in shape over three decades. This unique late example, of a fine twilled cloth, is much more fitted to her form, reflecting the fashionable world's current enthusiasm for tailor-made garments.

193 Detail: braid on jacket.

The Queen seems to have liked silk braid decoration on her outerwear as it is frequently seen in photographs.

In 1882 Queen Victoria suddenly decided to revive her private 'tradition' of wearing her wedding lace, apparently laid aside in 1858. Her usually excellent memory did not serve her well when she recorded in her Journal on 27 April: 'Wore for the first time my own wedding lace over black satin, and my own wedding veil, which I had not worn since my wedding day in 1840, surmounted by my small diamond crown'.[18] The occasion was the marriage at Windsor of her youngest son, Prince Leopold, to Princess Helena of Waldeck-Pyrmont: the Prince, who had inherited haemophilia through his mother, was to die within two years. In 1885 the wedding lace was unpacked again, but this time ornamented the bride rather than her mother. Princess Beatrice was Queen Victoria's youngest child, a great solace to her in the early days of her widowhood, and she was the only member of the family to be accorded this privilege. The Princess and her husband Prince Henry of Battenberg had agreed to live with the Queen after their marriage at Whippingham on the Isle of Wight. The Queen's wedding lace came out once more in 1893 when she wore it herself at the marriage of her grandson Prince George, Duke of York, to Princess Mary of Teck (later George V and Queen Mary) (illustration 209).[19]

Mrs Gieve submitted her last bill as Queen Victoria's dressmaker at the end of September 1889 and her place was taken by Mrs Martha Dudley. As with so many of the Queen's dressmakers, nothing is known of Mrs Dudley's establishment or her clientele. She does not appear to have sewn labels into her garments though this became an increasingly common practice amongst later nineteenth-century dressmakers and retailers. It has to be assumed that she was recommended to the Queen by one of the Women of the Bedchamber, who could vouch for her reliability and discretion. The ability to create eye-catching novelties was not what the Queen and many of her peers considered appropriate to their rank, and Mrs Dudley probably belonged to a large group of dressmakers who successfully met the needs of an older conservative clientele.

194 Handkerchiefs, 1890–1900. (MoL
57.38/25, 26, 27)

A number of decorative handkerchieves like
these survive and are associated with the
Queen's latter years. They perhaps started life
as presents, in matching sets. Several plain
white handkerchiefs, simply embroidered
with the Queen's cypher also survive.

195 Bonnet, 1887–8. (MoL 48.13)

This bonnet has traditionally been associated
with the Queen's 1897 Jubilee, but its solid
construction suggests 1887 as a more likely
date. The ribbon-trimmed white silk bonnet
is covered with net ornamented with small
black glass beads. It must have sat partly on
the top and back of the Queen's head (as in
illustrations 207, 211) with the fine black
machine-lace streamers falling down the back.
The bonnet has the printed silk label of
Perryman & Parsons sewn into its lining. It is
said to have been purchased from one of the
Queen's dressers after her funeral.

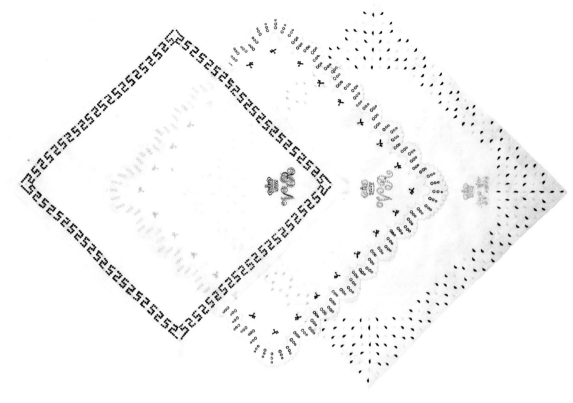

Only very occasionally did the Queen now patronise other dressmakers. Quantities of
fine silks continued to be acquired from major London mercers like Howell & James or
Lewis & Allenby (Regent Street), whilst outerwear was probably supplied by tailors like
Morgan & Co. or John Redfern (Isle of Wight), Meyer & Mortimer, or the furriers
Nicholay & Co. It is intriguing to see that the Queen patronised the makers of Princess
Mary of Teck's wedding dress, Linton & Curtis (Albermarle Street) in 1893, the year of
her marriage. Their bill, for less than £10, suggests that the Queen's acquisition was
small, and it was not repeated. Major London stores also feature more in these later bills:
Debenham & Freebody, Gorringe, Jay's, Liberty's, Marshall & Snelgrove, Robinson &
Cleaver, Woollands. Long-time suppliers like the mercers Halling, Pearce & Stone and
Lewis & Allenby were absorbed into the department stores Swan & Edgar and Dickins
& Jones in the latter years of the nineteenth century, and the Queen did not always
continue her patronage. Gundry & Co., who for seventy years had made her shoes, were
taken over in the last years of the reign by Joseph Box & Co. The number of suppliers
dwindled in the last decade of the Queen's life as she became much less active: the
quarterly totals still matched, or were less than, those at the beginning of her reign.

Over a period of time those around the Queen had had to adjust to her rigidly sombre
wardrobe and she continued to control, or to attempt to control, what they wore. Those
in her daily presence had no choice but to conform. Frequent periods of mourning
punctuated the long widowhood, for her extensive family was spread throughout
Europe and the Queen insisted that those in attendance upon her should also wear
mourning for the distant dead. 'I am in despair about my clothes', an exasperated Marie
Mallet (maid of honour from 1887 to 1891) wrote home from Balmoral in 1889:

no sooner have I rigged myself out with good tweeds than we are plunged into the deepest
mourning for the King of Portugal [Louis I], jet ornaments for weeks. And he was only a

first cousin once removed. So I only possess one warm black dress; the Sunday one is far from thick, it is a lesson never, never to buy anything but black!

Happily she could find humour in what must have been trying circumstances for one still in her twenties: 'I find I shall have to wear black feathers at the Drawing Room [in 1888] and black lappets so that I shall present a hearse like appearance. Can you lend me some black plumes for the occasion, if not I must write and order some.'[20]

The Queen's Ladies-in-waiting and Women of the Bedchamber were often widows or at least older married women who were more able to cope with the Queen's irksome restrictions, and it appears to have been the younger generation who sometimes fitted less comfortably into the royal household. Queen Victoria was certain to ensure that any transgressions were made known to the perpetrator, and a repetition of the offence was not expected. Marie Mallet, despite her private explosions, presumably complied. One of the Queen's letters preserved in the Royal Archives reveals how, terrier-like, she attempted to bring into line a slightly earlier maid of honour, Amy Lambart, through the offices of the Marchioness of Ely, one of her Ladies-in-waiting:

OSBORNE

Dear Jane,   Jan 2 1882

I wish Amy should know I thought since the Duchess of Roxburgh had spoken to her her dress decidedly improved – but I am anxious that there shd. be [no] <u>repetition</u> in new dresses of the very short sleeves – bodies with so little trimming – and too low, etc, etc, when she returns <u>again</u>, as I know it is remarked upon, and remarks are made by many – w[hich] as <u>my</u> Maid of Honour does not <u>do</u>.

I am so fond of her and know what a good straightforward steady girl she is, so devoid of all 'fastness' that I feel really anxious she shd. do nothing by her dress to lead people to think the contrary. I have always said this to everyone when people have remarked on her dress. <u>None</u> of her 'colleagues' dress in that style, she will observe.

The <u>shape</u> and <u>make</u> of the black dress I gave her is <u>quite</u> right; but white or grey if made in that style, will do quite <u>as well</u>. I am sure if she dressed a good deal looser it would be far better for her health. She did not dress so tight when she 1st came.

Ever yours affectionately V.I.

You did speak to her last year abt. her dress being too low, at Balmoral.

If she wd. try and remember before she comes back not to have very showy gowns in extreme of fashion. Not those very short sleeves – nor the bodies too low or too close fitting. Not short sleeves of a morning or tight fitting Jerseys or very tight fitting summer gowns wh. cling so very much. And altogether to let her dress be as much like other peoples as possible and never in any extreme of fashion.

The hair of course I very much regret and know other people have too – as it is not becoming – but I can only hope someday she will let hers grow again.[21]

Amy Lambart was already thirty when this letter was written and had been a maid of honour since 1877. Perhaps her marriage in 1884 to a royal equerry, the Hon. Henry Charles Legge, explains her unwillingness to forego the fashion niceties which so

196 Afternoon or dinner dress, 1890–1900. (MoL 66.79/12, Z2512)

Multiple pin-marks in the bodice of this dress suggest that it was worn for several formal occasions with a Garter ribbon firmly attached at shoulder and waist (as in illustrations 207, 209). The dress must date from the 1890s, perhaps after 1895, and has a second almost identical bodice, a sensible precaution repeated in a few other surviving dresses. The lace and chiffon parasol is inscribed 'Presented to the Queen by Her Majesty's oldest parliamentary subject C. P. Villiers 20 June 1897'. Charles Pelham Villiers (1802–98) was M.P. for Wolverhampton from 1835.

197 Detail of dress shown in illustration 196.

The plain black silk of this dress has been relieved by soft black chiffon pleating and the ingenious use of alternating bands of machine-embroidered organza and chemical lace (machine embroidery on a gauze ground which is removed by chemical means).

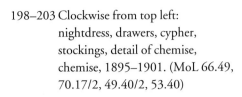

198–203 Clockwise from top left: nightdress, drawers, cypher, stockings, detail of chemise, chemise, 1895–1901. (MoL 66.49, 70.17/2, 49.40/2, 53.40)

All the Queen's underwear appears to have been distributed at her death to members of the Royal Household. It is now widely dispersed in public and private ownership and items pass through auction rooms. The Queen's cypher was always worked on each garment; the numbering system associated with the cyphers is not understood today but it is likely that the garments were ordered in quantities and then worn in rotation.

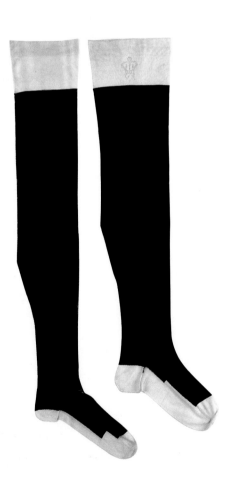

irritated her mistress. The outcome of the Queen's manoeuvrings is not known, but Amy left royal service on her marriage, possibly with some relief.

It was a special concession to the youthfulness of her maids of honour that Queen Victoria permitted them to wear white, grey, mauve and purple – the colours of half-mourning – except during an official court mourning, when all ladies in attendance on the Queen were required to don unrelieved black with jet jewellery. Harriet Phipps, another one-time maid of honour now risen to be a Woman of the Bedchamber, related to Marie Mallet in 1897 how:

> mauve has of late been forbidden to them [the maids of honour] in its fashionable pink tints ... I do mostly wear black as being so much on duty I can't afford to constantly change whites and greys ... I am sorry for you if H.M. is giving you a share of certain 'coloured' worries.

Marie, now married, had returned to the Queen as a Lady-in-waiting.[22]

In 1897 the anonymous author of a popular publication *The Private Life of Queen Victoria* reported just such struggles between the Queen and her female companions:

> The Queen always takes a great interest in the clothes of her Maids [of Honour], and never forgets a gown that has pleased her. As regards their dress, the ladies about the Court are obliged to dress well but very plainly, the Queen having a great objection to smart frocks, fly-away hats, and, above all, untidily-dressed hair. She often gives her Maids of Honour presents of jewellery, and frequently orders flowers for their personal adornment to be taken to their rooms.[23]

Marie Mallet's letters, as those of other ladies in the Queen's service, reveal many such acts of kindness and generosity. In November 1888, for example, 'The Queen has just given me a Balmoral Tartan Shawl and a very superior Cairn-gorm to fasten it with. I think I shall sport it at Ledbury & astonish the neighbours.'[24] The episode of Amy Lambart's hair seems not to have been a solitary instance, for something similar was referred to in the *Private Life*:

> the Ladies-in-Waiting and Maids of Honour have to avoid every kind of snare in the way of extravagant cut, loud colours, or remarkable style. For many years even the slightest fringe was 'taboo' at Court, and even now any such adornment has to be treated with great discretion or earn reprobation from the Sovereign.[25]

Parisian suppliers rarely featured during the Queen's widowhood. The great couturier Charles Frederick Worth claimed to have designed garments which the Queen wore, but if this was so she bought them unwittingly from another supplier. She had been a customer of both Swan & Edgar and Lewis & Allenby between 1838 and 1845 when Worth served his apprenticeship years in London. Later she patronised the important Parisian silk mercers Gagelin-Opigez when Worth was one of their employees. Might this have been the basis of Worth's claim? He set up his own business in Paris in 1858 and there are no direct payments to him. It seems unlikely that the Queen showed any great interest in the fashions which thereafter brought him fame and fortune.

The Queen continued to have finest of silks, but always in black. How well she patronised British textile manufacture is difficult to estimate. Irish poplins, Scottish shawls and tweeds, and Welsh flannels appear with some regularity in the quarterly

payments during her widowhood. Public patronage was more effectively bestowed by her daughters and daughters-in-law, who carried out a great many public duties on the Queen's behalf.

Many charitable or self-supporting organisations appeared in the second half of the nineteenth century devoted to assisting gentlewomen, either by training them to carry out plain needlework or embroidery or by helping to sell their handiwork. A number of these feature amongst the Queen's quarterly bills, acts of private charity probably drawn to her attention and encouraged by her daughters. Princess Louise was president of The Ladies' Work Society and directed her artistic gifts to designing embroideries for its members to work. It is not known whether she designed the striking mantle which the Queen acquired from this Society (illustration 208). Her older sister Helena, Princess Christian of Schleswig, was president of the School of Art Needlework, and probably through her influence this soon became the Royal School of Art Needlework. For nearly a century the school was an important training centre for embroidery. Both organisations were responsible for carrying out the ornate embroidery on twentieth-century coronation robes.[26] It is not known whether the Royal School embroidered any garments for Queen Victoria, but she did commission from them embroidery on heavy wool curtains for Windsor, and these are apparently still in existence. Other organisations which feature in the quarterly payments include the Royal Irish School of Art Needlework, The Working Ladies' Guild, the North Bucks Lace Association, and the Gentlewoman's Work Repository in Edinburgh.

As the Queen had continued to make public appearances only occasionally her subjects had to rely upon coins, postal stamps and popular prints for likenesses of their monarch. Photography provided alternative, less flattering images of the Queen, often with her children and grandchildren. Although brought up to conform with the Queen's conservative approach to fashion, they followed their own inclinations in adulthood. The Prince of Wales (later Edward VII), became a noted leader of fashion whilst his wife (the future Queen Alexandra), although considered far too thin by contemporary standards, dressed with an exemplary taste.

204 *The Four Generations* or *Windsor Castle*, 1899, by Sir William Quiller Orchardson (1832–1910). (Russell-Cotes Museum, Bournemouth)

A preparatory sketch for a large oil painting commissioned by the Royal Agricultural Society in 1897. With the elderly Queen are the Prince of Wales (later Edward VII), the Duke of York (later George V), and his son Prince Edward (later Edward VIII). Orchardson was lent one of the Queen's dresses and widow's caps, and these were in turn bequeathed to the London Museum by his widow in 1917. The fine silk dress is trimmed with machine-embroidered net with a design of bows and flower baskets. A small amount of crape on the dress shows that it had been worn by the Queen when mourning a distant relative.

205 Tulle cap, 1899. (MoL 33. 205/2)

The only one of the Queen's widow's caps known to survive. They were presumably disposed of when no longer fit for her to wear, or returned to her milliners for remaking. Regrettably at some point in its history the cap was washed: the dressing was removed from the tulle and the cap's original crisp appearance cannot be restored. However, it has provided valuable information for reconstructions.

206 Detail of dress shown in illustration 204. (MoL 33.205/1)

207 Queen Victoria, 1887, photograph by Hughes & Mullins. (Royal Archives)

Following the tiring succession of Jubilee celebrations, the Queen retired to Osborne and there posed for a series of official photographs in the dress she had worn for her procession to Westminster Abbey on 21 June 1887. Her dressmaker Mrs Gieve must be credited with this very smart dress of black with finely-patterned lace laid over white silk. Despite family pressure Queen Victoria had refused to wear her crown and robe of state for the thanksgiving service at the Abbey, and her crimson velvet and ermine mantle was instead draped over Edward I's coronation chair.

208 Mantle, 1887–97. (MoL 66.79/14)

The mantle is of a fine twilled black wool ornamented with narrow gold braid. Its authenticity is confirmed by a note recording that it was 'Worked by H.R.H. the Princess Louise's Work Society for Her Majesty the Queen Victoria, and constantly worn by the Queen'. This Society, properly titled 'The Ladies' Work Society' in Sloane Street was founded 'to provide employment for gentlewomen whose circumstances render it necessary that they should employ their leisure time more remuneratively'.

As Queen Victoria's figure thickened in old age the abiding image of the little old lady in black, 'the Widow of Windsor', became powerfully imprinted, so much so that even today, for many people, this is the only picture they carry of her. It is an image which in more recent years has been confirmed by the quantity of large-waisted black dresses and capacious underwear which survives in public and private possession, the garb of an elderly and rheumatic woman. It certainly exemplifies her last years but distracts from a broader consideration of a long and varied life.

In 1887 the Golden Jubilee celebrations, commemorating her fifty years on the throne, forced the Queen to make numerous public appearances over a period of two-and-a-half months. 'Now, Mother, you must have something really smart', the *Private Life* claims her son Prince Arthur, Duke of Connaught, implored her when the dress to be worn on the Jubilee day was under family discussion (illustration 207).[27] The Queen must have worn many 'smart' dresses during the celebrations. A number of samples of the dress silks survive, variations on a black and white theme suggesting that the family discussions had some impact on the Queen's wardrobe. For the banquet following a thanksgiving service at Westminster Abbey on 21 June 1887 she wore a dress embroidered with roses, thistles and shamrocks in silver, together with her massive diamonds.

The author of the *Private Life*, never identified but thought to have access to a well-informed source, added:

> About her own clothes the Queen never showed any particular taste, and nowadays she only fancies the plainest of gowns and mantles. Nevertheless, homely in cut as are Her Majesty's gowns, they are always made of the best material. It is an odd fad that induces the Queen to order every item of her toilette in duplicate. Most of her clothes now are made by the leading draper at Windsor, and the order for a cloak, hat or dress, always enumerates two as the number required.[28]

This rather suggests that the royal 'mole' was at Windsor, for although Caley's featured frequently in the quarterly clothing bills, London and other suppliers were always predominant. The anecdote regarding double ordering may also have a germ of truth. Indeed it was a practical and economical practice for an elderly woman not interested in fashion novelties. At least one of the surviving late black dresses has identical bodices, just as many men's suits in the past were supplied with two pairs of trousers. For a quarter of a century the Queen's resolutely sombre image probably influenced only a small number of widows, and the distinctive style of dress which she evolved for herself, it is true, merely echoed passing fashions.

The renewed public interest in the Queen after 1887 generated many magazine articles and publications about her. The writer Frances Lowe, pursuing the theme of royal playthings for an article in 1892, unexpectedly stumbled across Queen Victoria's collection of small wooden dolls, still carefully preserved from her teenage years (illustrations 83–6). This discovery led to a popular book about the dolls in 1894, a work which has proved a lasting favourite amongst doll lovers and collectors. Its charming coloured line illustrations captured the public imagination by revealing an intensely personal and human side to the apparently unsmiling Queen Empress. No wonder then that publishers sought further revelations of royal life and that *The Private Life of Queen Victoria* came into being in 1897. Given the lack of any other documentation about the Queen's clothing at the end of her life this publication is interesting for the claims which the seemingly well-informed writer advances. For example:

> Every woman cares for hoarding lace, fur, and feathers, but Her Majesty goes further than this, and almost without exception, her wardrobe woman can produce the gown, bonnet, or mantle she wore on any particular occasion. The Queen's collection of clothes would form the most accurate and interesting commentary on the modes of the past sixty years. Her Majesty also keeps with great care and pride a large number of articles worn by the late Prince Consort and by her mother the Duchess of Kent.[29]

The dresses that survive today partly bear out this claim although it is impossible to know exactly how much the Queen had preserved in her lifetime. It is true that her strong emotional ties to her family led her to preserve a great many keepsakes of happier times: the many tiny shoes of her children, for example, or small cubes of their christening cakes. These originate in the 1840s and are little different from the keepsakes of her subjects. The two dresses of the Duchess of Kent which still survive are from the 1850s and were presumably selected from her wardrobe after her death.[30] It is known that a number of Prince Albert's dashing uniforms survived well into the twentieth century, but only the incomplete Guards uniform is known to exist today (illustration 169).

If the Queen did preserve any of her dresses in the decades following the descent into black in 1861, then these did not survive her death. The large quantities of her late clothing – dresses, bonnets, capes, underwear or nightwear – seem all to have derived from dispersal during the 1890s or, much more usually, from a wholesale distribution of her wardrobe at her death. So distinctive is the size and cut of the Queen's dresses that they are readily authenticated. It is likely that her dressmaker Mrs Dudley used a master pattern, to save the fuss of fittings which the elderly Queen probably tolerated far less well in old age than she had when a young woman. The simple expedient of combining different materials and trimmings, with small variations on a basic design, almost certainly minimised this ritual. These dresses are generously cut for ease of wear, with little boning. Queen Victoria was now eighty, somewhat overweight and crippled by

209 Queen Victoria, 1893. (Royal Archives)

In 1897 this photograph was used as an official Jubilee portrait, but it had actually been taken on 6 July 1893 at the time of the marriage of Prince George, Duke of York, to Princess Mary of Teck, the last occasion on which the Queen wore her wedding lace. She had previously worn the lace at the marriage of Prince Leopold in 1882, and again a photograph taken at the time was issued in 1887 as an official portrait. The design shows up particularly well on its black satin ground. The Queen is also wearing her wedding veil with the small diamond crown made for her in 1870, and a portrait bracelet of the Prince Consort.

210   Queen Victoria and family, 1898–9,
unknown photographer.
(Royal Archives)

The birth of Prince George's eldest son
Edward in 1894 initiated a series of family
photographs over the next six years of the
four generations within the royal family. In
this photograph taken at Osborne, showing
the Queen with her son, grandson and great-
grandson, she wears a cape trimmed with
chiffon and braid, and a white straw hat
surmounted by white feathers.

rheumatism. All her clothes were therefore constructed so that they were easy to put on
and take off: chemises have button fastenings on the shoulders to allow them to be
dropped over the head and arms, and then fastened (illustrations 202–3); bodices all
have button fastenings (usually with a thread-worked covering) at the front, and a soft
ribbon inner waist-tie; skirts are ample and seem to have rested loosely on the hips rather
than to have nipped into the waist flesh. Many of the skirts have a button and loop just
above each knee so that the skirt could be raised to make walking a less hazardous
business. Almost without exception the bodices have a small watch pocket concealed in
the waist of the left front, whilst in the corresponding position on the right side is a
similar opening traversed by a cord bar. This seems to have served to secure such items as
reading glasses or keys, which were kept in a rectangular patch pocket on the skirt below.
Like any elderly lady Queen Victoria placed practical considerations before fashion.
Normally pockets were concealed in side seams below the hipline, but clearly these patch
pockets were much easier for the Queen to reach. One dress, however, said to date from
1901, still has pockets in the seams of the skirt. [31]

Many, but by no means all, of these 1890s dresses were trimmed with mourning
crape. The Queen's extensive family network, coupled with her own rigid adherence to
mourning etiquette, meant that crape was inevitable quite a lot of the time: she was not
now wearing it for Prince Albert, as some writers have assumed. As we have seen she
insisted that her immediate companions don black at these times too. One dress heavily
trimmed with crape is said to have been worn by the Queen in 1892 as mourning for the
Duke of Clarence, her grandson, who was already engaged to marry Princess Mary of
Teck. As with many of these late dresses, there is no documentary evidence for this claim,
and in fact this particular example is very similar to dresses worn by the Queen in an
1897 photograph, and in the 1899 portrait by Heinrich von Angelis.[32] Another crape-
trimmed dress, which claims to be the last dress worn by the Queen, seems in fact to date
from earlier in the 1890s, or perhaps even into the late 1880s. The process of dating these
dresses is difficult, and is not helped by the fact that none of the Queen's surviving
dresses or outerwear can be traced in photographs of her.

During the mounting of several of these dresses for photography it became evident
that the Queen's height had diminished strikingly by the last years of her life. It is not
surprising that this should happen, but it nowhere appears to have been noted. The
Queen had always been short of stature but, when faced with her commanding presence,
her household and ministers quickly forgot this. Her late 1890s' dresses suggest that she
was now about 4ft 7in.(1.40m), or 4ft 8in.(1.42m) at the most, as compared with a
height in 1837 believed to have been 4ft 11in. (1.50m).[33] This loss of height is very
natural in old age and is also revealed by the neat tucks made to shorten her drawers and
the sleeves of her nightdresses: such alterations were thought to have been made by later
owners, but from their proliferation it is clear that this was one of the tasks of her
wardrobe women in her last years (illustrations 198, 199). No mention seems to have
been made of this by the Queen's physician Sir James Reid, who otherwise kept a very
full and informative diary.[34]   The waists of the dresses now measure about 46in.
(117cm). She had never liked tight-fitting clothing and even her early dresses were
lightly boned and easy of fit. Whether she still wore stays in extreme old age is difficult to
judge, a problem that the quarterly clothing bills offer no help with. She had long given
up any form of exercise, had a hearty appetite, and ate rapidly. Sir James Reid appears
never to have been allowed to examine his mistress in all his twenty years of royal service

and was forced to make his diagnoses at a distance and on the Queen's information; she refused even the use of the stethoscope. When she died he discovered that she had a ventral hernia and prolapsed uterus, uncomfortable conditions which she had lived with without complaint.

The Diamond Jubilee in 1897, commemorating the sixtieth anniversary of the Queen's accession, again provided an opportunity for royal propaganda and for the Queen to make one of her rare public appearances in a carriage procession in London, and at a short thanksgiving service at St Paul's. She was no longer able to cope with more protracted celebrations.

The Queen's health declined slowly, but by 1900 she was noticeably frail. In April she had managed to make a visit to Dublin, and in July was present, on a very hot day, at a Garden Party at Buckingham Palace, her last grand public occasion. She determinedly continued her usual annual itinerary – Osborne in July, Balmoral in September, and Windsor in November. Her health was now a matter for grave concern. Nevertheless her death, at Osborne, on 22 January 1901 still came as a surprise to her family. She was eighty-one years old.

The Queen had prepared carefully for her own death. She drew up detailed instructions for her laying-out and funeral, and ensured that they were always in the possession of her principal dresser, Mrs Tuck, wherever the Queen was staying. Presumably Mrs Tuck had also been directed by the Queen to pack her laying-out necessities every time they moved on to a new residence. On the Queen's death her physician Sir James Reid was drawn into the laying-out proceedings: he was needed to help lift her body for the dresser and nurse, to put a satin dressing gown and Garter ribbon and star, etc, on the Queen, and he noted details of all that was done in the diary he kept. The Royal Family was not to know that the Queen was taking many personal mementos with her, in her coffin: 'rings, chains, bracelets, lockets, photographs, shawls, handkerchiefs, casts of hands – all souvenirs from her life – early, middle, and late', Sir James recorded. These were therefore placed at the bottom of the coffin, over a layer of charcoal, and included a dressing gown of the Prince Consort, and a cloak of his embroidered by Princess Alice. They were concealed by a quilted cushion, made to fit the coffin, on which the Queen's body rested.[35]

The Queen's wish to be buried alongside her beloved husband Prince Albert was duly carried out. Elaborate processions accompanied her coffin from Osborne, by carriage, yacht and train, the scarlet of the Guards' tunics and the white and crimson coffin drapes relieving the sombre black of the mourners. At Paddington there was 'no end of purple cloth stuck up on balconies … everyone in the crowds looking woebegone'.[36] For almost the whole population this was the first funeral of a monarch in their lifetime, and huge crowds had assembled along the route to watch this historic event.

The Queen's coffin lay in state in St George's Chapel at Windsor, surrounded by Guards and a huge array of floral tributes. Following a short service in the Chapel the last procession formed to accompany the coffin to the Royal Mausoleum at Frogmore where the Prince Consort lay. Only now was the marble effigy of the Queen, sculpted by Baron Marochetti in 1862, placed beside that of the Prince on the great granite sarcophagus which stands at the centre of the Mausoleum. Thus ended the longest reign in British history.

211 Queen Victoria, 1897, photogravure by Annan & Sons, after a photograph by Hughes and Mullins. (Royal Archives)

As in 1887 Queen Victoria made a special effort with her outfit for her Jubilee drive to St Paul's on 22 June 1897. In her Journal she noted 'I wore a dress of black silk, trimmed with panels of grey satin veiled with black net & steel embroideries, & some black lace . . . My bonnet was trimmed with creamy white flowers & white aigrette & some black lace'.

212 Dinner or evening dress, 1895–1900. (MoL 49.40/1)

The quantity of mourning crape on this trained dinner dress (right) indicates that the Queen was in mourning for a close member of her family, possibly Princess Beatrice's husband Prince Henry of Battenberg, who died in South Africa in 1896; or the Queen's second son Prince Alfred, Duke of Coburg, or his son 'young Alfred', both of whom died in 1899.

Select bibliography

Arch, N. & Marschner, J.
Splendour at Court, London 1987
Aspinall, A. (ed.)
(Geo IV) *The Letters of King George IV,*
1812–30, 3 vols, Cambridge 1938
(Pss C) *Letters of the Princess Charlotte,*
London 1949
(Geo III) *The Later Correspondence of George*
III, 5 vols, Cambridge 1962–70
(PoW) *The Correspondence of George, Prince*
of Wales 1770–1812, 8 vols, London
1963–71
Bury, S.
Jewellery 1789–1910, 2 vols, Woodbridge
1991
Cunnington, C. W.
Englishwomen's Clothing in the Nineteenth
Century, London 1937
Diamond, F. & Taylor, R.
Crown and Camera, Harmondsworth 1987
Duff, D.
Edward of Kent, London 1938
Esher, Viscount (ed.)
The Girlhood of Queen Victoria, 2 vols,
London 1912
Field, L.
The Jewels of Queen Elizabeth II,
London 1992
Ford, C. *et al.*
Happy and Glorious, 130 Years of Royal
Photographs, London 1977
Fraser, F.
The Unruly Queen: The Life of Queen
Caroline, London 1996
George, M. D.
Catalogue of Political and Personal Satires . . .
in the British Museum, vols VII, VIII, IX,
London 1942–9
Gernsheim, H. & A.
Queen Victoria, London 1959
Gibbs-Smith, C. H.
The Great Exhibition of 1851, London 1950
Ginsburg, M.
'The Young Queen and her Clothes', in
Early Victorian, Costume Society conference
proceedings, 1969, pp39–46

Green, T.
Memoirs of Her late Royal Highness Charlotte-
Augusta of Wales, London 1818
Grey, C.
The Early Years of HRH The Prince Consort,
London 1867
Halls, Z. & Holmes, M.
Coronation Costume and Accessories
1685–1953, London 1973
Hedley, O.
Queen Charlotte, London 1975
Hibbert, C.
George IV, 2 vols, London 1972
Hobhouse, H.
Prince Albert, His Life and Work, London
1983
Hone, W. (publisher)
Anon., *[A Description(?)] of the Royal*
Marriage Consisting of Original Memoirs of
Prince Leopold and Princess Charlotte,
pamphlet, London 1816
Huish, R.
Memoirs of Her Late Royal Highness Charlotte
Augusta, London 1819
Kinnersley, T. (publisher)
Anon., *The Life and Memoirs of Her Royal*
Highness Princess Charlotte of Saxe Coburg
Saalfeld, London 1818
Knight, Cornelia
The Autobiography of Miss Knight, ed.
R. Fulford, London 1960
Levey, S.
Lace: A History, Leeds 1983
Lloyd, C.
The Royal Collection, London 1992
London Museum
Catalogue no. 5: Costume, London 1933,
second edition 1935
Longford, E.
Victoria R.I., London 1966
Mallet, V.
Life with Queen Victoria, London 1968
Menkes, S.
The Royal Jewels, London 1986
Millar, D.
The Victorian Watercolours and Drawings
in the Collection of Her Majesty The Queen,
2 vols, London 1995
Millar, O.
(1969) *The Later Georgian Pictures in the*
Collection of Her Majesty The Queen,
2 vols, London 1969
(1992) *The Victorian Pictures in the*
Collection of Her Majesty The Queen, 2 vols,

Cambridge 1992
Morton, T.
Residences of the Victorian Era, London 1991
Morris, B.
Victorian Embroidery, London 1962
Oppe, A. P.
English Drawings: Stuart and Georgian
Periods in the Collection of His Majesty The
King at Windsor Castle, London 1950
Ormond, R.
National Portrait Gallery: Early Victorian
Portraits, 2 vols, London 1973
Patterson, S.
Royal Insignia: British and Foreign Orders of
Chivalry from The Royal Collection, London
1996
Plumb, J. H. & Wheldon, H.
Royal Heritage, London 1977
Private Life
Anon., *The Private Life of Queen Victoria By*
One of Her Majesty's Servants, London 1901
Roberts, J.
Royal Artists from Mary Queen of Scots to the
Present Day, London 1987
Rush, R.
A Residence at the Court of London, London
1987
Schramm, P. E.
A History of the English Coronation, Oxford
1937
Staniland, K. & Levey, S.
'Queen Victoria's Wedding Lace', in
Costume, the Journal of the Costume Society,
17, 1983, pp1–32
Stoney, B., Weltzien, H. C. & Bellaigue, S. De,
My Mistress the Queen, London 1994
Tanner, L. E.
The History of the Coronation, London 1952
Walker, R.
(1985) *National Portrait Gallery: Regency*
Portraits, 2 vols, London 1985
(1992) *Miniatures in the Collection of Her*
Majesty the Queen. The Eighteenth and
Early Nineteenth Centuries, Cambridge 1992
Woodham-Smith, C.
Queen Victoria, Her Life and Times, London
1972
Warner, M.
Queen Victoria's Sketchbook, London 1979
Watson, V.
The Queen at Home, London 1952

Endnotes

Endnotes

The following abbreviations are used:
PRO: Public Record Office
RA: Royal Archives

Full details of publications referred to in brief form are given in the bibliography (p185).

INTRODUCTION
Royal Clothing: its survival and display (pp10–25)

1 A. Harvey & R. Mortimer (eds), *The Funeral Effigies of Westminster Abbey,* Woodbridge 1994, pp21–8.

2 P. Chapman, *Madame Tussaud in England, Career Woman Extraordinary,* London 1992, pp36, 38, 63; Staniland & Levey, pp6, 23.

3 London Museum catalogue; Halls & Holmes.

4 J. Arnold, *Queen Elizabeth's Wardrobe Unlock'd,* Leeds 1988, pp174–5, 250–334.

5 *Catalogue of effects of her late Majesty Queen Caroline … sold by Mr Robbins … 20 February 1822,* RA Geo Box 10, no. 2. *A Catalogue of a Portion of the Expensive Wardrobe … late His Majesty George the Fourth's … Which will be sold by Auction by Mr Phillips … 16 December 1830,* Museum of London 38.294/1.

6 Louisa Louis (sometimes spelled 'Lewis') born Erback, Germany, 1771; died Buckingham Palace, 14 April 1838; buried St Martin-in-the-Fields, London (RA Z201/A3, Memoranda); Will of Louisa Louis, 1838, Museum of London 74.100/19. For Sir Robert Gardiner (1781–1864), see *Dictionary of National Biography,* London 1908. For Lady Gardiner (1784–1876), see W. A. Lindsay, *The Royal Household,* London 1898, pp106–7. Lady Gardiner was Woman of the Bedchamber to Queen Victoria from 1 July 1837 to 13 May 1859. A further dress which passed through the Gardiners' hands is that shown in illustrations 36 & 37 (Museum of London A15589). It is recorded as having passed from Sir Robert

to the family of Dr John Fisher, Bishop of Salisbury, who from 1805 supervised Princess Charlotte's education; it remained in their possession until 1897.

7 Museum of London 74.100/20–22.

8 Extract from Thomas Sully's manuscript journal, 22 March 1838 (provided by Hirschl & Adler Galleries, New York).

PROLOGUE
The Court of George III (pp26–33)

1 Hedley, p67; J. Brooke, *King George III,* London 1972, p278.

2 S. Llewellyn, 'George III and the Windsor Uniform', in *The Court Historian,* II, 1996.

3 I. Brooke, *Dress and Undress,* London 1958, p136. 'Mantua maker' was the term generally used in the seventeenth and eighteenth centuries to refer to a dressmaker.

4 Arch & Marschner, p40; Rush, p56.

5 Aspinall (PoW), II, p202 n1. The Earl of Albemarle, a childhood companion, recalled that one of Princess Charlotte's great enjoyments was to go out shopping with her governess Lady de Clifford (George Thomas, Earl of Albemarle, *Fifty Years of My Life,* London 1876, II, p293).

6 C. Barrett, ed., *The Diary and Letters of Madame d'Arblay (1788–1840),* London 1904–5, II, pp396–400.

7 Hibbert, I, p127.

8 Hibbert, I, p43.

9 Aspinall (PoW), I, p75.

10 Aspinall (PoW), II, pp490–1. Princess Sophia Matilda (1773–1844) was the daughter of George III's brother Henry, Duke of Gloucester.

11 Aspinall (PoW), II, p498.

PRINCESS CHARLOTTE
Girlhood, 1796–1812 (pp34–9)

1 Aspinall (PoW), III, pp126–7.

2 Aspinall (PoW), III, p151.

3 A 'rocker' was a nurse or attendant who rocked a child in the cradle. The post

originated in the Middle Ages, but by the late eighteenth century the duties of such nursery staff were probably more diverse.

4 Aspinall (PoW), III, pp146–8.

5 For a detailed study of this unhappy marriage see Fraser.

6 Museum of London 27.40/6; they are 4⅜in. (11.5cm) long.

7 Aspinall (Geo IV), II, pp142, 357; Fraser, p96.

8 E. Creston, *The Regent and His Daughter,* London 1932, p109; RA Geo Add MSS 37/6; A. J. C. Hare, *The Life and Letters of Frances, Baroness Bunsen,* London 1879, I, p71. 'Mr Canning' is presumably the politician George Canning (1770–1827).

9 RA 50134–50170.

10 RA 49255. Lady Elgin ('Eggy') was Martha Bruce, Dowager Countess of Bruce, a close friend of Queen Charlotte and a sensible, warm-hearted woman.

11 Aspinall (Pss C), pp ix, xii–xiii.

12 This set of letters is published in full in Aspinall (Pss C).

13 Aspinall (Pss C), p2.

14 Aspinall (Pss C), pp26–7. Three more novels were published before Jane Austen (*b.*1775) died in July 1817, just four months before Princess Charlotte herself – *Pride and Prejudice,* 1813; *Mansfield Park,* 1814; and *Emma* (dedicated to the Prince Regent, who had also fallen under Miss Austen's spell), 1816.

PRINCESS CHARLOTTE
Engagement, 1812–16 (pp40–9)

1 Knight, p118.

2 Aspinall (Pss C), p51.

3 Sarah Sophia, Countess of Jersey (1785–1867).

4 J. Raymond, *The Reminiscences and Recollections of Captain Gronow 1810–1860,* London 1964, p47. Writing to her brother the Tsar, the Grand Duchess of Oldenberg described the Princess as 'A little smaller than myself, well-covered, especially

– and too much – about the hips; white, fresh and appetising as possible with fine arms, pretty feet, large light blue lively eyes' (R. Walker, *Regency Portraits, National Portrait Gallery,* London 1985, I, p107).

5 Lady Rose Weigall, *A Brief Memoir of Princess Charlotte of Wales,* London 1894, p75. For the display figures for *In Royal Fashion* the Princess's distinctive profile was relatively easy to achieve, but it was impossible to create a full face which accurately reproduced her plump features (see illustration 43) without a distracting element of caricature.

6 The hair of the display figures was matched with a switch of the Princess's hair preserved in the Royal Collection at Frogmore.

7 Knight, p133.

8 For Mrs Louis's death in 1838 see p21.

9 Museum of London 27.40/4. The present dating is based on expert opinions from Anne Buck and Santina Levey.

10 Aspinall (Pss C), p197. A few months earlier the Regent himself had explained to his daughter 'Our station compels us no doubt to enter into matrimonial connexions guided by a superior sense of the duty which we owe to the country', Aspinall (Geo IV), II, p33.

11 Knight, p151.

12 British Library, Add MS 38261, pp28–9, 98.

13 The Princess was building up a set of prints illustrative of British history: the portrait of the Prince of Orange was displayed at Warwick House as part of this set (Knight, p151). Sir Thomas Lawrence was told by Colnaghi that 'she had made a large collection – all Sir Joshua's, Vandykes's, &c.' (G. S. Layard, ed., *Sir Thomas Lawrence's Letter-Bag,* London 1906, p109).

14 Knight, p168. Aspinall (Pss C), p148. 'Garth' was General Thomas Garth, a member of Princess Charlotte's household. Hone, p19, confirms the trousseau preparations in 1814.

15 Huish, p83.

16 Huish, pp86–7.

17 Knight, p166.

18 Another source adds that her 'shoes were beautifully studded with sparkling crescents, or half moons' (Kinnersley, p154). 'Patent lace' refers to the machine-knit net which had been produced in increasing quantities since 1790, and now mostly replaced the expensive hand-made net. As a British product it naturally found approval in royal and fashionable circles. This dress would have been similar to the Princess's wedding dress (illustration 48).

19 Aspinall (Pss C), pp xvii–xviii, 117.

20 Cornelia Knight was a victim of the Regent's wrath over the affair and he dismissed her from the Princess's service.

21 Aspinall (Pss C), pp152–3, 156.

22 Aspinall (Pss C), pp149, 168.

23 Aspinall (Pss C), p181.

24 Museum of London 66.79/1. The dress is made of a net created on an early net-machine of a type invented in the late eighteenth century.

25 Aspinall (Pss C), p191.

26 Aspinall (Pss C), p192.

27 Huish, pp176–7.

PRINCESS CHARLOTTE
Marriage, 1816 (pp50–65)

1 Aspinall (Pss C), p165.

2 Aspinall (Pss C), p197.

3 Knight, p206.

4 Aspinall (Pss C), pp193, 208.

5 Aspinall (Pss C), p201.

6 Hibbert, II, p94.

7 Aspinall (Pss C), pp219, 221. Princess Charlotte was incorrect in terming herself 'heiress presumptive'. Her father was the heir apparent.

8 Aspinall (Pss C), p224.

9 Kinnersley, pp255–6.

10 Hibbert, II, p945. Princess Charlotte had difficulties controlling her father's urge to set her up with a large and expensive

household: 'I have insisted vehemently upon no extravagance, waste, or debts', Aspinall (Pss C), p235.

11 Aspinall (Pss C), p231. Hone, pp38–41. Mrs Bean, 'milliner and dressmaker', was listed at 32 Albemarle Street (off Piccadilly) between 1820 and 1828.

12 Bury, I, pp48, 301.

13 Aspinall (Pss C), p220. Princess Elizabeth was the seventh child of George III. 'Bridge' was a partner in Rundle, Bridge & Co., the royal jewellers of Ludgate Hill

14 Aspinall (Pss C), p237. For details of the Princess of Wales's jewels see Bury, I, pp47–8.

15 Aspinall (Pss C), p237.

16 Aspinall (Pss C), p233.

17 Aspinall (Pss C), p227. Botany was one of Queen Charlotte's major hobbies and this probably sparked off her granddaughter's interest. In their brief time together at Claremont Princess Charlotte and Prince Leopold embarked on major agricultural and planting projects on the estate.

18 E. C. Corti, *Leopold I of Belgium,* London 1923, p36.

19 Aspinall (Pss C), p232. Robert Clive (1725–74), Governor of Bengal, had the house built for him between 1770 and 1772; it and the gardens were designed by Lancelot 'Capability' Brown and Henry Holland the younger. The purchase price of £66,000 in 1816 included the house, furniture, and 350 acres (Morton, pp36–41).

20 Huish, p260.

21 Camelford House was built by Thomas Pitt, 1st Baron Camelford (1737–93), a connoisseur of art and friend of Horace Walpole. It apparently had a splendid interior with particularly fine plasterwork.

22 RA 36773. PRO LC 5/8, f.109. Hone, p43, confirms that court hoops were not worn.

23 A pamphlet published in 1816 by W. Hone of 55 Fleet Street, *[A Description(?)] of the Royal Marriage,* provides further details of Princess Charlotte's trousseau and its

makers Mrs Triaud and Mrs Bean (Appendix 2a). This seems to have been the source used by at least one biographer, and further research may uncover similar pamphlets.

24 The skirt of the cloth of silver underskirt now associated with the Princess's wedding dress shows evidence of alteration. It was probably a full pleated skirt of the type worn over a court hoop, subsequently cut down for reuse under an altered court dress. The fact that it is much fuller than the present overskirt suggests that it possibly came from another dress associated with the Princess, ie not from either of the two dresses making up the present 'wedding dress'.

25 Museum of London 74.100/19; see p21, n6 above.

26 *La Belle Assemblée*, June 1816, pp224–5.

27 Huish, pp262–3.

28 *The Annual Register . . . for the Year 1816*, London 1817, p60. Hone, p43, records that the sword and belt had been presented to the Prince by 'her Majesty', presumably Queen Charlotte. The anonymous compiler of this pamphlet was also able to provide detailed descriptions of the dress of many of those attending the ceremony, and furthermore states that the Princess's wedding ring was 'stronger and larger than those usually worn' (p26).

29 Huish, p238.

30 RA 36773; PRO LC 5/8 f.109.

31 Aspinall (PoW), p498. Unfortunately the series of Queen Charlotte's accounts so valuable for information about her own wardrobe ceases to include these details after 1806–7. The last few accounts include London retailers who also supplied goods to Princess Charlotte and, later, to Princess Victoria – eg King & Co., mercers; D. & P. Cooper, mercers; Crook & Co., haberdashers; Thomas Gray, jeweller (British Library, Add MS 17881–3).

32 Huish, p292; Hone, p19.

33 *La Belle Assemblée,* June 1816, p225.

34 Aspinall (Pss C), p242. Princess Lieven (1785–1857) was the wife of the Russian

ambassador to London and a close friend of the Regent. Her considerable correspondence is a valuable source of information on contemporary society. A harsh critic, she was nevertheless one who admired Victoria's earliest appearances after her accession.

35 Aspinall (Pss C), pp242–3.

PRINCESS CHARLOTTE
Married Life and Death, 1816–17 (pp66–77)

1 Huish, pp304–5.

2 Museum of London 74.100/2.

3 Huish, p305. Hone, p41.

4 Huish, pp311, 338.

5 Aspinall (Pss C), p244.

6 Green, p369; Huish, p414.

7 Huish, p427.

8 Huish, pp450–1, 494.

9 Huish, pp491–2, 494.

10 Huish, p500. Lady Susan, a friend of long standing who had been one of Princess Charlotte's bridesmaids, was typical of the recipients of favours of this kind. The dress was very possibly that listed as no. 6 in Mrs Triaud's section of the Princess's trousseau (see Appendix 2a).

11 Huish, pp450–1. The Prince Regent similarly ordered 'all his state and household officers to wear costly dresses of home fabrication' (ibid.). Kinnersley, pp367–8; the Prince Regent also ordered Spitalfields silk for decorating rooms at Carlton House. Huish, p495, suggests that Princess Charlotte 'raised up a host of enemies against herself' by her refusal to use any foreign articles in her household or dress. This, he says, was construed by the Princess's enemies as 'affectation' and 'a love of popularity'.

12 Huish, p500.

13 Museum of London 74.100/1.

14 On 6 September 1816: Baron E. von Stockmar, *Memoirs of Baron Stockmar,* London 1872, p42.

15 Aspinall (Geo IV), p197. George, IX, cat. no. 12796. J. Richardson, 'The Princess Charlotte', in *History Today*, XXII. 2, 1972, p93.

16 Brighton Museum & Art Gallery, accession nos R.4813, R.4813/1. Together with other items with royal associations these shirts were donated to the museum by a descendant of the St James's apothecary John Nussey, apparently a supplier to George IV and Queen Victoria. He is not listed by Huish (p292) as one of the Princess's apothecaries in 1816 and the connection remains a mystery.

17 Museum of London 74.100/18. This list of robes, bonnets and caps, chemises, stockings and other underwear is neither inscribed nor dated and therefore the association with Princess Charlotte cannot be proven. It does list camisoles, bonnets and dressing jackets 'Pour La Princesse', but the billhead displays the arms of several French royal customers.

18 Hibbert, II, pp98–100. All documents relating to the Princess's pregnancy, labour and death were published in F. Crainz, *An Obstetric Tragedy,* Oxford 1977. The suggestion that the Princess suffered from porphyria (and that both her parents did too) was made in I. Macalpine and R. Hunter, *George III and the Mad-Business,* London 1969, p240ff.

19 Aspinall (Geo IV), II, p212.

20 Rush, p55–6. Huish, pp556–7.

QUEEN VICTORIA
Girlhood, 1819–37 (pp82–93)

1 Woodham-Smith, p34.

2 For example, £34 5s in 1823–4 (RA Add 0 57/B, f.71, f.123).

3 RA Add O 57/A, f.35.

4 H. Cathcart, *A Royal Bedside Book,* London 1969, p24. RA Add 0 57/B, f.73, f.144. In 1813 Jane Austen had also shopped at Crook & Besford, for a silk handkerchief (P. Byrde, *A Frivolous Distinction, Fashion and Needlework in the Works of Jane Austen,* Bath n.d., p18).

5 Cataloguing notes of J. Swann on accession no. D331 (royal loan).

6 RA Add 0 57/B, f.71, f.143; RA Add 0 57/C, f.4–5, f.74–6. Gundry & Co. were succeeded by Joseph Box & Co. (later taken over by Lobb & Co.) in 1898.

7 RA Add 0 57/B, f.71 , f.143; RA Add 0 57/C, f.4–5. PRO LC 13/2, f.4v, f.5r.

8 RA Add 0 57/B, f.145. Mrs Bettans is listed in London trade directories at 84 Jermyn Street from 1830 to 1845.

9 Museum of London 80.424/1.

10 A. Buck, 'The Costume of Jane Austen and her Characters', in *The So-called Age of Elegance,* Costume Society 1970, p41; RA Add 0 57/C, f.74–6, f.150, f.213–14.

11 Museum of London 69.132; S. Levey cataloguing notes.

12 Esher, I, pp62, 116.

13 Published by George Newnes Ltd, London 1894. RA Z118, *List of My Dolls.*

14 See Warner, pp46–55.

15 Museum of London 33.328; London Museum catalogue, p190, where dated at 1824; S. Levey cataloguing notes.

16 RA Add 0 57/C, f.74–6.

17 Another occasion when this dress could have been worn was the coronation ceremony of William IV on 3 September 1831. Princess Victoria should have taken part in the procession into Westminster Abbey, but when the King insisted that the Princess yield precedence to his brothers her mother refused to allow her to attend.

18 Museum of London 33.329; London Museum catalogue, p190, where dated at 1830.

QUEEN VICTORIA
Accession, 1837 (pp94–107)

1 D330 (royal loan).

2 Woodham-Smith, p139.

3 London Museum catalogue, p150; Longford, p76.

4 RA Privy Purse accounts. Woodham-Smith, p153. The Queen recorded in her Journal in January 1838 a conversation she had with Lord Melbourne concerning these

debts, 'about my dress etc., etc. which had never been paid'.

5 Esher, I, pp192–5.

6 RA Add A/11/18. The full history of Sir John Conroy's service in the Duchess of Kent's household and her daughter's profound hatred of this ambitious man is given in K. Hudson, *A Royal Conflict, Sir John Conroy and the Young Victoria,* London 1994.

7 Esher, I, p204.

8 Grey, p348.

9 See Stoney, Weltzien, & de Bellaigue.

10 PRO LC 13/2–4. The information contained in these volumes was first brought to public attention by Ginsburg. Other information drawn from the Lord Chamberlain's Office papers was used by Watson.

11 PRO LC 13/2, f.22v.

12 PRO LC 13/2, f.17v.

13 Hunter's warrant of appointment was issued on 11 August 1837 (PRO LC 13/2 f.4v).

14 Woodham-Smith, p148; A. J. C. Hare, *The Life and Letters of Frances Baroness Bunsen,* London 1879, I, p217.

15 *The World of Fashion,* July 1837, p171.

16 *The World of Fashion,* July 1837, p172.

17 This seems to be accurate, for the mantle (including its replacement fur cape) now weighs 21 lb (9.4kg); the present kirtle (made in 1851) added a further 6 lb 9⅜oz (3kg), but most of this weight would have been carried on the pelvic girdle.

18 *The World of Fashion,* October 1837, p227; Patterson, pp144–5.

19 PRO LC 13/2, f.11r, f. 40v, ff.45–54.

20 PRO LC 13/1, ff.146–7; PRO LC 13/2, f.11 £97 17s 6d. The present mantle is that made in 1837 apart from the later rabbit-fur cape.

21 D327 (royal loan); a warrant of appointment was issued to Peter Thompson on 11 August 1837 (PRO LC 13/2, f.4v).

22 Esher, I, pp226–7. The Queen did not wear uniform for her 1838 review, but did in

1839. Thereafter she was pregnant and does not appear to have worn uniform again until her military uniform was devised by Prince Albert in the 1850s.

23 Museum of London 33.77/1; London Museum catalogue, p127; Halls & Holmes, cat. no. 18.

24 *The World of Fashion,* February 1838, p28.

25 Museum of London 33.77/2; woven mark DANIN, a maker not currently known.

26 D. Liversidge, *Prince Charles: Monarch in the Making,* London 1975, p130.

27 Esher, I, p294; II, p127.

28 Esher, II, pp152, 189.

QUEEN VICTORIA
Coronation, 1838 (pp108–17)

1 PRO LC 13/2, f.44v: 'We must know what the several Robes, etc., you require are to cost, because the charges have to be compared with those which were made at the last coronation, and the whole expence to be incurred must be ascertained in order that Parliament may vote what may be necessary'.

2 PRO LC 13/2, f.45v.

3 Esher, I, pp356–64.

4 Tanner, pp25–38.

5 Schramm, p110; to avoid confusion the terminology used in the present text is that used in the Office of Robes ledgers.

6 E. C. Ratcliffe, *The English Coronation Service,* London 1936, p149.

7 Esher, I, p356.

8 Esher, I, p361.

9 PRO LC 13/2, f.60. By 'cloak' the Duchess really meant a processional mantle.

QUEEN VICTORIA
Marriage, 1840 (pp118–23)

1 A detailed account of the design and making of Queen Victoria's wedding lace, together with its use on her dresses throughout her lifetime, is given in Staniland & Levey. Nothing further has been discovered in the intervening years.

2 Esher, I, pp367–8.

3 Staniland & Levey, pp28–30.

4 *The World of Fashion,* March 1840, p66, mentions that 'among the morning dresses of the Queen's trousseau is one of very beautiful design, entirely made of Honiton lace, with handsome flounces, and worn over white silk'.

5 Staniland & Levey, p23. PRO LC 13/2, f.7r, given in August 1837. No additional payments can be traced in the Queen's Privy Purse Accounts (Royal Archives).

6 A small square of white satin purporting to come from the Queen's wedding dress was pinned, at a later date, into the book of dress cuttings associated with Mrs Bettans (Museum of London 80.424/1). The book contains the business card of 'L. Clark' of Gravesend who may have compiled the collection when an apprentice with Mrs Bettans.

7 PRO LC 13/2, f.91r.

8 Esher, II, p318.

9 Esher, II, p320.

10 Esher, II, p321.

11 Woodham-Smith, pp205, 207.

QUEEN VICTORIA
Married Life and Family, 1840–50
(pp124–39)

1 Museum of London 54.121/10.

2 Stoney, Weltzien & de Bellaigue, pp19–20; R. Fulford, ed., *Dearest Mama, Letters between Queen Victoria and the Crown Princess of Prussia, 1861–4,* London 1968, p192.

3 PRO LC 13/2, f.7r, August 1837.

4 Museum of London 66.79/21. PRO LC 13/2, f.100–64.

5 Mary Bettans, 84 Jermyn Street, recorded in trade directories 1830–45.

6 The senior partner (and perhaps founder of the firm) was Mme Maradan Carson in 1837. François Vouillon, a junior partner, is listed as a mercer in contemporary trade directories. The warrant in 1837 was awarded to Mlle Marie Laure Vouillon, late partner and successor to Mme Maradan Carson (PRO LC 13/2, f.2v).

7 Journal entry 14 February 1838, Esher, I, pp283–4.

8 Griffiths & Crick were awarded a warrant in November 1837 (PRO LC 13/2, f.16r). The advertisement for Mrs Geary's products was discarded when this journal was bound; however, her advertisements are to be found in many contemporary commercial publications, always referring to her royal connection. Warrant issued 6 November 1837 (PRO LC 13/2, f.13v).

9 For Planché's varied career see *Dictionary of National Biography,* London 1909, XV, pp1281–3. In 1834 he had published one of the earliest studies of the subject, *The History of British Costumes,* and in 1838 *Regal Records, or a Chronicle of the Coronation of the Queens Regnant of England.*

10 See Warner, p99, for Queen Victoria's Journal sketch of the costumes. The page's tunic has been on loan to the museum as a childhood garment of Edward VII (D151).

11 RA Y 90/48.

12 D. Millar, 'Quadrilles & All Kinds of Surprises: Queen Victoria's Costume Balls I' in *Country Life,* 10 October 1985, pp1024–6.

13 The painting was completed in 1846; see O. Millar (1992), pp141–2.

14 Woodcuts of the *bal* were included in the very first issue of *The Illustrated London News,* and Planché published a *Souvenir of the Bal Costumé,* London 1843, showing over fifty of the costumes worn by the most distinguished guests.

15 PRO LC 13/2, ff.126–41: payments to Mrs Bettans dwindle from 1842 and the last payment, for only £2 2s (when previously these had usually been well over £100, and sometimes over £200) was made in March 1844. The last date inscribed in the dress-cuttings book (Museum of London 80.424/1) is June 1843.

16 Mrs S. Erskine (ed.), *Twenty Years at Court,* the Correspondence of The Hon. Eleanor Stanley, London 1916, p39.

17 Ibid., p171.

18 V. Surtees, *Charlotte Canning,* London 1975, p135.

19 Advertisement in *Boyles' Court Guide,* London 1835, p781. Curling & Co., Woodstock Street, New Bond Street, 1828–1902.

20 Watson, p18.

21 See C. Walkley and V. Foster, *Crinolines and Crimping Irons,* London 1978, pp50–69.

22 Stoney, Weltzien & de Bellaigue, pp1–26.

QUEEN VICTORIA
Public Life, 1851–61
(pp140–53)

1 Museum of London 33.199; S. Levey and N. Rothstein cataloguing notes. The shoes and gloves originally worn with this dress have not survived.

2 RA Queen Victoria's Journal 13 June 1851; D. Millar, 'The Prettiest Effect Possible: Queen Victoria's Costume Balls II', *Country Life,* 17 October 1985, pp1092–3; Ginsburg, p45.

3 PRO LC 13/3, f.31.

4 Woodham-Smith, p349.

5 Longford, p316–17.

6 Victoria R, *Leaves from a Journal,* London 1961, p110.

7 Stoney, Weltzien & de Bellaigue, p19.

8 Museum of London 33.137; N. Rothstein cataloguing notes. The dye used for this dress has been identified as lichen purple, an extremely fugitive dye which can fade rapidly (research report of G. W. Taylor, 13.12.1996).

9 Stoney, Weltzien & de Bellaigue, p17. In March 1861 a bill amounting to £5 5s was settled with J. Bernall (or Burrell?), crinoline maker, PRO LC 13/3, f.105.

10 Ibid., p21.

QUEEN VICTORIA
Widowhood, 1861–1901 (pp154–73)

1 Gernsheim, p65.

2 Museum of London 54.137/1.

3 The Queen and her family adopted deep mourning for the Duchess of Kent. A number of portraits and photographs of the Queen at this time show her in dress that is still very fashionable but trimmed with crape or other black ornaments.

4 PRO LC 13/3, f.116.

5 Watson, pp145, 156.

6 Longford, p386.

7 R. Fulford, ed., *Dearest Child, Letters between Queen Victoria and the Princess Royal, 1858–61,* London 1964, pp199-200.

8 Gernsheim, p65.

9 D. C. Coleman, *Courtaulds, An Economic and Social History,* Oxford 1969, I; A. Adburgham, *Shops and Shopping,* London 1981, pp58–69, 180–1.

10 S. Robinson, *A History of Dyed Textiles,* London 1969, p33.

11 Watson, pp159–60.

12 G. Battiscombe, *Queen Alexandra,* London 1980, p43.

13 P. Cunnington and C. Lucas, *Costumes for Births, Marriages and Deaths,* London 1972, p248.

14 Grey, p348.

15 Watson, pp175–7.

16 PRO LC 13/3, 31.3.66.

17 Warrant of appointment of Mary Frances Perryman and Caroline Elizabeth Parsons 'as milliners to the Queen', 4 October 1882; supporting her application Emilie Dittweiler, the Queen's dresser, commented that 'they have both been with her [Miss Unitt] and have worked for the Queen for many years', PRO LC 13/4, ff. 271, 269.

18 Staniland & Levey, p12

19 Ibid, pp13-15. Photographs taken in 1882 and 1893 showing the Queen in her lace-trimmed dresses were issued in 1887 and 1897 at the time of her jubilees and are often incorrectly dated to these years.

20 Mallet, pp18, 32.

21 RA Vic Add A/7/352. The Jersey costume had a revealing tight-fitting bodice to the hips, and was fashionable between 1879 and 1891. It was named after the celebrated actress and beauty Lily Langtry (1853–1929), known as the 'Jersey Lily'.

22 Mallet, p60.

23 *Private Life,* p175.

24 Mallet, p25.

25 *Private Life,* pp67–8.

26 Halls & Holmes, pp53, 58, 61.

27 *Private Life,* p68.

28 Ibid.

29 Frances Lowe, *Queen Victoria's Dolls,* London 1894; *Private Life*, p69.

30 Museum of London 33.129, 33.131 (royal loans), London Museum catalogue, pp151–2.

31 Museum of London 33.277; it may, however, date to earlier in the 1890s.

32 Museum of London C2291, London Museum catalogue, p159; this dress is very similar to a dress with two bodices at the Gallery of English Costume, Manchester, also ascribed to 1892 (acc. no. 1963.294). Both dresses, however, are very like that in Heinrich von Angeli's 1899 portrait (O. Millar, 1992, cat. 8).

33 It seems impossible to be absolutely certain of the Queen's height. For the photographs in this publication the figures have been set at 4ft 11in. (1.50m), a height that seems appropriate to the dresses. *The World of Fashion's* claim, in 1837, that she was 5ft 2in. (1.57m) – perhaps obtained from the robemaker John Hunter – could possibly be flattering journalistic licence. The painter Thomas Sully recorded the Queen's height as 5ft 1in. (1.55m) in 1838 in his journal. Regrettably the measurements which Sir George Hayter, who knew the Queen well, recorded beside preparatory sketches for his large painting of the marriage ceremony (in the British Museum) do not resolve the problem (O. Millar, 1992, p108). No other references to the Queen's height have been located.

34 M. Reid, *Ask Sir James,* London 1987, pp191–221.

35 Ibid., pp215–16. Sir James's descendants own a photograph which reveals that the Queen went to her grave wearing one of her inimitable widow's caps (ibid., opp. p192).

36 It was the Queen's wish that royal purple rather than black be used; a small square of the purple cloth drapery from Buckingham Palace has been inserted into the dress cuttings book (Museum of London 80.424) by a later owner.

Appendix 1

Family tree showing the immediate families of Princess Charlotte and Queen Victoria, edited to show the direct line of descent to Her Majesty the Queen.

GEORGE III
(1738–1820)

m

Sophia Charlotte of
Mecklenburg-Strelitz
(1744–1818)

GEORGE IV
(1762–1830)

m

Caroline of
Brunswick
(1768–1821)

Charlotte
(1796–1817)

m

Leopold of Saxe-Coburg-
Saalfeld, brother of
Victoria, Duchess of
Kent, later Leopold I,
King of the Belgians
(1790–1865)

m

(2) Louise, d. of King
Louis Philippe of France
(1812–50)

issue

Frederick, Duke of York
(1763–1827)

m

Frederica, Princess Royal
of Prussia (1767–1820)

WILLIAM IV,
Duke of Clarence
(1765–1837)

m

Adelaide of Saxe-
Meiningen (1792–1849)

issue, died young

Edward, Duke of Kent
(1767–1820)

m

Mary Louisa Victoria
of Saxe-Coburg-
Saalfeld (1786–1861)

m

(1) Prince Emich
Charles of Leiningen
(1763–1814)

VICTORIA
(1819–1901)

m

Prince Albert of
Saxe-Coburg-Gotha
(1819–61)

Augusta
(1768–1840)

Emich Charles Ernest,
Duke of Leiningen
(1804–56)

m

Marie, Countess of
Klekelsburg (1806–80)

issue

Elizabeth
(1770–1840)

m

Landgrave of
Hesse–Homburg
(1769–1829)

Feodore
(1807–72)

m

Ernest, Prince of
Hohenlohe-Langenburg
(1794–1860)

issue

Victoria, Princess Royal
(1840–1901)

m

Frederick Crown Prince
of Prussia, later Frederick
III, German Emperor
(1831–88)

issue

EDWARD VII
(1841–1910)

m

Alexandra of
Denmark
(1844–1925)

Alice (1843–78)

m

Louis IV, Grand Duke
of Hesse-Darmstadt
(1837–92)

issue

Alfred, Duke of
Edinburgh, Duke of
Saxe-Coburg
(1844–1900)

m

Marie of Russia, d. of
Alexander II (1853–1920)

issue

Helena
(1846–1923)

m

Christian, Prince of
Schleswig-Holstein
(1845–1917)

issue

Albert Victor,
Duke of Clarence
(1864–92)

GEORGE V
(1865–1936)

m

Mary of Teck
(1867–1953)

Louise
(1867–1931)

Victoria (1868–1935)

EDWARD VIII
(1894–1972)
Duke of Windsor
Abdicated 1936

GEORGE VI
(1895–1952)

m

Lady Elizabeth
Bowes-Lyon
(*b.* 1900)

---

3 other sons and
1 other daughter

ELIZABETH II
(*b.* 1926)

m

Philip,
Duke of Edinburgh
(*b.* 1921)

Ernest,
Duke of Cumberland,
King of Hanover
(1771–1851)
m
Frederica of
Mecklenburg-Strelitz
(1778–1841)
issue

Augustus, Duke of Sussex
(1773–1843)
m
morganatic wife
issue

Adolphus, Duke of
Cambridge (1774–1850)
m
  Augusta of Hesse-
  Cassel (1797–1889)

Mary
(1776–1857)
m
Duke of Gloucester
(1776–1834)

Sophia (1777–1848)

2 other sons and
2 other daughters

George,
Duke of Cambridge
(1819–1904)

Augusta (1822–1916)
m
Frederick,
Duke of Mecklenburg-
Strelitz (1819–1904)

Mary Adelaide
(1833–97)
m
Francis, Duke
of Teck (1837–1900)

Louise
(1848–1939)
m
John Campbell, Duke of
Argyll (1845–1917)

Arthur, Duke of
Connaught (1850–1942)
m
Louise of Prussia
(1860–1917)
issue

Leopold, Duke of Albany
(1853–84)
m
Helena of Waldeck-
Pyrmont (1861–1922)
issue

Beatrice (1857–1944)
m
Henry of Battenberg
(1858–96)
issue

Maud (1869–1938)

PRINCESS CHARLOTTE'S TROUSSEAU

Anon., *[A Description(?)] of the Royal Marriage Consisting of Original Memoirs of Prince Leopold and Princess Charlotte*, pamphlet published by W. Hone, London 1816, pp38–41.

Page 38

NUPTIAL DRESSES
OF HER
ROYAL HIGHNESS PRINCESS CHARLOTTE.

1. The Wedding Dress, composed of a most magnificent silver lama, on net, over a rich silver tissue slip, with a superb border of silver lama embroidery at the bottom, forming shells and bouquets; above the border a most elegant fulling, tastefully designed, in festoons of rich silver lama, and finished with a very brilliant roleau of lama. The body and sleeves to correspond, trimmed with most beautiful Brussels point lace, in a peculiarly elegant style, &c. The *manteau* of rich silver tissue, lined with white satin, trimmed round with a most superb silver lama border, in shells, to correspond with the dress, and fastened in front with a most brilliant and tasteful ornament of diamonds. The whole of the dress surpassed all conception, particularly in the brilliancy and richness of its effect. Head-dress, a wreath of rose-buds and leaves, composed of the most superb brilliants.

2. A superb gold lama dress, with an elegant border of lama, over a white satin slip. The body and sleeves embroidered to correspond; trimmed with an elegant blond net, in vandyke; also a most magnificent gold tissue manteau, lined with a rich white satin, and trimmed round with a beautiful gold border in net-work and shells, and fastened in front with diamonds.

3. A silver lama dress, richly embroidered on net, with a superb border over a white satin slip; body and sleeves elegantly trimmed with a rich silver blond lace. The manteau to suit, composed of a rich silver tissue, lined with white satin, and trimmed round with a beautiful silver lama border, fastened in front with diamonds.

4. A very superb blue and white figured silver tissue dress, trimmed with a full elegant trimming of lama on net, tastefully interspersed with silver orange blossoms, and corn-flowers; the body and sleeves elegantly trimmed with lama and silver blond lace.

5. An embroidered gold muslin dress, with an elegant Indian gold border; above the border two flounces of most beautiful Mechlin lace; the body and sleeves richly trimmed with Mechlin lace. This dress had a particularly attractive effect.

6. A very superb Brussels point lace dress, trimmed with point lace over a slip of rich white satin. This dress cost 800 guineas.

7. A rich white satin dress, elegantly trimmed with blond lace, with a beautiful satin and net trimming above the blond; the body and sleeves very full and handsome, with blond lace.

8. An elegant sprig book-muslin dress, trimmed with rich Mechlin lace, over a white satin slip.

9. A rich figured satin dress, elegantly trimmed with blond lace.

10. A travelling dress of rich white silk, elegantly trimmed with flounces at the bottom, and superb Brussels point with ruffs and cuffs to correspond.

11. A rich white satin wedding pelisse, trimmed with a most beautiful ermine for the occasion.

12. An elegant white satin hat, tastefully trimmed with blond lace, and a beautiful plume of ostrich feathers.

The above were executed by Mrs. Triaud, of Bolton-street.

Page 39

The following were made by Mrs. Bean, of Albemarle-street.

1. A most superb Brussels point lace dress, over white satin, the pattern at the bottom carnations and buds, above which is a beautiful flounce, a quarter deep, of point lace; the body and sleeves richly trimmed to correspond.

2. A rich gold sprigged dress, with a long train, trimmed round with two rows of lama, of a very rich and beautiful pattern; above which is a heading of white satin and lama intermixed; the sleeves lama over white satin, with a most tasteful band and bow to correspond.

3. A very rich evening primrose satin dress, with a deep flounce of blond lace, of a very beautiful tulip pattern, above which is a broad embroidery of pearls, in grapes and vine leaves; the top and sleeves ornamented with pearls to correspond.

4. A beautiful pink flounced satin dress, with a rich garniture of white satin and blond; the sleeves tastefully ornamented with blond to correspond.

5. A Prussian blue and white striped satin dress, with a beautiful garniture; above which is a rich broad blond lace, tastefully looped up in the form of shells.

6. A full dress over a rich white satin, ornamented with silver, the garniture silver leaves intermixed with full puffings of tull; this forms at the bottom a tasteful scollop, above which are large bunches of silver double lilacs, the sleeves striped with silver, and finished at the top with a narrow wreath of corresponding flowers.

7. A pink silk dress, trimmed with two rows of a most beautiful bell trimming, composed of tull and ribbon; the sleeves tull over pink, ornamented at the top with a handsome full blond.

8. A spotted muslin morning dress, trimmed with four flounces of most beautiful English lace; sleeves and top to correspond, with lace ruff.

9. A sprigged India muslin morning dress, with two rows of Valenciennes lace; let in above each, is a scolloped flounce, trimmed round with Valenciennes lace; the body and sleeves richly trimmed, with full cuffs and ruff.

10. A train dress of net, richly embroidered with a beautiful border of roses and buds a quarter and a half deep round the train, the embroidery coming up to meet the waist; body and sleeves richly worked to correspond; the whole dress lined with rich white satin.

11. A rich violet satin dress, elegantly trimmed with a beautiful broad point lace, a most superb heading of broad double-edged point; body and sleeves richly trimmed with satin and point to correspond.

12. A rich white striped gauze dress, of a most beautiful pattern, made expressly for her Royal Highness, trimmed with two rows of beautiful blond lace, satin and full trimming above the blond; body and sleeves to correspond; slip of lilac satin.

13. A rich blue striped gauze dress, richly trimmed with broad blond, in quite a new and elegant style; the body and sleeves trimmed with satin and blond to correspond.

Page 40

14. A rich black Chantilla lace dress, the pattern of which was grapes and vine leaves; above the border, a full flounce put on in deep scollops; the body and sleeves trimmed to correspond.

15. A superb blond lace dress, elegantly trimmed with blond and satin over a white satin slip.

16. A rich twilled sarsnet morning dress, with a rich garniture of white satin and silk; the body made high, and trimmed with satin; a rich Mechlin lace ruff.

17. An elegant worked India book muslin dress, with long sleeves of a most beautiful pattern, richly trimmed at the bottom, with a double flounce of Mechlin lace, over a slip of evening primrose satin.

18. A fine mull muslin dress, worked in shells, with two rows of lace, and three flounces of beautiful English lace, between a trimming of work to finish; the body and sleeves richly trimmed.

19. An elegant violet and white striped satin pelisse, lined with white satin, trimmed with leaves of violet, and white blond cuffs and collar; bonnet to match, with a beautiful plume of white feathers.

20. A rich green ruff sarsnet pelisse, lined with white, and elegantly trimmed with green and white satin.

21. A beautiful primrose silk high morning dress, trimmed and worked in a most unique style of elegance.

22. An elegant white satin dress, superbly ornamented with point lace, of a very beautiful shell pattern, and headed with wreaths of roses and lilies; sleeves very full, composed of point and satin, the body to match.—This dress has a very new and elegant appearance.

23. Very beautiful clear India muslin dress, most elegantly worked in lace work and satin stich, forming bunches of wheat ears and corn flowers; at the bottom a waved border of the same, finished with very full rows of elegant English lace; short sleeves, composed of rows of satin, and lace body to correspond, made low to meet the waist, with a satin slip, which forms a very elegant dress.

24. A curious striped India muslin dress, tucked with small tucks, next to which is a broad muslin lace let in, and below it another row of tucks, finishing at the bottom with a full flounce of muslin; lace sleeves, beautifully worked on India muslin, and striped with Mechlin footing; body to match.

25. Morning dress of fine mull muslin, trimmed with English footing; lace let in at the bottom alternately with work; full long sleeves, with lace cuffs; collaret of lace.

26. A blue satin dress, tastefully trimmed with satin and net; sleeves very full; body made low, with a very pretty cape, trimmed to match the dress.

MILLINERY.

Six beautiful white satin and blond lace bonnets, elegantly trimmed; some with beautiful plumes of ostrich feathers, and others with large bunches of flowers.

Six elegant English lace caps, trimmed with the most beautiful English laces that could be procured.

Two Valenciennes lace caps, trimmed with Valenciennes lace, forming a coronet round the top, which has a very pretty effect.

Page 41

A Brussels point lace mob cap, with beautiful rich trimmings of point lace.

A very superb cap of Brussels point, quite a new shape: this cap is most elegantly trimmed with point, and the new double-sided satin ribbon.

A Mechlin lace cap, beautifully trimmed with Mechlin lace, and lined with white satin.

An elegant Mechlin lace mob cap lined and trimmed.

There are several other elegant morning dresses of muslin, tastefully decorated with lace, and a variety of other handsome articles of millinery. The whole of the dresses and lace are of British manufacture, with the exception of the Brussels, Mechlin, and Valenciennes laces, which ornament the full dresses. All the silks and satins used in these dresses were purposely manufactured in London.

WEDDING DRESSES.

THE QUEEN.

A beautiful gold tissue, trimmed with a mixture of gold and silver, having two flounces of brilliant silver net-work, richly embossed with stripes of gold lama, and a superb head to the flounces of silver lama border. The whole had a most novel, grand, and magnificent appearance.

PRINCESS AUGUSTA.

An elegant silver lama dress, beautifully embroidered and trimmed with lama flouncing, worn over a rich white satin petticoat. A most superb silver and blue tissue robe, richly ornamented with lama trimming and silver roses; body and sleeves to correspond. Head dress, feathers and diamonds.

PRINCESS MARY.

An elegant silver lama dress superbly embroidered, with rich silver vandykes, and lama flouncing drawn through each vandyke, headed with a beautiful silver trimming of roses, worn over a rich white satin petticoat. An elegant silver and pink tissue robe trimmed to correspond, and fastened at the waist with a diamond clasp; body and sleeves of silver lama and blond lace. Head dress, feathers and diamonds.

PRINCESS SOPHIA OF GLOUCESTER.

An elegant robe of gold tissue, superbly ornamented with silver lama; silver tissue sleeves, tastefully intermixed with gold. Her Royal Highness wore a profusion of diamonds and feathers.

MARCHIONESS OF WINCHESTER.

Silver stitched lama petticoat, over white satin, with two superb flounces of lama, headed tastefully with net and silver; robe of pink satin, trimmed with a fulling of white satin, and embroidered with silver of a very beautiful pattern sash to match, studded with silver, and confined in front with a diamond clasp. Head dress, feathers and diamonds; necklace diamonds. This dress had a most brilliant and splendid effect.

THE MARCHIONESS OF CHOLMONDELEY'S

dress was very conspicuous for its singular elegance.—A superb silver lama dress, with a border beautifully wrought with silver li-

Appendix 2b

R. Huish, *Memoirs of Her Late Royal Highness Charlotte Augusta,* (London 1819) pp260–2

This list does not appear to be directly derived from Appendix 2a and is included for comparison and for the additional details it provides.

After the visit to Camelford-House, the Queen and Princesses proceeded to inspect the wedding dresses of the Princess Charlotte, which consisted of the following:

1 The wedding dress was a slip of white and silver atlas, worn under a dress of transparent silk net, elegantly embroidered in silver lama, with a border to correspond, tastefully worked in bunches of flowers, to form festoons round the bottom; the sleeves and neck trimmed with a most rich suit of Brussels point lace. The mantua was two yards and a half long, made of rich silver and white atlas, trimmed the same as the dress to correspond. After the ceremony, her Royal Highness was to put on a dress of very rich white silk, trimmed with broad satin trimming at the bottom, at the top of which were two rows of broad Brussels point lace. The sleeves of this dress were short and full, intermixed with point lace, the neck trimmed with point to match. The pelisse which the royal Bride was to travel in, on her Royal Highness leaving Carlton-House for Oatlands, was of rich white satin, lined with sarcenet, and trimmed all round with broad ermine. Her Royal Highness had also the following dresses made up upon the happy occasion:-

2 A dress of white net, embroidered in gold lama, with an elegant order over white satin; the mantua of an extremely rich gold brocade, with blown roses, richly woven in very thickly all over the dress, and trimmed with broad gold lace.

3 A dress of transparent net, worked in bright and dead silver; the border, twelve inches deep, in scollops; at each scollop was placed a bunch of barley-corn, in bright and dead silver the sleeves to match trimmed with point lace over white satin.

4 A silver tissue dress, trimmed with a rich trimming of silver lace and Brussels point.

5 A gold India-worked muslin, in small spots, very thick, and deep border to correspond, and trimmed profusely with Brussels point lace.

6 Another dress, similar to the former, only in sprigs.

7,8 Two Brussels point lace dresses, with border and trimming of point lace to match; the one cost 360 guineas, the other 300 guineas.

9,10 Two dresses of British blond net, elegantly trimmed with blond, and another to wear over satin slips. There were, beside, several dresses of plain satin, handsomely trimmed with lace and net.

11 A morning dress of fine muslin, with three rows of broad Valenciennes lace, the flounce surmounted with broad footing to match; lace ruff, four breadths of the same, and cuffs to correspond.

12 A fine India muslin dress, with Mechlin lace; flounces, cuffs, and ruff of the same, and a lace cape, trimmed twice round.

13,14 Two worked dresses for the occasion; very rich scalloped borders of four rows, quilled with net at the top of each row. Laced and worked muslin ruffs and cuffs to match.
Several other dresses, nearly similar.

Appendix 3

THE DUTIES OF QUEEN VICTORIA'S DRESSERS

ROYAL ARCHIVES Z20262 Letters, etc. *Relative to Household Appointments*

The duties of Her Majesty's dressers are: <u>in the first place</u> scrupulous tidiness and exactness in looking over everything that Her Majesty takes off, never omitting to mend or to give to the Wardrobe maid to mend thins which require it, at once – to look over the bonnets, gloves, caps, cloaks, etc, etc before Her Majesty puts them on. <u>2ndly</u> to see that everything is right and in its place before Her Majesty gets up, goes to bed, or dresses so that there can be no confusion or anything missing. <u>3rdly</u> to take note when anything is getting torn or dirty and to have others got. <u>4th</u> to think over <u>well</u> everything that is wanted or may be wanted when Her Majesty goes anywhere, likewise when Her Majesty goes to London to hold a Court etc. to be certain that every thing is in its right place. <u>5th</u> The dressers have the charge of the Wardrobe and all that belongs to it, whether dress, shawls, jewels or whatever Her Majesty uses I the wardrobe; for all these things they are responsible. <u>6th</u> If they are in doubt about anything they should at once ask Her Majesty. <u>7th</u> To see that all Her Majesty's clothes are kept properly and in their places and in proper drawers appointed for them.

The dressers have to look after the Wardrobe maids to see that they do their duty and that their health is properly attended to, etc, etc.

Index

References to illustrations are by **page number** (in bold), not by illustration number. References with 'c' annotations (eg 13c) are to caption material not directly related to the illustration. References with 'n' annotations (eg 13n) are to endnotes, and refer to the page on which the reference occurs.